GARLAND STUDIES IN

Entrepreneurship

STUART BRUCHEY

Allan Nevins Professor Emeritus
American Economic History
Columbia University

GENERAL EDITOR

A Garland Series

One Hundred Years of Energy

Public Service Company of Colorado and Its Predecessors, 1869–1969

Ellen Kingman Fisher

Garland Publishing, Inc.
New York & London
1989

Library of Congress Cataloging-in-Publication Data

Fisher, Ellen Kingman.
One hundred years of energy : Public Service Company of Colorado and its predecessors, 1869–1969 / Ellen Kingman Fisher.
p. cm. — (Garland studies in entrepreneurship)
Bibliography: p.
ISBN 0-8240-3362-0 (alk. paper)
1. Public Service Company of Colorado—History.
2. Electric companies—Colorado—Denver—History.
3. Gas companies—Colorado—Denver—History.
I. Title. II. Series.
HD9685.U7P825 1989
333.79'32'06078883—dc20 89-16868

Printed on acid-free, 250-year-life paper

Manufactured in the United States of America

One Hundred Years of Energy

Public Service Company of Colorado
and Its Predecessors, 1869–1969

CONTENTS

ILLUSTRATIONS

PREFACE

The one hundred year history of the Public Service Company of Colorado and its predecessors is a study of a particular energy production and distribution business which was a microcosm of the national utility industry. The people involved in the industry were as important a part of the history as the product they developed and sold. They, like their companies, reflected the mores of the day. Without the drive, ambition and innovation of industry, entrepreneurs, managers, and scientists there would have been no power companies and society today would be vastly different.

This is the history of the state's largest utility, Public Service Company of Colorado, its origin, evolution and contribution to the region's development. The energy it supplied changed the way Coloradans lived, worked, and played. It is an entrepreneurial story which seeks to identify key people in the company and describe their impact on the enterprise.

The utilities contributed measurably to the standard of living and were, in turn, influenced by rising consumer expectations. The inventors and manufacturers continually created new uses for energy and society responded with an almost insatiable hunger. Energy development was an integral part of humanity's quest for material well being, responding with increasingly sophisticated machines and appliances. People and energy early on formed a symbiotic relationship.

Because Public Service Company is an on-going business it is very conscious of its public image. For that reason, many records were unavailable. However, because of the company's prominence there is an abudance of information in government documents, in the files of the Colorado Public Utility Commission, in court records, and in a variety of newspapers and periodicals. In addition, there were many people in the company who were willing to take time to give first-hand information about the organization for which they have high regard.

Robert T. Person, chairman of the board of directors until 1985, read the initial chapter and cleared the way for gaining access to information in the Company. After his retirement he generously reviewed the entire manuscript and elaborated on a number of significant points. He spent many hours in interviews which were not only informative but enjoyable for the author.

William "Fitz" Fitzmaurice, Manager of Public Relations and Corporate Communications, and his assistant Bobbye Foster coordinated the use of records. Robert J. Hugo, Administrative Assistant of Engineering and Planning; Milton McBride, Nuclear Fuel and Analysis Manager; and Robert E. Kelly, retired vice president of the gas department read chapters and provided additional information. Peg McMahan, MaryAnn Hamm, and Shirley Taylor also offered helpful suggestions.

Outside of the Public Service Company Harry A. Galligan, Jr., Executive Secretary of the Public Utilities Commission of the State of Colorado generously furnished important information. He also gave invaluable insight into the relationship between the PUC and PSC. Mary Gibson, historian for the Electrical Workers' Union III shared her unpublished manuscript and spent several hours explaining labor relations with PSC. Her paper provided information that was otherwise unavailable.

Other people contributed information including James R. McCotter, William P. Denious, III, and Lee

Olson. The staffs of the Colorado Historical Society, Denver Public Library, Colorado State Archives, and Colorado Judicial Library were also very helpful.

Without the support of of my family this history never would have been written.

One Hundred Years of Energy

CHAPTER 1

DEVELOPMENT OF EARLY GAS COMPANIES

Colorado's utility industry traced its roots to a time when Colorado was not yet a state and Denver was teetering between success and failure. Those who chose to stay in Denver realized there was often as much money to be made in town building as in mining. The men who struggled to form the first gas company to provide manufactured gas for street lighting were motivated by a mixture of profit and community service. Several ventures were proposed before one actually went into operation. Eventually a group of business entrepreneurs were successful in establishing the Denver Gas Company, a forerunner of the Public Service Company of Colorado.

In 1858 the rumor of gold on the eastern slope of the Rocky Mountains lured 100,000 fortune seekers to the region that would be called Colorado. Within a year three quarters of those people had returned home with their optimistic "Pikes Peak or Bust" signs replaced with "Busted." Some of the prospectors remained and one of those, John Gregory, was lucky enough to find gold in May, 1859. Again the clarion call went out and thousands arrived near the confluence of the Platte River and Cherry Creek. Two town companies, Auraria and Denver, were platted on opposite banks of Cherry Creek. The two merged in 1860, assuming the name of Denver. The small town evolved quickly from a rough mining camp into a central locale in which to buy supplies.

Denver's earliest energy company was established in 1860. Named the Arapahoe County Gas Light Company, its stated purpose was to manufacture and distribute coal gas to the residents of Denver. The firm, with future mayor Richard Sopris as president, probably sought to do nothing more than establish its priority under the laws of Kansas Territory as a utility.[1] A market for gas, either for heating or illumination, did not exist at the time. When at some future date demand was sufficiently large to justify the expense of erecting retorts and laying mains, Sopris and his associates intended to be owners Following the creation of the Colorado Territory in 1861, other enterprises vied for the opportunity to provide coal gas to Denver residents. The Occidental Gas Light Company secured a thirty-year exclusive franchise in 1864[2] and two years later the legislature extended a twenty-year franchise to the Denver Gas

Company.[3] *It was William N. Byers, editor of the Rocky Mountain News,* and enthusiastic town builder, who chartered the Denver Gas Company to manufacture gas and lay pipes to supply Denver. Both ventures failed to erect retorts or install mains, but their mere existence indicated continuing local interest in an energy source for illumination. The history of many of these early companies is unknown. Some companies are listed in official registers as having been incorporated, but there is no record of their actually doing business of any kind.[4]

Early in 1867 the *Rocky Mountain News* announced that the territorial lawmakers were considering the chartering of another gas company.[5] The newspaper encouraged the legislature to choose a concern that had the capital and ability to provide gas for Denver at an early date. Presumably, a successful company would encourage investment in other fields. ThE journalist angrily suggested that Denver did not need any more "dog in the manger" operations that wanted a franchise for financial gain without the intention of developing a company.[6] There may have been a conflict of interest between Byers the *News* editor and Byers the president of the Denver Gas Company. His company may not have been immediately able to lay pipes and transmit gas, but he was unwilling to give up exclusive control of the franchise.

There were more broken promises. On 27 December 1867, a new company, the Colorado Land and Mineral Association[7] made several commitments to Denver, one of which was to operate a plant to manufacture gas in the city and the outlying additions in Arapahoe County. The capital stock was $100,000 divided into shares of $100 each. The company, chartered for twenty years,[8] was given permission by the city to lay mains under the streets, but no construction was undertaken.[9]

Because no company had yet manufactured gas, entrepreneurs continued to be interested in the gas franchise. In the summer of 1868 a flamboyant Frenchman, Colonel William Heine, arrived from the East Coast with $100,000 and several partners to invest in a plant to manufacture gas. Heine had been one of the commissioners of minerals for the 1867 Paris Exposition.[10] He came to Colorado through the encouragement of J. P. Whitney, a Boston financier, who had represented Colorado at the exposition, exhibiting ore samples to drum up interest in the territory.[11] Heine requested an ordinance from city council to place pipes under streets in order to distribute gas throughout the community. Council enthusiastically granted his company, the Denver Coal and Gas Light Company, the right to dig up city streets. Three months later Heine changed the enterprise's name to Colorado Coal and Gas Light Company, optimistically widening the territory he planned to serve even before the enterprise was functioning. City fathers breathed a sigh of relief, believing that this company, backed by substantial French capital, would soon be ready to provide manufactured gas.[12]

There were signs of progress as well as problems with the gas venture. Colonel Heine arranged for a supply of coal from the Austin coal bank in Erie, but legal problems halted further development. The difficulty lay in fear of a possible lawsuit by one of the previously incorporated gas companies. Each enterprise wanted exclusive right to do business in Denver. None was willing to give up easily the valuable right to supply gas. The *Rocky Mountain News* pleaded with those concerned to solve the problem, so that one company could begin building.[13] Colonel Heine eventually proceeded with plans to build a gas plant despite the legal uncertainties.

Gas had captured the attention of French

investors. Financiers speculated that a gas plant would attract attention to Colorado and encourage others to invest in enterprises, such as construction, railroad building, treating ores, coal mining, gold, silver and copper mining, manufacturing, farming, stock raising, and colonizing. The *Rocky Mountain News* was delighted that investors were willing to put their money in a Colorado utility despite the fact that capital invested in Denver earned a lower profit than investments in other cities. Manufactured gas would make the area a desirable place for prospective residents and investors to come.[14]

Visions of a great municipality danced in the minds of editor William Byers of the *News*. The operation of a gas plant would provide a market for coal which could be brought from Colorado's coal mining areas. The demand for transporting coal would lead to another benefit, the arrival of railroads to carry the fuel. Denver would become a hub for the overland route from the eastern cities. It could become a major link in the transportation system between the Atlantic and the Pacific coasts. Attracting a larger population would bring excellent schools of all grades taught by professional men and women, and, "all the fashionable world would vie hither to spend the summer months, leaving, of course, hundreds of thousands of dollars in their trail."[15] In fact, such enthusiasm convinced many people in the East that Denver's streets were lighted long before they were.[16]

October was not only a month for dreaming, but also one of action. A committee of people who wished to hasten gas service subdivided the city into sections and systematically collected data on how many gas burners each business and resident desired.[17] The company, in order to keep the cost of gas fittings low, needed an accurate count of potential customers. Selling burners and chandeliers was separate from manufacturing and conveying gas. Colorado Coal and Gas Light Company wanted to control the selling of fittings to make additional profit.[18]

Prospective consumers were told that gas would be supplied by 1 August 1869 at no more than $5.00 per 1,000 cubic feet. This was higher than the prevailing price of $2.50 a 1000 cubic feet in many large European cities and the average of $4.00 for the same volume in many places in the United States. The charter, however, allowed a company to charge up to $6.00 during the first twenty years of its existence, $5.00 for the next ten, and $4.00 a thousand thereafter.[19]

Colonel Heine then set about to find a site on which to build a gas plant. A 43-acre tract between Wynkoop street and the Platte River seemed desirable and his offer of $5,000 was accepted by the owners. The *Rocky Mountain* News reported that Heine's purchase was a bargain because the land was worth twice the price he paid.[20]

After an auspicious beginning, Colonel Heine's scheme had a mysterious ending. The *News* added to the folklore of the day by reporting that Heine counted on a wealthy French woman, Madame Edouard, for his funds. She, in turn, was to take as security a mortgage on his company. A story circulated that while on her way to Denver she was kidnapped by an agent of the Union Pacific, who forced her to put her gold in railroad bonds. Heine was apparently unable to continue his venture without these promised funds.[21]

A plausible, but less romantic explanation was that Heine, lacking the necessary funds, skipped town rather than face the humiliation of being called disreputable. When Heine left in 1869 William Byers angrily observed that the businessmen who had asked for exclusive privileges for the gas franchise had sought them for speculation only. Their motive was to hold the franchise for future profit, not to carry out the contract to serve the people of Denver, Colorado.[22]

Despite three years of unsuccessful efforts the desire to provide gas for Denver was still alive. In 1869 two groups, the Denver Gas Water Company and the Denver Gas Company, requested an exclusive franchise to supply gas to the city[23] The Denver City Council reviewed the proposals for price, soundness of business, and type of gas. They chose the Denver Gas Company, incorporated on 13 November 1869, granting the company a fifty-year franchise, without any provision for compensation to the city.

There had been another company with the same name incorporated on 18 May 1866. The law at that time stated that a business would be defunct if it did not commence operations within two years. After almost two years the initial Denver Gas Company was not manufacturing gas, but on 10 January 1868 the enterprise made an agreement with the city to supply gas on or before 1 August 1869 at a price not to exceed $5.00 per thousand cubic feet. The Denver Gas Company was still not able to fulfill its commitment so another Denver Gas Company was chartered. Colonel James Archer was the head of the new company and William Byers the secretary. They bought the charter of the company incorporated in 1866.[24]

Colonel Archer succeeded where others had failed. A native of Belfast, Ireland he had sailed to America at the age of 32 to engage in an iron business in St. Louis. As the Kansas Pacific Railway built a line to Denver, Archer visited the community and, like others, saw great prospects for the small settlement at the edge of the Rockies. He had accumulated modest wealth and was willing to invest some of his money to improve the town as well as to enhance his fortune.[25]

On 13 November 1869 Archer met with seven local capitalists. The men who would back the enterprise to manufacture fuel for illuminating Denver's streets were leading entrepreneurs and community builders. William N. Byers, was editor of the *Rocky Mountain News* and a consummate town booster. Louis Bartels was a merchant, rancher and banker. Walter Scott Cheesman, a druggist, would become a builder of railroads and water utilities. John Evans was a medical doctor, founder of the University of Denver and second Governor of Colorado Territory. David Moffat was a banker and would also become a railroad builder. Lewis N. Tappan was a prominent merchant. D. Tom Smith was a freighter.[26]

The lawmakers were so eager to establish a functioning gas company that they granted the company a fifty-year charter that required no remuneration to the city.[27] The day after Denver City Council approved their proposal the capitalists opened a subscription drive to raise $100,000 for their enterprise. James Archer was listed as president, William Byers as secretary, and David H. Moffat, Jr. as trustee in charge of the new company's account at the First National Bank.[28]

By early 1870 a gas company was in place, located at the corner of I and Wewatta streets, close the the future site of the Union Depot. Building the plant to manufacture gas was a major construction project. There were two rooms for retort ovens to heat the coal, plus a purifying room. The retorts alone contained 18,000 fire bricks which were set in clay. A gas storage vault was made of 150,000 bricks put together with 45 barrels of cement.[29]

Loaded wagons crossed the plains from different parts of the country with supplies. The gas holder, which would contain the gas after it was manufactured, came from Cincinnati, the pipe and cement from Louisville, Kentucky, and a secondhand iron frame structure came from St. Louis where a local company had outgrown its facilities. Excited residents watched as 120 tons of cast iron and sixteen tons of wrought arrived in their small town. Meanwhile, samples of coal were tested to determine their suitability for making gas. Louis Bartels worked in Denver while James Archer supervised the coal testing in St. Louis.[30] Because of high ox cart freight rates, the men delayed ordering pipes for underground transmission until the scheduled arrival of the railroad at the end of 1870.[31]

Skeptics had no faith in the gas works. As the date for production neared in 1871 rumors circulated that the retorts had failed, the pipes had leaked, and Colorado coal had not yielded a suitable gas. A newspaperman rushed to the scene to see if the stories were true. He found men busily working under the light of gas from the purifier. The reporter noted, "Gas is going to be supplied, and in a very few days [we] will see that result fully realized."[32] For once the doubters were wrong. By 1872 glass-enclosed gas jets, mounted on posts were in place lighting the town's business section and some residential areas. At last, Denver was "lighted" by gas.

By 1873 the Denver Gas Company had installed ten thousand gas burners and there was a demand for more. In order to keep pace with the demand the company added to the capacity of its plant.[33] Every symbol of progress was a cause for a local celebration. On 18 November the community dedicated the addition to the gas works. The solons of the city turned out in full regalia. After a banquet the mayor, city council members, and other dignitaries were led down into the empty iron gas reservoir to view it from the inside. The *Rocky Mountain News* joked that "Beyond all doubt there were more solid feet of gas assembled there at that time than will ever be confined there again."[34]

By the time a plant was established in Denver the technology of manufactured gas had been developing for about seventy-five years. Scotsman William Murdock realized that gas could be put to effective use as early as 1792. Twenty-two-year old Murdock had joined James Watt and Matthew Boulton in 1777 at their engineering plant at Soho in Birmingham, England. After two years James Watt sent Murdock to Cornwall to oversee the fitting of steam engines. While in Cornwall Murdock experimented with the distilling of coal. He heated coal in an airless retort to temperatures of between 1,000 and 1,200 degrees centigrade to produce gas which was then collected and purified. The retorts in the early days were usually made of clay and the efficiency of gas making was dependent on the stoker's ability to keep the heat at the proper temperature.[35] In 1792 Murdock produced gas in a huge iron retort, and then transported it through seventy feet of copper pipe to light his home and office. As he struck a match to light the first lamp his family and co-workers jumped back in fear, waiting for a deadly explosion. Instead, a steady and bright flame appeared making his experiment a success.

Murdock moved back to London in 1803, continuing his work to improve the manufacture and storage of gas. He also experimented with gas and steam engines. His work brought him great recognition. In 1820 he was asked to light Pall Mall in London.[36]

Not everyone approved of lighting city streets, in England or America.[37] When Baltimore in 1816 gave the Gas Light Company permission to light the city streets there was talk of little else. Many residents were proud that their city was the first in America to install commercial gas lights, but there were also vocal critics. Some people thought that God had planned to divide the day into dark and light making it almost irreligious to have light in the evening. Law enforcers feared that unsavory elements of society would spend more time in crime and debauchery, because there would be less fear of the night. Others objected to the stench of the gaseous fumes, assumed by many to be unhealthy.[38] Most doubters, however, seemed to be simply opponents of change. Fortunately, there are always those who are willing to take risks and go forward. So it was in Baltimore, and with that example, other cities followed, lighting their own streets.[39]

Despite continued improvements, gas lighting was plagued with problems. It gave off heat, was cumbersome, and was expensive. In addition to the inherent problems of gas, the new science of electricity offered stiff competition as an illuminant, furnishing safer, steadier light with less heat. To remain competitive the gas industry offered inducements such as lower prices for service and free gas jets. But, it was improved technology rather than price cutting that gave gas a reprive.[40]

In 1885 German scientist Carl Auer von Welsbach invented a gas mantle increasing sixfold the light which could be produced.[41] This new mantle was made by dipping the woven fabric into a metallic solution for a short time. When the lamp was lighted the woven material was burned away, leaving the metallic meshwork to give off a concentrated light.[42]

With the Welsbach mantle, gas light was cheaper than electric incandescent light, thus temporarily delaying being outmoded by electric lighting.[43]

Denverites were anxious to light their streets with gas in order to make their surroundings more pleasant and to attract new residents. As a result, they were willing to grant franchises with few restrictions. The utility companies virtually created their own rates, regulations, and length of service.[44] Town capitalists felt that the future of the city depended on utility services of gas, transportation, communication and water. It was evident very early that the future of the city and the gas company were intertwined.

The developmental decade of the 1860s had presented challenges to the Colorado Territory. Gold, the resource that meant riches to some prospectors and merchants had become less accessible. In addition, Indian hostilities made life in Colorado Territory unsettled. The 1870 census reflected the reluctance of people to move to the territory. Colorado had gained 4500 people and Denver only ten in a decade.[45] To stay alive the region needed economic diversification, which is exactly what the 1870s brought.

In the 1870s silver mining as well as other promising activities began in Colorado. Homesteaders staked out agricultural colonies, and cattle raising expanded at a rapid rate. Most important railroads reached Denver by 1870. Local businessmen raised enough capital to build the Denver Pacific Railroad Company, linking Denver with the Union Pacific in Cheyenne, Wyoming. The railroad encouraged other train systems within the state as well as an expansion of the wagon roads. It was now more convenient to journey to Colorado and also easier to travel from place to place within the territory.[46]

Perhaps statehood was the greatest event of the decade for Colorado. Several requests to become a state had been made to no avail. In 1875 it became politically expedient to reconsider Colorado's status as a territory. The Republican party realized that presidential candidate Rutherford B. Hayes might need additional electoral votes to beat a Democratic opponent. To gain three potential votes Republicans pushed through an enabling act for statehood which was passed in Washington on 3 March 1876. Coloradans ratified their constitution on 1 July 1876 and exactly one month later President Grant brought the "Centennial State" into the union.[47]

People came to Colorado in increasing numbers especially those who sought a salubrious climate.[48] Health seekers did not necessarily bring wealth to the state, but they did come, attracted by the clean, clear air and beautiful surroundings. Those who came to Colorado in 1872 arrived in a city supplied with gas through nine and one half miles of gas mains.[49] Residents boasted about Denver Gas Company's progress in laying pipes and erecting lamp posts throughout the business and residential sections of the city.[50]

The expanding demand for gas allowed the company to lower rates in 1877. On 1 October the price of gas was reduced from $5.00 to $3.50 per 1,000 cubic feet, and $3.00 for those who paid their bills promptly. The zealous young company further increased business by publicizing its good service, and the cheapness, cleanliness, and safety of its products.[51]

One of the major benefits of holding a franchise was the ability to bid on the lucrative Denver city street lighting contract. During territorial days franchises were granted by the legislature, but in 1867 the United States Congress denied territories the right of granting private charters or special privileges. After December 1867 companies were established under general state laws and were granted franchises by local councils. Since the time Colorado became a state, franchises have not been granted for longer than twenty years.[52] Whether that provision negated Denver Gas Company's fifty year franchise was to be a matter of debate in future years.

In 1869 the city made an agreement with the Denver Gas Company to provide illuminating gas of good quality to light the streets of Denver and to provide light poles. The fifty-year contract began 1 January 1870.[53] Thereafter the company claimed an exclusive contract with the city, as well as a perpetual franchise, until it was forced to change some provisions in a 1927 franchise renewal. Despite company claims, the contract to light city streets was renewed much more frequently than every fifty years and did not appear to be exclusive.

At the 7 April 1875 meeting of the city council a councilman reminded everyone that the agreement with Denver Gas Company expired in November of that year.[54] On 4 October the city council's Committee on Gas and Gas Lamps recommended that a new contract be given the Denver Gas Company. Members believed that it would be unfair to give a rival company the use of street right-of-ways after James Archer and his company had expended capital on construction and service[55] and the Denver Gas Company was granted a three-year contract.

Three years later other companies submitted bids to either compete with the Denver Gas Company or gain the exclusive rights for themselves. All interested parties brought bids before city council on 19 December 1878. The lawmakers sent the various propositions to a committee for review and recommendations.[56] At the committee meeting the issue was hotly debated, and two applicants jumped up and angrily shouted at each other, one accusing the other of harshly using Chinese labor to keep costs down.

The committee, because of disagreement among its members, had been making a thorough study and reported on gas prices in other cities. They had contacted twenty four communities in Kansas, Iowa, Illinois, and Missouri asking for information about the cost of making gas. Comparing the eighteen responses, the committee found Denver's prices to be reasonable. The committee, by a vote of eight to four, recommended that the Denver Gas Company be granted another two-year contract for lighting the city streets.[57]

The tempting rewards of an expanding gas market brought Denver Gas its first serious rival. Others had been dissuaded by the Denver Gas Company's political clout and a clause in the city charter which required any challengers to indemnify the city against the costs that might arise in defending any claims brought by Denver Gas. United Gas Improvement Company of Pennsylvania was willing to risk the suits that might follow. They offered to furnish gas lighting to residents at $2.00 per 1,000 cubic feet compared to the prevailing price of $3.00, and to light the city's streets at $27.00 per post which was $13.00 less than service by Denver Gas Company. United Gas Improvement Company set up its business in 1883.[58] Any suits against it or the city were not recorded, nor is the fact that it ever manufactured gas.

By the mid-1880s the city was not as anxious to have utilities as it once had been. As proposals came before city council, Denver began to exert more control over utilities. When the city granted People's Gas Light Company a franchise on 11 April 1887 (to supply gas at $1.50 per 1,000 cubic feet) city council reserved the right to set rates after fifteen years, but still did not charge a franchise fee.[59]

The first regulatory device in Colorado was the franchise which gave the rate-setting powers to the issuing bodies. However, local governments generally confirmed rates that the utilities established. As people realized the vast profits that could be made from the gas business, they began to put pressure on the governmental unit to charge yearly franchise fees, or, in other words, a percentage of revenues for the privilege of doing business in cities. Denver, as in most communities was only willing to impose a franchise tax after it felt confident that the utility could provide adequate service.[60]

Franchises were a good beginning in the regulatory process but they had many inherent problems. For example, city leaders rarely had the training or background to know how to establish a rate that was fair to the consumer as well as the vender. In some cities the government meekly acquiesced to all utility demands, while in other there was a combative relationship. Obligations were often imposed on utility companies with the thought that the harder the bargain, the fairer it was to the consumer. People in adjacent neighborhoods often paid different rates because of different regulations.[61] The fact that franchises were granted for a long period of time--usually twenty years--with inflexible rules created other problems because conditions changed over time, making some of the restrictions that were appropriate in one decade unsuitable the next.

Franchises had been used as the only means of regulation during the utilities'promotional stage which spanned the time of early energy use and town development. Society was so anxious to have city services that the local governments were willing to give grants, tax relief, minimum control and permission to use city streets without getting a revenue return for the city. People were anxious to obtain new energy technology to save labor, and make economic progress, but also to gain status. Having the first gas or electrically-lighted house in the area made a person the envy of the neighborhood.

Cities were just as eager for new technology as individuals. Communities sought energy development as a source of pride. To be "first" or "best" was an aspect of city boosterism, important in every part of the country. For example, Baltimore boasted about being the first American metropolis to have streets lighted by gas. Years later, Denver actively publicized its reputation as the "city of lights." In the early West new technology attracted business and people to sparsely-populated land. Lighting utilities also showed that the presumably-primitive Western towns were as modern as the well-established, more refined cities of the East. They were part of the effort to prove that the West was as good as the East.

If progress and pride were two elements of utility development, profit was a third. Entrepreneurs realized that there was money to be made in the utility business, and vied for the right to establish an energy company. In Denver, companies were incorporated years before they could provide service. When Denver Gas Company finally distributed gas, customers forgot their willingness to strike any deal and began complaining about high rates and erratic service. In order to respond to these complaints, cities issued a franchise to more than one company, hoping that competition would improve service and rates.

Competition rarely solved the problem. City life was disrupted as two or more companies ripped up the streets to lay pipes. They created a maze of underground conveyances. The gas suppliers engaged in a rate war while laying pipes side by side. Destructive rate wars weakened the companies by reducing income below expenses, and also discouraged investment in utilities. Most cities, like Denver, retreated from encouraging competition and turned to promoting merger and sole franchises. The resulting confusion taught the city that competition did not necessarily bring good service. Denver learned as had other cities that utilities operate more effectively as a monopoly.[62] City council, therefore, changed its tactics and encouraged consolidation. Councilmen ushered in a monopolistic era.

There were several reasons why it was inevitable that utilities became monopolies. First, the utility business took a heavy outlay of capital, management, and labor which most small enterprises could not afford. The majority of money went into plant and equipment creating a high ratio of fixed investment to total assets. Second, it was more practical to have a centralized system with a relatively large service area, because the greater the volume of gas and electricity sold the less expensive it was to produce each unit. A utility was, and is, a decreasing cost industry.[63] Small concerns had difficulty competing with their bigger brothers and, therefore, mergers were quite common, particularly from 1898 through 1902.[64]

In Denver, competing gas companies joined to form the Denver Consolidated Gas Company in 1891. The new company issued $1,500,000 in bonds to fund improvements and make their service as efficient as possible in an effort to avoid competition from electricity. The consolidation of the gas companies was reported without fanfare and, on the surface, there were no battles or litigation. Merger was a matter of necessity to compete against electricity.[65]

When the Denver city council granted a franchise to the Denver Consolidated Gas Company in 1891, it did not impose rate regulations, nor did it mention a responsibility for quality or any other requirement for the privilege of using city rights of way. The city lost any advantages gained during the era of competition.[66] The mere size of a consolidated company, or monopoly, gave it more power to bargain with governing bodies. Their influence was so great that some said these corporations ran the local government.[67]

NOTES--CHAPTER 1

1 *Rocky Mountain Herald*, 9 June 1860, p. 1.

2 Clyde King, *The History of the Government of Denver, with Special Reference to Its Relations with Public Service* (Denver: The Fisher Book Co., 1911), p. 63.

3 Certificate of Incorporation of the Denver Gas Company. Colorado. *Certificate of Incorporations*, Book AB, p. 364, (Colorado State Archives, Denver, Colorado).

4 An early law (Jefferson Territory 1859) stated that, "any corporations organized or attempted to be organized . . . shall cease to exist by the non-user of its franchise for two years at any one time." Provisional Laws and Joint Resolutions passed at the First and Called Sessions of the General Assembly of Jefferson Territory held at Denver City, J.T. November and December 1859 and January 1860. Section 21 (Omaha, N.T.: Robertson & Clark Printer, 1860), p. 217. It is not clear whether this provision was extant in future laws (Colorado Territory or State).

5 The Consolidated Gas Light Company of the City of Denver. *Colorado Session Law*, 11 January 1867, p. 121. Clyde L. King, in his book *The Regulation of Municipal Utilities* (New York: D. Appleton and Company, 1912), p. 78, wrote that at first, franchises for public service were granted by a special act of the State Legislature. Sometime in 1867 Congress denied Territories the power to grant private charters or special privileges. After that, companies were incorporated under general laws and obtained their franchises from local councils.

6 *Rocky Mountain News*, 5 January 1867, p. 1.

7 The company was incorporated by Charles A. Cook, B. M Hughes, Jasper P. Sears, Jr., Jerome DeHarpert, and James H. Jones.

8 Certificate of Incorporation of the Colorado Land and Mineral Association. Colorado. *Articles of*

Incorporation and Book C of *Incorporations*, p. 327, (Colorado State Archives, Denver, Colorado).

9 Jerome C. Smiley, *History of Denver* (Denver: Times Sun Publishing Co., 1901), p. 473.

10 Smiley, *History of Denver*, p. 474 and *Rocky Mountain News*, 15, July, 1868, p. 4.

11 Robert G. Athearn, *The Coloradans* (Albuquerque: University of New Mexico Press, 1976), p. 88, *Rocky Mountain News*, 22 July 1868, p. 4, *Colorado Tribune*, and *22 Rocky Mountain News*, 5 August 1868, p. 1.

12 *Rocky Mountain News*, 5 July 1868, p. 4.

13 *Rocky Mountain News*, 5 August 1868, p. 1.

14 *Rocky Mountain News*, 17 October 1868, p. 4.

15 Ibid.

16 *Rocky Mountain News*, 15 November 1869, p. 1.

17 *Rocky Mountain News*, 20 October 1868, p. 4.

18 *Rocky Mountain News*, 17 October 1868, p. 4.

19 Ibid.

20 *Rocky Mountain News*, 23 October 1868, p. 4 and 24 October 1868, p. 4.

21 *Rocky Mountain News*, 15 November 1869, p. 1.

22 Ibid.

23 On 14 October 1869 Colorado The Denver Gas Water Company incorporated. Certificate of Incorporation of The Denver Gas Water Company *Articles of Incorporation*, Book D of Incorporations, (Colorado State Archives, Denver, Colorado).

24 Smiley, *History of Denver*, pp. 473-474, *Rocky Mountain News*, *15 November 1869*, *p. 1*, King, *The History of the Government of Denver*, p. 63, and Charles Varnum and J. Frank Adams, *Franchises and Special*

Privileges of the City and County of Denver (Denver: 1907), p. 51.

25 *Colorado Tribune*, 27 August 1882, p. 1 and Lyle Dorsett, *The Queen City: A History of Denver* (Boulder: Pruett Publishing Company, 1976), p. 79.

26 *Public Service Company of Colorado, Providing Energy for More than a Century*, (Denver: Public Service Company of Colorado, 1976), p. 2.

27 "Brief History of Public Service Company," (unpublished paper, 1 December 1931, Public Service Company Record Center, Denver, Colorado), p. 1.

28 *Rocky Mountain News*, 15 November 1869, p. 1.

29 *Rocky Mountain News*, 13 July 1870 and 25 October 1870, p. 4.

30 *Colorado Tribune*, 29 June 1870, p. 2 and *Rocky Mountain News*, 25 October 1870, p. 4.

31 "Brief History, p. 3.

32 *Rocky Mountain News*, 25 January 1871, p. 3.

33 *Rocky Mountain News*, 19 November 1873, p. 3.

34 Ibid.

35 Edward Hungerford, *The Story of Public Utilities*, (New York: G. P. Putnam Sons, 1978), pp. 115-16.

36 "Lighting and Lighting Devices," *The New Encyclopaedia Britannica*, 1978, 10, 958.

37 Hungerford, *Story of Public Utilities*, pp. 115-16 and Eliot Jones and Truman C. Bigham, *Principles of Public Utilities* (New York: The MacMillan Company, 1931), pp. 7-9.

38 Jones and Bigham, *Principles of Public Utilities*, pp. 9-10.

39 Hungerford, *The Story of Public Utilities*, p. 125.

40 Harold C. Passer, *The Electrical Manufacturers 1875-1900, A Study in Competition, Entrepreneurship, Technical Change, and Economic Growth* (New York: Arno Press, A New York Times Company, 1972), p. 196.

41 Ibid.

42 George Bush, *Future Builders: The Story of Michigan's Consumer Power Company* (New York: McGraw Hill, 1973), p. 42.

43 Passer, *The Electrical Manufacturers*, p. 197.

44 King, *A History of the Government of Denver*, p. 62.

45 Suzanne Schulze, compiler, *A Century of the Colorado Census* (Greeley, Colorado: University of Northern Colorado, 1976), revised edition 1977 with Robert Markham, p. 1960-7.

46 Carl Ubbelohde, Maxine Benson, and Duane A. Smith, *A Colorado History: Revised Centennial Edition* (Boulder, Colorado: Pruett Publishing Company, 1976), pp. 120-26.

47 Marshall Sprague, *Colorado: A Bicentennial History* (New York: W.W. Norton & Company, Inc., 1976), pp. 74-75.

48 Athearn, *The Coloradans*, pp. 93-95.

49 King, *A History of the Government of Denver*, p. 152.

50 *Denver Tribune*, 28 December 1872,, p. 4.

51 *Rocky Mountain News*, 6 September 1877, p. 4.

52 Clyde L. King, *The Regulation of Municipal Utilities* (New York: D. Appleton and Company, 1912), p. 78.

53 Contract between the Denver Gas Company and the City of Denver, Denver. *Charters and Ordinances of the City of Denver, pp. 207-210., (Colorado State Archives, Denver, Colorado)*and Varnum and Adams, *Franchises and Special Privileges*, p. 52.

54 Denver. City Council Proceedings, 7 April 1875. (Colorado State Archives, Denver, Colorado).

55 Letter from the Committee on Gas and Gas Lamps to the Honorable Mayor and City Council of the City of Denver 4 October 1875 (State Archives)

56 *Rocky Mountain News*, 20 December 1878, p. 4.

57 *Rocky Mountain News*, 9 January 1879, p. 4. Other companies were A. H. Watkins of Boston to supply naptha gas for $32.50 per post per year and Cincinnati Globe Gas Light Company to provide a gasoline light equal to any gas for $32 per post per year.

58 King, *A History of the Government of Denver*, p. 152.

59 Ibid., p. 153.

60 Paul W. MacAvoy, ed., *The Crisis of the Regulatory Commission, an Introduction to a Current Issue* (New York: W.W. Norton & Co. Inc., 1970), p. 3.

61 Martin T. Farris and Roy J. Sampson, *Public Utilities: Regulation, Management and Ownership* (Prospect Heights, IL: Waveland Press, Inc., 1973), p. 14.

Authors Martin T. Farris and Roy J. Sampson have divided utility development into five stages: promotional, sompetitive, monopolistic, regional, and cooperation.

62 King, *A History of the Government of Denver*, pp. 153-54 and Farris and Sampson, *Public Utilities*, pp. 13 and 14.

63 Ibid.

64 Thomas C. Cochran, *American Business in the Twentieth Century* (Cambridge, MA: Harvard University Press, 1972), p. 17.

65 "A Brief History of Public Service Company," p. 13.

66 King, *A History of the Government of Denver*, p. 63 and 152.

67 Writers Program, Colorado, "Public Utilities in Denver" part III. "Denver's Gas and Electricity," (Colorado Historical Society, Denver, Colorado), pp. 20-21.

CHAPTER 2

WHITE MAGIC--THE NEW TECHNOLOGY OF ELECTRICITY

In the 1880s Denver Gas Company not only faced competition within its own industry but from a much more threatening rival--the new technology of electricity. The citizens of Colorado were entranced with Edison's invention of the incandescent electric light. Some people feared the "white magic" but many keenly anticipated installing the novel lighting system. Electricity's uses, however, were not limited to lighting. Ingenious scientists developed the electric motor to power all sorts of machinery. Electricity made the world more modern, created new industrial wealth, new convenience, new enjoyment, and a new tempo of life.[1]

The development of electricity has had a long and interesting history. The science of electricity started in the Middle Ages when curiosity about the magnetic compass led to the discovery of electromagnetism. Englishman William Gilbert went beyond the theory of magnetism to describe the force between two objects charged by friction. He was the first to distinguish magnetism from electricity. Gilbert's startling experiments drew attention from the scientific community, and research on the new force, which Gilbert termed electricity, was quickly expanded.[2]

Interest in electrostatic effects gradually increased during the next two centuries. In 1733 Charles Francois de Cisternay Dufay, a gardener for French King Louis XV, described different forces of electricity which American scientist and statesman, Benjamin Franklin, later labeled with "+" and "-" signs. Franklin showed that lightning and electricity are identical. Believing that water and metals attracted lightning, he attached a key to his kite string in 1752. As the kite soared to the dark thunderclouds overhead the metal drew electricity from the sky. Franklin was overjoyed with the success of his experiment although he risked death from a lightning strike proving his theory. His continued investigations produced practical devices, such as the lightning rod.[3]

Scientists quickly put electricity to use. Samuel F. B. Morse began tinkering with electricity to transmit sound. In 1837 he petitioned Congress to support his electric telegraph, but the government did not approve money for his project until 1843. With those funds Morse built his first line and the telegraph was an immediate success. For thirty-five years cities depended on it for communication. Businesses eagerly installed the new device, sometimes employing their own operators. The telegraph made police and fire protection more responsive resulting in safer cities. The military also depended on the telegraph to wire orders and messages, hastening maneuvers and knowledge of the enemy.[4]

People began to consider rapid communication a necessity rather than a luxury. However, the telephone rather than the telegraph ultimately became the primary mode of electrical communication. By 1837 it was known that vibrations could be translated into electrical impulses,[5] although it was not until Alexander Bell patented the telephone in 1876 that the sound of a voice was transmitted over electric wires on a significant scale. More than an inventor, Bell was an entrepreneur who realized the potential of allowing people to talk to each other at a distance. After the first commercial switchboard was installed in 1878 people clamored for telephones. Local service expanded to include long distance in 1881.[6] Once again electrical energy technology changed the style of people's lives. It speeded communication, saved lives, bonded friendships, and made sweeping changes in the methods of doing business.

The next important stage in electrical development was lighting. Sir Humphrey Davy, an English scientist, had produced light in 1808 by forming an arc with current passing between two slender pieces of charcoal. As a power sources he used an expensive 2000-cell voltaic battery which made arc lighting too costly for general consumption. In 1870 the dynamo was improved to provide a reasonable method of power supply. The dynamo, which is also called an electric generator, converted mechanical energy that was produced by a steam or water turbine, or internal-combustion engine, into electrical energy. The dynamo culminated forty years of continued research to develop a practical energy source.[7]

Arc lighting's first market was city streets. Improvement of the arc light and the dynamo constituted a system that rivaled gas lighting by the 1880s. To compete with gas arc lighting had to be inexpensive, reliable, and efficient. Charles F. Brush was the man chiefly responsible for meeting these challenges. Working in Michigan in 1879, he devised large generators that produced reliable, constant current that was suitable for lighting. His generator powered sixteen lights, a wonder at the time. He also devised an arc light that burned for eight hours before the charcoal filaments had to be replaced. Although it was significant progress, having to replace the carbons so frequently was expensive and inefficient. With determined research, Brush and other engineers improved the life span of the arc light and invented generators with a capacity of more than sixteen lights.

By 1885 arc lights provided lighting in many cities. Advances continued in the 1890s. The cost of the lights were reduced, so that all-night lighting became common in many large cities between 1895 and 1902. The arc light remained more appropriate for street than for home lighting because of its intense brightness.[8]

The enthusiasm with which people greeted each new form of lighting proved that they were eager to use an efficient illuminant. The potential home market was there, but an inventive entrepreneur was needed to produce a better light. That man was brilliant Thomas Alva Edison. Invention came easily and early for Edison. Although he dropped out of school at the age of seven he had the ability to assimilate large amounts of knowledge simply through observation of his surroundings.

Edison's experiments began at an early age, when as a small child he went into his family's barn and set it on fire just to see what the flames would do. His father was furious, but Edison learned from the experiment as he did each one thereafter. By the time he was twenty, his experiments resulted in a long list of patents.

As a young man he manufactured various electrical devices, until by 1876 he had acquired enough money to devote all his time to inventing.[9] After seeing the exhibit of dynamos and arc lights at the Philadelphia Centennial Exposition, Edison boasted that he would invent a light that was safer and less expensive than either the electric arc light or gas for home use. He decided that there were bigger rewards in incandescent lighting than in other fields of electrical development. Edison's motives were both economic and pursuit of excellence. His goal revealed a man who invented not only for pure scientific results and for the betterment of mankind, but also for commercial success. He relished the challenge of being the first to devise a low-cost practical lighting system.[10] Edison was thirty in 1877 when he began experimenting with incandescent lighting.

As he experimented, Edison kept in mind his objective of competing with gas. He designed an incandescent light to give off sixteen-candle power as gas jets did at that time. He also planned a central supply of electricity in order to avoid the necessity of batteries in each home. This led to a central station system designed like a central gashouse with a distribution system of pipes running to homes and businesses. Finally, as with gas, electricity was distributed in such a manner that individual lights could be independently controlled.[11]

Edison invented a high-resistance filament to reduce the cost of copper conductors, as well as a highly efficient dynamo that reduced energy lost as heat. To show consumers how much electricity they consumed, Edison fashioned a meter which made the new technology less suspicious to the consumer, and allowed them to control how much electricity they used. Edison believed that from watching the meter, businesses and households would economize and lessen the need for capital investment in generating and transmission equipment.[12] After he invented the various components, Edison first demonstrated his incandescent light in October 1879.

Other inventors were also working with the exciting new field of electricity. Two major contributors were Elihu Thomson and George Westinghouse. Elihu Thomson moved to Philadelphia from Manchester, England in 1858 at the age of five years. After finishing school he became a high school chemistry teacher with a strong interest in electricity. He and a colleague, Edwin J. Houston, began working together conducting electrical experiments in 1875. Three years later Thomson traveled to Paris, and while waiting at a Paris railroad station he noticed an arc lighting system that was operated on a commercial basis. This system gave him the incentive to plan his own arc-lighting system when he returned to the United States.[13]

Thomson produced a better system than that of Charles Brush by designing a regulator that kept the current of the dynamo constant. Thomson's generator also consumed less energy. Furthermore, he kept improving his product while Charles Brush's interest turned to other things. Thomson and Houston designed a system that was promising enough to interest a group of wealthy Eastern businessmen. The capitalists agreed to fund the two scientists' efforts to form a large, profitable business. They organized the American Electric Company on 16 July 1880. Three years later, this became the Thomson-Houston Electric Company. Thomson-Houston marketed its arc lighting system on the strength of technical excellence, and by 1897 the company had become a dominant force in the lighting business.[14]

George Westinghouse was another inventor who went on to become a leader in the electrical manufacturing business. He began experimenting with machinery while working for his father in the family machine shop in Schenectady, New York. In 1867, at the age of twenty-one, Westinghouse invented a device to put derailed trains back on the track. Two years later he developed his well-known air brake which made railroads considerably safer. He followed that invention with technical contributions for handling and transporting gas over long distances.[15]

Westinghouse became a strong advocate of the alternating current system of transmitting electricity, which was generally scoffed at by scientists. The system most used was direct current in which the electrons of the current move in one direction along a wire. With alternating current the direction through the wires changed (for example, 120 times every second for house current). The voltage, or force of electricity, could be increased or decreased, unlike direct current, by putting it through a transformer. Alternating current could also be sent long distances at high voltages and then reduced near the place of consumption.

In January 1886, Westinghouse established the Westinghouse Electric Company, which manufactured the first commercial alternating current (AC) system to supply electricity of incandescent lighting. AC was superior to Edison's direct current because it required less copper, had a stronger, and more efficient generating system, and was more flexible in producing different voltages for transmission and consumption.[16] A well-publicized battle started between Edison's direct current electrical system and Westinghouse's alternating current.[17] Both General Electric, established in 1892 from the merging of the Edison Electric Company with the Thomson-Houston Company, and Westinghouse dominated the electrical lighting and equipment business for many years.[18]

In addition to electricity for communication and lighting, converting electrical energy into mechanical energy with an electric motor, opened boundless opportunities as a power source and a substitute for human labor. Many profitable commercial applications evolved with the development of the electric motor. Electric motors eventually raised America's industrial efficiency nearly fifty percent.[19]

Cities expanded upward with electric elevators and outward with electric streetcars. The combined effect of steam engines and electric motors on individual life styles and mobility was significant and changed the face of cities. By the turn of the century there would be more electric cars on an urban street than horse-drawn buggies.[20]

The proliferation of electric motors also changed businesses and homes. Steam could only be produced by big engines in large plants, but electricity from central generators could run small electric motors hundreds of miles away. Factories no longer had to be large or close to the source of power generation.[21] In the home electricity ran vacuum cleaners, washers and sewing machines, freeing the housewife from long days of housework. Electricity liberated her physically, so that she had time to work for social freedom. The development of power technology began to make a class difference between those who had electricity and those who did not. It also built a socio-economic chasm between the industrial countries and underdeveloped nations. On a global basis innovative energy development continued to be woven into the pattern of the world's social development.

Denver was one of the first cities in the world to adopt electric lighting.[22] Its development was similar to that of gas with many companies being formed to seize the opportunity of making money with a new technology. There was a difference between the development of gas and electricity because Denver did not grant an exclusive franchise during the beginning stages of electrical development as it had with gas. City council passed a resolution welcoming all bids to furnish the city with electric lighting. Council's only restriction was that the companies could not obstruct the city rights-of-way.[23] The city had still not learned how to allow the treasury to profit from utilities. The city was so eager to have electricity that it imposed few restrictions. As with gas, the hope was that competition would keep prices down and provide residents with good service.

Soon after Thomas A. Edison tested his incandescent lighting system businessmen established the Colorado Edison Electric Light Company, in March 1880, to supply the people of Denver with electric lighting. The company submitted a proposal to the Denver city council requesting the right to use city thoroughfares.[24] The company realized that people might be reluctant to switch from gas to an unfamiliar technology. Therefore, in order to entice people to learn about electricity, company backers set up a fancy exhibition plant at 390 Curtis Street in the middle of the business district. Notice was spread around town that an electric show would take place the evening of 21 April 1880. A curious crowd gathered, watching appreciatively as the twinkling light appeared in a small glass globe.[25] Some onlookers were so impressed that they wanted to sign up for electric service immediately.

Proponents of electricity such as William Byers of the *Rocky Mountain News*, advocated installing electric street lights instead of gas, because the early generating techniques did not produce a steady flow of gas and the lights flickered.[26] The city lighting contract did not expire until 1885, however, and the Denver Gas Company was ready to fight to retain its lucrative business. The gas company defended its product claiming that electricity was impractical and no more than a faddish toy that needed to be improved.

Because of the competition between gas and electricity, the Denver city council asked its gas committee to study the various proposals. The *News* encouraged the members not to be caught in a morass of old thinking when considering adopting the new technology. The committee members were enthusiastic about electricity after their research, and reminded reluctant members of the council that there was once a debate about the merits of whale oil compared to manufactured gas.[27]

On 24 January 1881, the night that the gas committee was to report to city council, a large and noisy crowd had gathered to listen to the proceedings. During the meeting Colonel James Archer, president of the gas company, became quite vocal. He announced that he had just been on an East Coast trip to investigate the use of electricity. Although he did not argue against the new technology itself, he did insist that Edison was continuing his research on incandescent lighting and further improvements would make the Colorado Edison Light Company's present proposal before city council obsolete in short order. Archer recommended that the City stay with gas until Edison's most current work was complete.

The shoulder-to-shoulder crowd murmured to each other as the red-faced Archer continued arguing against replacing gas. He was so loud that Alderman Davis asked that the gas man be arrested. When the chief of police jumped to his feet to carry out the request Archer quickly calmed down.[28] Despite Archer's plea the city council adopted the resolution of 2 February 1881 which permitted any company to receive a franchise for supplying electricity to business establishments and residents in the city, as long as the public thoroughfares were not obstructed,[29]

The Denver *Tribune* was enthusiastic about electricity, and reported that some councilmen were supporting gas rather than electricity only through loyalty to individual men rather than practicality.

> The Gas Company gave Denver a valuable and metropolitan improvement at a time when the future of the city was in doubt. . . The electric light is an invention modern and brilliant and the people of the West are always among the first to encourage and promote scientific and natural advance. 30

After clearing the way for any electric company to obtain a franchise city council prepared to take another vote. At the 9 February 1881 meeting councilmen were ready to vote on the electric committee's proposal favoring electricity over gas to light city streets. Six aldermen voted yes and six voted no and it was up to the mayor to break the tie. James Archer, head of the gas company, sat by with a threatening demeanor. The mayor allegedly "looked the great gas mogul in the eye, and then calmly and with a prayer on his lips voted against electricity, . . ."[31]

It was not the first or the last time that a utility man would intimidate a politician. With that tie-breaking vote the contract to light the streets remained with the Denver Gas Company until the new contract ran out in 1885.

In February, 1881 a rival to the Edison company announced its intentions to build an electric plant to sell to the city arc lighting generated by Brush equipment. Entrepreneurs established a company on 21 February 1881.[32] To persuade people that arc lighting was superior the Colorado Electric Company advertised successful projects of Brush electric lighting in the United States and Canada.[33] The company founders arranged for a demonstration on 29 March 1881 to further educate Denverites. Company representatives attached a Brush light to the top of a church tower at Fourteenth and Lawrence streets. The 2000-candle power lamp brightened the area for what seemed like miles. In the glow of the electric light Professor Sidney Short from the University of Denver lectured, explaining the merits of the Brush system.[34]

Colorado Electric Company convinced the Denver City Council that its system was best. Even though gas was officially the lighting device for Denver streets, the company was allowed to build towers with arc lights in various sections of the city.[35] The eight 150-foot to 210-foot towers each supported six 3000-candlepower arc lights. During their years of use utility company employees maintained these lights by going up the towers in a small cage hooked on a cable. This burdensome method of changing lights took an inordinate amount of time, and eventually the towers were removed and poles with electric globes were placed on each street corner.[36]

The entrepreneurs who established the Colorado Electric Company were men willing to invest in an untried technology, with the usual mix of motives of making the city more prosperous and earning a profit for themselves. Initial investors in the Colorado Electric Company were William G. Fisher (pioneer department store owner), Walter S. Cheesman, Frederick O. Vaille (organizer of Denver's first telephone exchange; fourth in the United States), James Duff (manager for English capital in the Windsor Hotel and other large enterprises), Edward W. Rollins (member of a large investment firm), Nathaniel M. Tabor (son of H.A.W. Tabor--who had made a fortune in mining), Thomas G. Johnston, and Charles C. Ruthrauff.[37] The company had a capital stock of $200,000 divided into $100 shares and fully subscribed.

Colorado Electric Company built a central station located at 21st and Wewatta Streets. The company intended to transmit electricity for electric lights and power, and would also lease electric apparatus. The plant generated electricity with two 35-horsepower Brush-Swan direct-current dynamos driven by a 250-horsepower Wright steam engine. The fly wheel weighed nine tons and measured seventeen feet in diameter. "Old Sally," as the engine was called, provided electricity directly to businesses and to several substations.[38]

After the plant was built, Colorado Electric Company advertised an extravagant demonstration of its arc lighting to take place at Denver's train station. After several postponements the event which people were eagerly awaiting finally happened on a hot night in July, 1881. A crowd of between 8,000 and 10,000 onlookers gathered at Union station in the dark to see the "light of the future." With a flick of a switch the depot became brilliantly lighted, and the throng of people expressed delight and approval.[39]

The Brush Company had sent William J. Barker to Denver to install and operate their machinery.[40] Barker was born in London on 21 December 1855. His father, superintendent of a shipdock, died in 1867 and his mother five years later. Young Barker and a companion joined a ship's crew to sail to America, earning their way working as cabin boys. When the ship's engineer became ill Barker took his place. After the two young men arrived in the United States they rode a freight train to Cleveland where they picked apples to make their living. While in Cleveland, Barker studied electrical engineering in order to get a better job. His hard work paid off when he was hired as a engineer in a powder mill, and his experience there led to a job with the Brush Electric Company.[41]

After Barker proved that he was a capable employee, Brush sent him to set up a new plant in Denver. There Barker installed the first generator for electric lighting in the West and the third in the nation. Although he had planned to return to Cleveland, the young engineer liked the bustling town of Denver so much that he remained, becoming the Colorado Electric Company's chief engineer, and later its superintendent. His plant, which lighted the relatively small town of 35,000 people, was considered one of the finest in the country.[42]

He stayed with the company as it changed in 1889 to the Denver Consolidated Electric Company, then the Denver Gas and Electric Company in 1899 and through the merger of this company with the Lacombe Electric Company in 1906. Barker was appointed vice president and general manager when Frank Frueauff became president of the Denver Gas and Electric Company in 1907. After 1908 he became resident head of the company while Frueauff worked in New York. Barker gained a national reputation as "one of the most progressive minds in the industrial worlds."[43] He and another town promoter, Mayor Robert W. Speer, believed in the promotional benefits of street lighting, and the two worked well together.

As part of his responsibilities with the Denver enterprise, Barker was president of other utilities such as the Summit County Power Company which supplied part of western and northern Colorado with power. He was also vice president of the Western Light and Power Company which furnished another section of northern Colorado with energy. His managerial responsibilities in the power industry stretched to Cheyenne, Wyoming as well as various parts of Colorado. In Denver, Barker was active in community organizations such as the Denver Chamber of Commerce and Colorado Manufacturer's Association. He was also a leader in the movement toward cooperation between public utility corporations and the general public.[44]

The economic climate of the community served by the Denver Gas Company was improving in the 1870s and 1880s. Colorado's population had increased to 194,327 at the end of the 1870s[45] and in the 1880s the development of railroads, the pacification of the Indians and several mineral discoveries in the San Juan Mountains brought settlers to the western slope of the state.[46] Business enterprises were multiplying as rapidly as the population.

Until the gas contract for lighting city streets expired in 1885 electricity was used mostly for demonstration purposes. Few homes and businesses had elected to install the modern technology. Daniels and Fisher department store was one of the trendsetters. With its own storage batteries serviced by the electric company, it was the first Denver business to utilize the new arc lighting system. There were also a few wealthy Denver residents who wanted to impress guests with electric lighting for special occasions. The hosts asked the company to set up a temporary lighting system on the day of their party. The electric company cooperated knowing that a beautifully lighted home would encourage others to purchase service. The morning after a festive soiree the company retrieved the apparatus and transported it back to the plant.[47]

Denver was won over to electric lighting for several reasons. Electricity was cheaper than gas, it lighted more completely, eliminating the dark areas which existed between the areas each gas lamp post covered, and electric lights did not have to be turned on one at a time.[48] The lighting of Denver streets with electricity marked the close of a pioneer era, one portrayed by lamp lighters who walked down the city streets at dusk pushing a wheelbarrow and ladder. They rested their short ladder on each iron lamp post, climbed up, and struck a match to the hissing gas. Electricity brought an end to this time-consuming but colorful tradition.[49]

In late summer 1881 Colorado Electric Company strung electric wires throughout the cities. Rather than erecting their own poles, crews attached the wires to telephone company poles. It was faster and required fewer poles, but double stringing often resulted in complaints from telephone customers who were annoyed by the static caused when wires rubbed together.[50] Denver was a maze of wires and poles for decades until utilities put many of the main lines underground.

When electricity replaced gas for lighting streets many entrepreneurs recognized that there were also vast untapped residential and commercial markets.

The prospect of making a fortune in the electric business inspired other companies to enter the field and compete with the Colorado Electric Company. The Denver Electric Illuminating Company was incorporated in 1886; the Denver Light Heat and Power Company was established in 1893; the Montclair Light Company was founded in 1890; and the Denver Highlands Electric Company, and the South Denver Electric Light and Power Company both were incorporated in 1891. The intense competition meant that profits were almost impossible because of the cut-rate pricing needed to win customers. As a result, the city government encouraged companies to consolidate. The Colorado Electric Company merged in 1889 with the Denver Light Heat and Power Company under the new name of the Denver Consolidated Electric Company, with $1,000,000 in capital.[51]

Consolidation was further stimulated by the Panic of 1893 which hurt the finances of small electric and gas companies in and around Denver, making them vulnerable for takeover.[52] The 1893 depression also brought labor and management disputes, but these problems were largely overshadowed in Colorado by the repeal of the Sherman Silver Purchase Act when the government demonetized silver, thereby eliminating a substantial market for Colorado's silver. The price of silver dropped and the economy of the state suffered tremendously. The nineties were uneasy years for Colorado.

By 1895 Denver Consolidated Electric Company had accumulated the stocks, bonds and equipment of the Denver Electric Light and Power Company and the Western Electric Construction Company. With those mergers all electric operations for Denver and close surroundings were under one enterprise. It also consolidated the four major systems of electrical production. Before the 1895 consolidation, branches of Thomson-Houston, Brush, Westinghouse and Edison were all competing for a share in the electrical business in Denver. When Denver Consolidated Electric Company became the dominant electric company it meant a temporary end to price cutting of Denver's electrical service.[53]

Westerners were quick to adapt electricity to their way of life. Coloradan Irving Hale, who was active in the late nineteenth century development of the state's electricity, said that Colorado had more money invested in electrical plants *per capita* than any other state in the nation.[54] Hale believed Denver's system of electric streetcars was one of the most complete nationwide. The tramway system had been converted to electricity by 1893. With electricity, transportation was able to expand in the city to serve more people, but the city also spread out along the streetcar tracks. Telephone service and electric lights were, by 1900, available to most Colorado cities with populations greater than 3,000 people. Colorado also put electricity to good use in mining, agriculture, quarrying, and manufacture.[55]

In the 1890s electricity made a marked difference in Colorado mining operations. For a decade the electric companies had neglected the potential of using electricity in mining, because they were preoccupied with developing other markets. Most miners cast a skeptical eye at trying a new technology that seemed more like magic than a practical method.[56]

One man was the exception. He was an entrepreneur from Telluride who challenged the Westinghouse Electric Company to come up with electrical applications for mining and by doing so, made history in Colorado. Lucien Lucius Nunn was born in rural Ohio and educated at Harvard University. When he was twenty, he decided to seek his fortune in Leadville, Colorado, not in mining, but in the restaurant business.[57] He worked unsuccessfully for some time before deciding to give up in Colorado and move to the warmer climate of Arizona. He packed his belongings in a small bag and headed southwest, but when he arrived in the Colorado town of Durango, he was afraid to continue his journey because of Indian unrest. Nunn decided to settle in Durango and again tried to earn money in a restaurant, but for the second time, was a failure. At that point he had so little money that he had to proceed to a new town on foot.

In his second attempt to move he got as far as Telluride in the mountains of Colorado, a town where he would make his fortune. He began by working at several new occupations--as a cabinet maker, a builder, and a miner--and at each he was a success. After accumulating a comfortable amount of capital, he established the Illim Gold Mining Company, and in the meantime, he added two more jobs to his resume, that of banker and lawyer. In fact, in 1888, he owned the county's only bank.[58]

Nunn was a stockholder in the Gold King Mine located in the high mountains south of Telluride. The mine was going broke because there was no more timber to burn, and coal was prohibitively expensive to run mining equipment. Nunn decided to save the mine by replacing the operation with electricity. Miners in the area were at least acquainted with the principle of electricity, but the direct current system had proved unsuccessful since it lost power over longer distances and it was expensive. L L. Nunn, had heard that George Westinghouse was experimenting with a type of electricity called alternating current. Nunn was never one to shy away from trying something new, especially if it might save his investment.

With the strength of character of his role model, Napolean Bonaparte, L. L. Nunn, the five-foot one inch Coloradan, took $100,000 worth of gold pieces east to meet with the Westinghouse board of directors. His goal was to convince them to spend money building a power plant for his Gold King Mine. Nunn was persuasive. Within a few weeks Westinghouse was designing equipment, at a cost to the company of fifteen million dollars, and shipping it to Ames, Colorado, twelve miles south of Telluride. The Westinghouse engineers left their laboratories to put their machines together in the beautiful alpine community. Part of the package offered by Nunn was a laboratory in the mountains where large companies like Westinghouse could test lightning arresters, tranformers, wire and insulators.[59]

The project was not only pioneering but daring work. Often by himself, Nunn had to chop down trees for poles on which to string second-hand wire.

He had to scrape together funds to build the other facets of the project. He constructed a water-powered plant and the world's first known high tension, long-distance electric power transmission line. When the project was finished the water wheel generated a 3,000-volt current that was transmitted for three miles. It was the first time electricity was consumed outside a relatively close radius of the point of its generation.[60]

Nunn eventually extended the line to seventeen miles. At some points workers strung the wire on mountains 13,000 feet high. Because of the steepness of the mountains some of the wire was at a 45 degree angle, and some pole holes were literally drilled into solid rock. During the summer the wires attracted lightning, which sometimes struck as many as one hundred times an hour. Winter snowfalls were so deep that snow occasionally reached the top of the poles.[61]

Thanks to Nunn and Westinghouse, on 20 June 1891 the alternating current electricity system for mining began, reducing the power bill for the Gold King mine from $2,500 a month to $500.[62] Some say that Nunn and the Ames plant saved Colorado mining. All the readily accessible gold had been taken out of the mountain before 1890, and the new electrical machinery allowed the miners to get to the less accessible ore. Electric mining machinery proved reliable and helped miners eke out a slim profit; something they were unable to do with traditional production methods.[63]

Nunn had used water to produce electrical power, a natural resource abundant in the mountains of Colorado. To produce hydroelectric power, water from a stream or reservoir was captured by waterwheels and used to turn turbines connected to generators. The higher the fall, the more electricity generated from a given volume of water.[64]

Hydroelectric generation had its drawbacks. There were a limited number of sites that would provide uninterrupted water flow. In addition, engineering considerations of hydroelectric power such as variation of the stream flow, and feasibility of constructing dams and reservoirs, made the cost and efficiency of hydroelectrics more difficult to determine than steam power. Nevertheless, there were many advantages to hydropower. Water was a renewable resource, even though limited in the arid West. A hydroelectric plant was economical, because it required no fuel or cooling system. The simplicity of the system required little maintenance and meant a long life span of the equipment.[65] Hydroelectric plants required less capital investment up front and were not as damaging to the streams as other power plants.[66] The Denver *Times* in 1898 estimated that one quarter of the electric power in Colorado was derived from water.[67]

Mining was not the only industry in Colorado to profit from the use of electricity. Pumping water with electricity enabled farmers to cultivate agricultural land located above streams. Grand Junction was a good example of creative use of electricity in the 1890s. The Colorado River, then called the Grand, came out of a canyon east of the town. Ditches carried water to only a small part of the available agricultural land. Behind the mouth of the canyon there was excellent land but no practical way to dig ditches through the canyon to get the water. Building an electric pumping station to bring water up to a level where canals could be built, solved the problem. Steam power would have been prohibitively costly but electricity generated by nearby water turbines was economical.[71]

Electricity benefited the eastern part of the state as well. Water was often absorbed through the sandy soil making it difficult to use for irrigation. Engineers proposed using electrical pumping stations to force water through hoses to spray on large amounts of land. Each electric pumping station could cover approximately forty acres of land for cultivation.[69]

In addition to its agricultural functions electricity was used in the Colorado stone quarrying industry in the nineteenth century. Electricity supplied power for many aspects of the business. Electric percussion drills engraved and divided blocks, while electric hoists, derricks, and cranes conveniently handled the enormous rocks. Colorado's excellent building stone was used in the state and in other regions adding to the diversity of the state's economic base.[70]

Colorado also found electricity helpful in its manufacturing enterprises during the 1890s. Electric current, supplied by central stations, ran electric motors for individual tools or machines. With a central supply of electricity, manufacturing plants did not have to be large, and the smaller units could be located close to various markets.[71]

Colorado personified the nation in its poor economic condition during the 1890s. Electricity aided agriculture, rescued mining, and made other industries more viable. With the help of electricity Colorado's economic decline was not as severe as it might have been.

On 17 April 1894 the Denver City Council awarded the city's street lighting contract to Denver Consolidated Electric Company. The company agreed to light city streets for $10 a month per light pole, using incandescent lights in some areas and arc in others. (Arc lighting and incandescent lighting were developed simultaneously, leapfrogging each other in popularity as new technology developed to improve each system.) Previously, the right to inspect company operations had been restricted, but the new contract stipulated that city representatives could inspect all operations and facilities of the company pertaining to the street light. The portion of the business devoted to private customers remained private. In 1895 the one-year contract was renewed without a time limit. Denver paid $200,000 a year for its street lighting for many years.[72]

In Colorado, electric ecompanies had been consolidated in 1889 and gas companies in 1891. The time would soon come to combine the two technologies. Utilities had served the Denver community for almost thirty years. They had been built through the vision of men who had the courage and daring to engage in untried ventures, men who were true pioneers working with primitive technology. Without their capital and innovation, the extraordinary development of Colorado's commerce, mining, agriculture and transportation would not have been possible.

Between 1875 and 1900 America was ripe for the further development of manufacturing enterprises for several reasons. People migrated to cities providing a large market for a variety of goods. The national population grew enormously, supplying the expanding businesses with both labor and capital. Businesses grew, unhindered by the restraints of effective labor unions, and were smiled on by the laissez-faire government which was receptive to industry, without imposing few regulations. Business dealings were further enhanced by improved communication systems. The United States was becoming an industrial society with electricity at its base. Entrepreneurs in every field were eager to capitalize on industrialization and the continually increasing standard of living.[73]

NOTES CHAPTER 2

1 Matthew Josephson, *Edison* (New York: McGraw-Hill Book Co., Inc., 1959), p. 266.

2 Percy Dunsheath, *A History of Electrical Power Engineering* (Cambridge, MA: The MIT Press, 1962), p. 25.

3 Thomas J. Fleming, *The Man Who Dared the Ligtning, A New Look at Benjamin Franklin* (New York: William Morrow and Co., Inc., 1971), pp. 3-11.

4 Harold I. Sharlin, *The Making of the Electrical Age: from the Telegraph to Automation* (London, New York: Abelard Schuman, 1964, c. 1963) pp. 1135.

5 Ibid., p. 37

6 John Brooks, *Telephone the First Hundred Years* (New York: Harper and Row Publishers, pp. 47, 53 and 89.)

7 Harold C. Passer, *The Electrical Manufacturers 1875 1900, A Study in Competition, Entrepreneurship, Technical Change, and Economic Growth* (New York: Arno Press, New York *Times* comapny, 1972), pp. 712 and Eliot Jones and Truman C. Bigham, *Principles of Pubglic Utilities* (New York: The MacMillan Company, 1931), pp. 3132.

8 Passer, *The Electrical Manufacturers,* pp. 1721 and pp. 6364 and Dunsheath, *A History of Electrical Power Engineering,* p. 125.

9 Josephson, *Edison* (New York: McGraw Hill Book Co., Inc., 1959), p. 156.

10 Ibid., p. 177.

11 Ibid., p. 179.

12 Passer, *The Electrical Manufacturers,* p. 185.

13 Ibid, pp. 2527 and p. 57.

[14] Ibid., pp. 19230.

[15] Ibid., p. 138 and p. 164.

[16] Ibid., p. 170.

[17] Thomas C. Cochran, *American Business in the Twenthieth Century* (Cambridge, MA: Harvard University Press, 1972), p. 21.

[18] Passer, *The Electrical Manufacturers*, p. 177.

[19] Josephson, *Edison*, p. 432.

[20] Ibid.

[21] Sharlin, *The Making of the Electrical Age*, p. 7.

[22] "Brief History of Public Service Company of Colorado," 31 December 1931. A manuscript found in the records of Public Service Company of Colorado., p. 1.

[23] *Rocky Mountain News* 4 February 1881, p. 8.

[24] *Clyde L. King, The History of the Governhment of Denver with Special Reference to Its Relations with Public Service* (Denver: The Fisher Book Co., 1911), p. 154.

[25] "Brief History of Public Service Company," p. 5.

[26] *Rocky Mountain News*, 4 February 1881, p. 8, and Citizens Historical Association of Indianapolis, Manuscript No. 2B979 DS #16 F149.

[27] *Rocky Mountain News*, 25 January 1881, p. 8.

[28] Ibid.

[29] *Rocky Mountain News*, 4 February 1881, p. 2.

[30] Denver *Tribune*, 11 February 1881, p. 1.

[31] *Rocky Mountain News*, 10 February 1881, p. 8.

32
"Brief History of Public Service Company," p. 1.

33
Rocky Mountain News, 4 February 1881, p. 8.

34
Rocky Mountain News 30 March 1881, p. 6.

35
Writers Program, "Public Utiities in Denver," p. 21 and "Brief History of Public Service Company," p. 5.

36
Public Service Company of Colorado: A Hundred Years of Progress (Denver: Public Service Company of Colorado, 1969), p. 4.

37
Public Service Minute Book 35141, Public Service Company of Colorado, Denver, Colorado.

38
Public Service Company of Colorado, a Hundred Years of Progress, p. 4.

39
Rocky Mountain News, 17 July 1881, p. 8.

40
William J. Barker, Compiled and Published by His Associates of Many Years in Denver Gas and Electric Light Company (Denver: 1922), pp. 1114.

41
Ibid., p. 14.

42
Denver *Times*, 15 February 1922, p. 1.

43
Wilbur Stone, *History of Colorado*, IV (Chicago: The S. J. Clarke Publishing Co., 1919), p. 24.

44
Denver *Post*, 15 February 1922, p. 1.

45
Susanne Schulze, compiler, *A Century of the Colorado Census* revised edition 1977 with Robert Markham, (Greeley, CO: University of Northern Colorado, 1976), pp., 196067.

46
Carl Ubbelohde, Maxine Benson, and Duane A. Smith, *A Colorado History: Revised Centennial Edition* (Boulder, CO: Pruett Publishing Company, 1976), p. 181.

47
Public Service Company, a Hundred Years of Service, p. 7.

48
"Brief History of the Public Service

Company," p. 7.

[49]Ibid.

[50] *Rocky Mountain News*, 2 October 1881, p. 3.

[51] "Brief History of Public Service Company," p. 5.

[52] Public Service Company Minute Book 35141, Public Service Company of Colorado Denver, Colorado.

[53] Public Service Company Minute Book 35117, Public Service Company of Colorado, Denver Colorado. Incorporaters were: Dennis Sullivan, David H. Moffatt, Joseph A. Thatcher, Henry M. Porter, William G. Fisher, James B. Grant, Edward Eddy, Henry P. Wolcott, Edward W. Rollins, William H. James, Michael E. Smith, Nathaniel M. Tabor, Charles H. Smith, Charles Boettcher, Finis P Ernest, W. H. H. Cranmer, Richard Pearce, and Frank C. Young.

[54] Irving Hale, "Influence of Electricity on Colorado's Progress, c. 1890, p. 153. Denver Public Library, Western History Room, Denver, Colorado.

[55] Ibid.

[56] Ibid.

[57] Denver *Post*, 5 October 1975, p. 29.

[58] San Luis Valley Historical Sociaty, XIV, no. 4, p. 3.

[59] Denver *Post*, 5 October 1975, p. 33.

[60] *Pueblo Chieftain*, 31 January 1960, p. 3. c. and P. N. Nunn, "Pioneer Work in High Tension Electric Power Transmission," *Cassier Magazine*, XXVII (January, 1905), 171.

[61] *Pueblo Chieftain*, 31 January 1960, p. 3.c.

[62] Denver *Post*, 5 October 1975, p. 33.

[63] *Rocky Mountain News*, 19 April 1959, p. 6c and Denver *Post*, 5 October 1975, p. 29 and p. 33.

[64] Edwin Vennard, *The Electric Power Business*, second

edition (New York: McGraw Hill Book Co., 1970), p. 278.

65 *Ibid., p. 283 and "Energy," The New Encyclopaedia Britannica*, 6, 623.

66 Louis J. Goodman, John Hawkins, and Ralph N. Loved, (eds.), *Small Hydroelectric Projects for Rural Development, Planning and Management* (New York: Pergamon Press, 1981), p. 7.

67 Denver *Times*, 31 December 1898, p. 1.

68 Hale, "Influence of Electricity," p. 158.

69 Ibid., p. 154.

70 Ibid., p. 158

71 Ibid., p. 159.

72 *Western Electrician*, XII (5 August 1893), 71.

73 Cochran, *American Business in the Twentieth Century*, p. 21.

PART II

THE DOHERTY YEARS

1899-1923

CHAPTER 3

HENRY L. DOHERTY

In the late nineteenth century many gas and electric companies were merging to reduce the fierce competition between the two technologies to provide lighting for city streets and homes. In Denver the gas and electric companies had consolidated among themselves in the 1890s, but the two technologies had not yet combined by the time Henry L. Doherty arrived in Denver from the Midwest in 1898. Sent by his employer, Emerson McMillin, a stockholder in the gas company, Doherty succeeded in combining Denver's gas and electric enterprises. Denver's utilities have had many strong leaders, but none was more colorful than Henry L. Doherty, the quintessential entrepreneur. Brash, bold, innovative, and successful, he helped the gas and electrical utilities come of age in Colorado and in the rest of the United States.

Doherty gained his business experience as a youth working for Emerson McMillin, the "light king of the country."[1] There is little wonder why the two men were compatible, since both were innovative geniuses who, despite their limited formal education, put great value on learning. Emerson McMillin quit school in 1854 at the age of ten to work in an steel plant where his father was manager. He worked at a variety of tasks quickly mastering all of them. Even as a boy he was creative and won a prize for designing a new type of pit which increased the heat output of charcoal by twenty-five percent.[2]

McMillin left home during the Civil War to serve in the army. As a soldier Emerson McMillin filled his knapsack with books to teach himself engineering in his spare time. It was the beginning of a long tradition of self education and, at the end of his life, he claimed to have devoted five hours a day over fifty years to such study. The first twenty-five years he focused on the sciences, and the second twenty-five on history, political and social sciences, foreign languages, music and art.

After leaving the army McMillin went to work for a gas company. His employers were impressed by his hard work, intelligence, and inventiveness. He devised a new purification method which improved the quality of manufactured gas and in 1889 gained great fame by consolidating four rival gas companies in St. Louis, Missouri. His success earned him the confidence of financial leaders who were willing to invest in his projects. As he worked for others he began accumulating the funds to buy his own gas plants. In 1891 he established a banking company in New York which specialized in the consolidation of gas companies. In ten years' time, by 1901, the Emerson McMillin Company had capital of over four million dollars.[3]

Henry L. Doherty began his utility career working for McMillin's Columbus (Ohio) Gas Company. Doherty was the son of a college-educated engineer and inventor who worked as the superintendent of the waterworks in Columbus, Ohio. When Frank Doherty died in 1882, he left his widow, Anna (McIlvaine), and four children with little money. Henry Doherty chose to quit school at the age of twelve to help support his family, and discovered that working as an office boy at the gas plant was much more exciting than going to school. Reading machinery catalogues at the company he learned everything he could about gas and electricity.[4] As he said, "I bought books, joined societies, dressed as well as I could afford, mingled when possible with engineers and scientific men."[5] He was determined to get ahead in a business he loved.

At the Columbus Gas Company Doherty worked in various departments, and in six years was named assistant manager. During that time he devised a way to lay pipes around obstacles without creating a trap for sediments. His invention and hard work brought him to the attention of Emerson McMillin, and in 1896 McMillin sent Doherty to the Madison (Wisconsin) Gas and Electric Company. Neither the electric nor gas departments in Madison was making money, and Doherty's job was to make them profitable.

When he arrived in Madison Doherty found that most housewives preferred to cook with coal rather than gas, and in his usual manner he tried to analyze the basic problem. After much questioning he determined that many housewives considered gas stoves inefficient and even dangerous. When he examined the different brands of stoves, Doherty agreed with them, and proceeded to rebuild the gas stove to make it more efficient and reliable.

Doherty trained salesmen to sell the new stoves and to sign up new gas customers for cooking and heating. He promised to pay the salesmen bonuses as an incentive to sell as much as they could. Servicemen were also trained to repair the stoves quickly. Doherty organized the Housewife League which arranged for cooks to go into neighborhoods to teach housewives to use gas to cook tasty and economical meals. He gave away prizes to encourage attendance and in a short time half the homes in Madison had gas stoves.[6]

Doherty also made valuable recommendations to the Madison electric department. His research revealed that only thirty percent of the electricity generated by the company was reaching the customer. Doherty instructed the engineers how to redesign the transformers, which moved the utilization factor up to eighty percent. He also promoted the use of electricity by setting up a campaign to install lighted signs to advertise businesses,[7] an idea which was well received by commercial enterprises. He had created different markets for gas and electricity to enable each to make a greater profit.

McMillin was so pleased with Doherty's success that he named him general manager and chief engineer of the entire utility empire. In that capacity Doherty established the American Light and Traction Company which was one of the earliest utility holding companies.[8] Doherty spent most of his time traveling to different cities to restructure the utilities owned by McMillin.

Doherty launched his career when America's economy was expanding. In the time following the Civil War new consumer demands were created while old ones were changed by economic growth, increasing population, territorial expansion, growing individual and national incomes.[9] In addition, the abundance of new technology being developed in a pro-business atmosphere provided many people the opportunity to become wealthy. There was an ideal climate for entrepreneurs. Doherty was typical: egocentric, untraditional, and ambitious. Some labeled these entrepreneurs robber barons, but whatever the label they helped shape the country in the nineteenth and early twentieth century.

Luck probably played some part in Doherty's success in the energy field but most was due to his ability to seize opportunities in an industry based on new technology and expanding demand. Rescuing Madison, Wisconsin's gas and electric company and then combining numerous utilities earned him a national reputation. Never content without challenges, he sought new adventures in the engineering, financial, and management spheres of business.

Doherty was always a believer in using professionals and hiring the best men available. In 1902 he spoke about the importance of carefully choosing employees:

> I think every gas company should be more careful in the selection of its employees. Many branches of work can employ men who have been specially trained for their engineering positions,

> and while this is hardly possible for the gas business, yet we can hire men who have the necessary education, and these we must teach for our particular business. We are running a business and not a school, and it seems to me highly important that where possible we should hire men who have been educated for general engineering work, and not men to whom we must teach the very rudiments of arithmetic in order to fit them for the problems which they must solve every day to improve our operating efficiency. . . . 10.

On the other hand he believed in training to improve employees' abilities. For example, in Denver he formed one of the nation's first industrial training schools where engineers who had just graduated from school could gain practical experience in the business.[11] Beginning in 1903 college graduates came to Denver from all parts of the nation to be trained. In the 1920s he established the Doherty Men's Training School with a two-year curriculum on engineering and utility subjects. After completing the course the graduates usually went to work in one of Doherty's organizations.[12]

Doherty represented the old school of entrepreneurial, almost dictatorial management. Yet, he sensed the need for well-trained, professional managers long before the new style became commonplace. The mindset of these new college-educated managers with a social conscience was never fully embraced by Doherty, but he knew that professional and scientific management was necessary in the increasingly larger utility companies. New executives were expected to be more professionally competent managers. They employed advisors to make decisions based on long-range planning.[13]

Doherty expected superior performance from employees. Work was the first priority in his life and he thought others should feel the same way. He often traveled by train with a male secretary and it was not unusual for him to awaken in the middle of the night to dictate a letter or even to make a telephone call to a startled employee.[14] Although he was reputed to give suggestions rather than issuing orders, his employees knew well that suggestions were expected to be heeded. He set high standards which employees were to follow.

He was a mentor to executive and subordinates alike. In fact, the "Doherty Spirit" was a term used to encourage everyone around him to seek success.[15] He made good use of his free time spending spare moments on projects of self improvement. Some of Doherty's spirit is captured in his "Doherty grams":

> Never give orders--give instructions.
>
> When a business enterprise starts out, it should always be with the idea of making a greater contribution to the public than the profit it may derive.

> Get a man to believe in you, get the public to think a certain way, and you have unloosed a dynamo of power.
>
> Given the will to learn, life and industry are better than all the colleges of Christendom.
>
> Make a game out of your work.
>
> Good humor is absolutely essential to good mental health.
>
> The greatest dividend in human life is happiness. 16

Doherty said that if he could choose his own epitaph it would read: "Here lies a man who spent his principal energies trying to develop men."[17] Vice president Alton Jones recalled that Doherty felt that anyone could hire a man who was a success, but the real success was in the development of men capable of achieving success. For that reason some of his employees described Doherty a "maker of men."[18]

Not only a leader in his own enterprises, Doherty was a moving force in national associations. In 1899 he was president of the Northwestern Electric Association, and, in 1901, president of the National Electric Light Association. As its presiding officer he instituted beneficial changes and considerably increased the membership rolls.[19] In 1902 Doherty assumed the job of president of the Ohio Gas Light Association. The same year he was picked as one of the American members of the organizing board of the 1904

World's Fair representing the World's Congress of Electricity.[20] At the end of World War I he was one of the men who established the first cooperative petroleum organization, called the American Petroleum Institute. He was its vice president between the years 1919 and 1924 and was a director until 1931. Doherty was a member of numerous other organizations.[21]

During his lifetime Doherty received many awards. He was the first recipient of the Beall Gold Medal given by the American Gas Light Association in 1898 for his paper, "Gas as Fuel." He also received the Walton Clark Medal of the Franklin Institute in 1930 for his contributions to the development of the manufactured gas industry, and an honorary degree of Doctor in English from Lehigh University in 1931. In 1937 he received two honors: the Anthony F. Lucas Gold Medal of the American Institute of Mining and Metallurgical Engineers, for distinguished achievement in improving the practice of finding and producing petroleum; and an honorary L.L.D. degree from Temple University. He was made a trustee of the same institution in 1938.

Humanitarian endeavors were also on his resume. He worked to rid Manhatten Island of mosquitoes, and he was the first chairman of the national committee for the President's [Franklin D. Roosevelt] Birthday Ball, a fund raiser for those who suffered from infantile paralysis.[22]

Not only a manager and leader, Doherty was also an innovator. He had a long list of progressive and practical inventions to his credit with more than 150 patents on the combustion process and apparatus.[23] His early gas appliances, developed at Madison, for example, were adopted by many manfacturers. One of Doherty's most significant contributions to the gas industry was his support of the Welsbach lamp which made most other gas lamps obsolete, and enabled gas to stay competitive with electricity for lighting for a short period of time. Not only did he help develop and market the lamp but also invented a system to handle, wash, dry, and clean the glassware and brass.[24]

By 1905 the demand for his skills was so great, and his innovative ideas were so daring, even for McMillin, that he struck out on his own and founded the firm of Henry L. Doherty and Company in New York city to consult in the reorganization, management and financing of public utility companies.[25] To house his new venture he rented the smallest office in the prestigious Sixty Wall Street Building, a building which he bought and redesigned nineteen years later.[26]

He and his three associates, two of whom came from Denver, convinced enough financiers to buy operating control of the Denver Gas and Electric Company from McMillin who relinquished control but kept some of his shares. Doherty at the time was 35 years old, but already had 23 years of experience in the utility business. He and his colleagues were knowledgeable, aggressive young men who were used to dealing with large sums of money and could attract investors particularly from Europe.[27]

Doherty had already established a formula for success during his years of consulting with various utilities:

> launch extensive promotional campaigns to sell wider use of product, gas and electric
>
> obtain capital for needed modernization
>
> train engineers and administrators to run the plant and train a sales staff
>
> raise rates in keeping with service delivered, improving profit, attracting new investors for further improvements. 28

The next five years his business grew so rapidly that he extended its activities and in 1910 established a holding company along with six other men, including Denverites Frank W. Frueauff and William J. Barker. He was an advocate of the holding company system, believing that it was more efficient than smaller units of operation. The nucleus of the new company was the Denver Gas and Electric Company, the Spokane (Washington) Gas and Fuel Company, and the Empire District Electric Company of Joplin, Missouri. With the experience of service many cities with the Henry L. Doherty Company, Doherty came to believe that the difference between those small cities that grew and those that withered was the quality of the services such as gas, electricity, water, communications and transportation. He believed that America's destiny for expansion lay on the foundation of good service for cities. For that reason he named his holding company Cities Service.[29] "Progress through Service," is the Cities Service motto, and its logo is an emblem using a Greek delta within an expanding circle. The three sides of the delta represent "industry," "integrity," and "imagination." The three elipses of the expanding circle represent "engineering," "finance" and "sales." The circle was used to signify the growing character of the Cities Service enterprise.[30]

Henry L. Doherty and Company remained in business and was the fiscal agent for Cities Service Company.[31] Cities Service grew tremendously after a Doherty drilling crew unexpectedly discovered crude oil while looking for natural gas in 1914,[32] and thereafter, the major focus of the business turned from gas and electricity to oil.

Doherty rarely missed an opportunity to improve his own enterprises, or to prove a point. He and his associates had realized correctly that, although Colorado had many assets, it needed water to prosper.[33] In 1909 the East Denver Municipal Irrigation Company was organized to construct an irrigation system east of Denver as well as to improve the Antero reservoir and Highline Canal. Proponents had previously tried unsuccessfully to raise the money necessary to finance construction of the project. Finally, they asked Henry Doherty to underwrite the project, which he did.[34]

When the Antero irrigation project was completed in 1913, Denver celebrated. The Denver *Republican* recorded the event under headlines that read, "Denver Hails its Prophet of New Industrial Era."[35] A thousand businessmen attended a luncheon, including the mayor, the governor and Doherty's own business executives. Everyone applauded enthusiastically when Doherty rose to speak. He said that he was convinced that Colorado had as much potential for growth and prosperity as any other state in the country. The fact that almost all his employees in Denver were Coloradans, he said, attested to the talent in the state. Doherty also pointed out that there were enough funds within Colorado to support any major capital venture, and reprimanded those who were unwilling to capitalize the Antero project. In his speech, he urged the men to be progressive and enterprising in their outlook. He gave the businessmen two examples to encourage them to invest in the state.

> . . . amongst your number you have many who cannot be convinced that the thing to do is to grab opportunities. If anybody would start any sort of constructive movement in his state there are men who seem to feel that it is their duty to pull it down. If you will stop and think, one man pulling backwards can do more to hold things back than twenty men pulling forwards. It is like having one horse in a team that pulls back and it is marvelous what that horse can do in preventing the whole team from carrying the load uphill. 36

Not only did Doherty chastise those individuals who impeded progress, but he also remarked that legislation designed to protect, often stifled business interests.

The second lesson of the day was brought to mind, he said, in light of the jubilee in Germany celebrating the twenty-five year reign of emperor William II:

> The German emperor has done a marvelous thing. When he ascended the throne he found a

> country that was rapidly deteriorating--that was sending people to practically every nation in the world; the people left the country to go elsewhere for bread. The German emperor adopted a constructive policy toward business, commerce and industry; he encouraged everything he could. 37

Doherty pointed out to the audience that Germany had made advances improving employment without great resources, because there was citizen support for an enterprising leader. The moral of his story was obvious: to get ahead the businessmen of a community must encourage progressive ideas and take risks.

Doherty had used his money to prove that the financing of the Antero canal would be of value to the community. The goal was not necessarily to make money but to improve the economic climate of Colorado. It is difficult to know whether Doherty invested in Antero to make a profit, to improve the state's prosperity, or to prove the point that progressive ideas were being stifled in Colorado. Perhaps it was a combination of all three, but in any event he set himself up as an example of someone who took risks and successfully helped the state. 38

Although Henry L. Doherty never ran for political office he was involved in trying to shape political decisions to the advantage of his business. When President Theodore Roosevelt claimed that a gigantic national trust existed which controlled the power organizations, Doherty defended the industrial leaders by saying:

> Naturally there had to be a community of interests in order to secure the immense amount of capital necessary to carry out the plans for power plants, and in the future these same power companies will be one of the country's aids in helping to conserve the coal and water supply. 39

He spoke out against President Roosevelt's insinuation that trusts were filled with dishonest men who wanted to take advantage of the public. Roosevelt, in Doherty's opinion, hurt the country's prosperity by damaging the reputation of the corporations, and thereby making its difficult to raise money in the United States as well as in foreign countries.

Doherty, who did not want the industry regulated by the government, maintained a campign against regulation for most of his life. In 1916 as the main speaker at the National Electric Light Association meeting in Philadelphia he again railed against control:

> There is everywhere a tendency to regulate the profit of the electric companies and to cut them so short that so far as the immediate future is concerned there is no encouragement to go ahead in the active development of our work. But most of us in the electrical business are optimistic and we are sure that the good sense of people will prevail. We must teach the public that the electrical industry is entitled to the same degree of profit that would be realized in other lines of business which accept the same risk. 40

He would eventually lose the battle to resist government regulation.

Doherty always had various financial schemes for raising capital. He sought funds from foreign investors, but often relied on local sources. At the age of twenty four Doherty gave a speech expressing the idea that a company's stock should be sold to prominent people in the community. Not only would it raise capital, but it would give influential men a stake in the business and lead them to a favorable attitude toward the company. It was a matter of combining public opinion with finances.[41] Doherty also sold stock to his employees, and in 1912 he established a profit-sharing plan for employees in the Cities Service system.[42]

After World War I Doherty relied increasingly on selling stocks and debentures to employees who worked for Cities Service subsidiaries. He used pressure tactics on employees and customers to invest at an overpriced rate for the stocks. Doherty used every device he could conjure up to sell stocks and bonds.[43] Some of his competitors said that his initials "HLD" stood for Henry Lacks Dough for a new venture. He was warned by other utility owners about the risks of his financial practices, although they were neither illegal nor uncommon at the time.[44] His complicated financial dealings were one reason the Federal Trade Commission investigated the utility industry. His aggressive tactics contributed to the Federal Security Act of 1933, by which the Securities and Exchange Commission was given control over all the securities sold in interstate commerce.

Doherty had been a bachelor until 1928 when he secretly married a thiry-eight year old widowed nurse, Grace Eames, who had tended him during one of his long bouts of crippling arthritis. Doherty adopted her daughter Helen and held a lavish coming out party for her during the height of the Depression. By many this seemingly profligate spending on an extravagant party by a utility leader during hard times fanned the fire of the anti-utility sentiment.[45]

Denver's utility was one of those that would be broken away from Cities Service after his death in 1939.[46] Henry L. Doherty had always taken particular pride in his association with Denver. Why Denver became his crown jewel is not entirely clear. It may have been timing. When Doherty came to Denver he had had experience elsewhere and was willing to go beyond just combining the gas and electric companies to experiment with scientific management and training schools. It also may have been that by the time he had arrived in Denver he had accumulated enough capital that he could afford to seek independence from McMillin. Doherty may, by that time have gained enough confidence to try daring ideas, ideas that even worried his mentor McMillin. Another possibility is that the political climate was agreeable; that there were not excessive restrictions placed on his financial experimenting. Or, perhaps he happened to find exceptional businessmen such as Frank Frueauff and William Barker with whom to work. He may even have believed that Denver, for whatever reason, was going to blossom and be the regional center of a larger territory.

Whatever his reasons, Doherty tried out his new ideas in Denver and he considered his work in Colorado a springboard for the Cities Service Company. Because of his successful experiments and his ability to promote new ideas through his membership in trade associations, other utilities often adopted those ideas.[47] He once remarked: ". . . Denver has the model gas and electric plant of America. All other gas and electric plants which are growing and improving have adopted the Denver method."[48]

All entrepreneurs add both negative and positive aspects to a company's history. Doherty made tremendous contributions to technology, management training and the development of utilities. And, while he may have been the ultimate wheeler-dealer, he worked within the ethical standards of his time. Perhaps one can say of the tycoons of the early part of the century, to them the end justified the means.

NOTES--CHAPTER 3

1
Denver *Times*, 7 June 1899, p. 8.

2
"Emerson McMillin", *The National Cyclopaedia of American Biography: Being a History of the United States*, XXIV (New York: James T. White & Company, 1935), p. 170.

3
Ibid.

4
"Henry L. Doherty," in Robert L. Schuyler and Edward T. James, eds., *Dictionary of American Biography* XXII (New York: Charles Scribner's Sons, 1958) Supplement Two., p. 155.

5
W. Alton Jones, *"The Cities Service Story." Cities Service company: A Case History of American Enterprise*. (New York, San Francisco, Montreal: The Newcomen Society in North America, 1955), p. 10.

6
William D. Ellis, *On the Oil Lands with Cities Service* (Tulsa, OK: Cities Service Oil and Gas Corporation, 1983), pp. 60-62.

7
Ibid., p. 62.

8
Schuyler and James, *Dictionary of American Biography, p. 154.*

9
Alfred Chandler, "Entrepreneurial Opportunities in Nineteenth Century America," Explorations in Entepreneurial History, I (1963/1964), 106.

10
Progressive Age, XX (1 April 1902), 128.

11
Alton Jones, *"The Cities Service Story"*, p. 13.

12
Denver *Post*, 18 July 1925, 18 September 1927, p. 11., and 13 November 1927, p. 14.

13
Thomas C. Cochran, *American Business in the Twentieth Century*, (Cambridge, MA: Harvard University Press, 1972), p. 17.

14 Robert T. Person, interview, 10 September 1984.

15 John W. Leonard, et al, eds., *Romance of American Petroleum and Gas*, II (New York: J. J. Little & Ives Company, n.d.), p. 350.

16 *Literary Digest* LXXCII (2 June 1923), 56

17 Jones, "*The Cities Service Story*", p. 22.

18 *Progressive Age*, XXVI (1 October 1908), 570.

19 Ibid.

20 Ibid.

21 "Henry L. Doherty," *The National Cyclopaedia of American Biography: Being the History of the United States*, XXXIV (New York: James T. White and Company, 1948), p. 12. Doherty belonged to the American Association for the Advancement of Science, The American Institute of Electrical Engineers, American Society of Heating and Ventilating Engineers, American Society for the Promotion of Engineering Education, American Gas Institute, Franklin Institute, Canadian Electrical Association, New York Academy of Sciences, International Congress of Investors, International Peace Forum, American Society of Mechanical Engineers, and American Academy of Political and Social Science.

22 "Henry L. Doherty," *National Cyclopaedia*, pp. 12-13.

23 *Progressive Age*, XXVI (1 October 1908), 570. The Doherty bench fuel economizer for the use in manufacture of gas was patented in 1906. His 1907 patent was the gas washer cooler system of preparing and condensing manufactured gas. Doherty also improved methods for distillation of petroleum and the gasification of coal, as well as the recovery of byproducts. He also improved the meters by which gas was measured. In 1899 he raised support to put purifiers out of doors rather than purifying houses. In his paper (1900) on "Equitable Competitive Uniform Rates," he established a method of charging that was accepted by the industry as the standard.

24 *Progressive Age* XXVI (1 October 1908), 570.

In addition he invented a carrying device for glass chimneys, a way of "blowing dust from the check plates of the bunsen tubes and ingenious bypasses and devices for distant control of lamps for shop windows, signs and theatrical uses."

25 "Henry L Doherty," *The National Cyclopaedia of American Biography*, p. 12.

26 Ellis, *On the Oil Lands*, p. 150. In New York Doherty purchased his office building on Sixty Wall Street and wanted to tear it down to build a larger skyscraper, but the city would not give him a permit to do so. Since Cities Service Company controlled four acres behind his Sixty Wall Street office Doherty decided to build on that ground, but to connect it to his present building in order to retain the Wall Street address. The 64-story Wall street Tower, the world's third tallest structure, was built during the Depression. When completed people entered Sixty Wall Street, rode the elevator to the fifteenth floor then crossed over to the new edifice whose technical address was Sixty Pine Street.

27 Ellis, *On the Oil Lands*, pp. 68-69.

28 Ibid., p. 62.

29 Ibid, p. 72. The company was incorporated in Delaware 2 September 1910.

30 Jones, *"The Cities Service Story"*, p. 27.

31 Ibid., p. 72.

32 *Literary Digest* LXXVII (2 June 1923), 56.

33 Denver *Republican*, 21 June 1913, p. 1 and 6-7.

34 E. L. Mosley, "History of the Denver Water System," Chapter VI, 1910-1919, pp. 50-66. (unpublished paper, Colorado Historical Society, Denver, Colorado).

35 Denver *Republican*, 21 June 1913, p. 6.

36 Ibid., p. 6.

37 Ibid, pp. 6-7.

[38] Ibid.

[39] Denver *Post*, 11 May 1909, p. 2.

[40] *Electrical Review and Western Electrician*, LXVIII (22 April 1916), 705.

[41] Ellis, *On the Oil Lands with Cities Service*, p. 70.

[42] *Progressive Age* XXX (15 May 1912), 451.

[43] *News Week* II (5 August 1933), 22.

[44] "Henry L. Doherty," *Dictionary of American Biography*, XXII, p. 155.

[45] Ibid., and Ellis, *On the Oil Lands with Cities Service*, p. 136.

[46] "Henry L. Doherty," *Dictionary of American Biography*, XXII, p. 155.

[47] Ellis, *On the Oil Lands with Cities Service*, pp. 62-63.

[48] Denver *Post*, 11 May 1909, p. 2.

CHAPTER 4

THE DENVER GAS AND ELECTRIC COMPANY

In 1899 Denverites began to hear rumors of plans to unite the Denver Consolidated Gas Company and the Denver Consolidated Electric Company. Twenty-eight year old Henry L. Doherty had arrived the year before to inspect the gas plant for his employer, Emerson McMillin, and to talk to businessmen and politicians. McMillin instructed Doherty to begin quietly negotiations to merge the two companies, believing that with reduced overhead they could raise new capital, improve plants, and make more profit under consolidated management.[1] The customers feared, however, that a merger would create a perpetual light and heat monopoly with the ability to charge exorbitant prices. They also objected to secret negotiations.

There was a great deal of behind-the-scenes maneuvering to insure that there was support for approval of the merger. Stockholders from both companies had to vote in favor of the plan, and then the Denver City Council had to approve the incorporation of a new enterprise. John H. Poole, general superindendent of the Denver Consolidated Electric Company, and Dennis Sullivan, a prominent Denver politician, traveled to the East to lobby for consolidation. Merging the gas and electric companies was a local issue, but there was more at stake than building a "light trust." According to a Denver newspaper, prominent Denver politicians wanted to reestablish a political machine after their former strength had been fragmented during the 1898 election. Senator Edward O. Wolcott was the leader of the aspiring politicos and before any decision was made he had to give approval. The men went to Washington, D.C. to speak to Senator Wolcott, who, according to the Denver Times, favored setting up a group of politically influential men to push through the merger. At home, speakers went out to various civic organizations to rally enthusiasm for the plan.[2]

The well-organized political machine won the day. The state legislature approved the incorporation of the Denver Gas and Electric Company to serve the counties of Denver, Arapahoe and and Jefferson, as well as the rest of the state. A twenty-year franchise created a virtual monopoly in the lighting business for the city of Denver.[3] The company was restricted only by the terms of its franchise and was otherwise unregulated by local and state government.

A thirteen-member board of directors had legal responsibility for the company.[4] Emerson McMillin, one of the principal stockholders, announced that he would direct the new company from his office in New York, with George Thompson as the on-site manager. The law firm of Wolcott and Vaille of Denver did the legal work for the company.[5] The McMillin Company proposed a capital stock issue of $3,500,000 and bond issue of $5,500,000. Stockholders of the merging gas and electric companies had the option of selling the stocks they held at par value or of converting their holdings to stocks or bonds of the new company. Of the $3,500,000 in capitalization only $1,300 was paid in cash, the balance of $3,498,700 was issued for gas and electric property.[6] The Denver Times cynically reported that there would be a slush fund of $1,205,000 which would be adequate to pay the politicians. Although consumers were cynical about the merger and the control of the lighting business it would bring, the new company gained a measure of credibility when it announced a rate reduction in June 1899. Gas for lighting was lowered from $1.75 per 1,000 cubic feet (with a discount of 25-cents for higher consumption), to $1.50 per 1,000 cubic feet (with a 15-cent discount to large consumers). Gas for fuel was reduced to $1.15 (with a discount of 15 cents for higher consumption). Changes in the electrical rates were discussed but not implemented.[7]

At the same time the rates were reduced a new board of directors was elected.[8] Two of the directors were former presidents of the old companies: James B. Grant of the gas company and Edward W. Rollins of the electric company. Charles W. Waterman represented the Wolcott and Vaille law firm on the board, and George Thompson, a former resident of New Haven, Connecticut, who had worked in the lighting business for fourteen years, again assumed the role of president.[9]

Another Denver Gas and Electric Company employee, Frank Frueauff, played an important role in the company's development. Frueauff held the position of secretary with the new company, the same job he had with the Denver Consolidated Electric Company.[10] Born 29 March 1874 in Columbia, Pennsylvania, Frueauff moved to Colorado as a small child when his family located in Leadville. They later moved to Denver where Frank attended Denver High School (now East High School).[11] After graduating, Frueauff went to work as a meter reader and lamp clerk for the Denver Consolidated Electric Company, and moved up to bookkeeper, cashier, and then secretary. After four years as secretary for the Denver Gas and Electric Company Frueauff became vice president in 1904 and president in 1910.[12]

Frank Frueauff went on to be one of Henry L. Doherty's most trusted business associates. He was a director and officer of Henry L. Doherty and Company and of Cities Service Company.[13] As vice president of the latter enterprise he was associated with 142 corporations throughout the United States. The Henry L. Doherty Company, parent organization of Cities Service, operated approximately 225 public utilities properties in twenty-six states. Under Frueauff's direction the utility and oil companies earned about $100 million annually.[14] In addition to business Frueauff was very active in community affairs in both Denver and New York.[15]

In 1900 the City of Denver was suffering financial difficulties in attempting to keep up with rapid growth. Some people vehemently professed that, had the city not given away the the utility franchises, the coffers would not be depleted. They suggested the implementation of a franchise tax to remedy the problem, but the utilities strongly disagreed, letting the mayor know that they considered a franchise fee blackmail for use of city streets.[16] Thomas L. Patterson, owner of the morning newspaper, the *Rocky Mountain News*, (and later also owner of the evening Denver *Times*) lobbied for a franchise fee to help the city. Trained as a lawyer, he used his considerable writing ability to expose the abuses of the gas and electric concerns, as well as those in the water and transportation businesses. He also took to the stump, both nationally and locally, to fight corporate greed.[17]

Patterson criticized the Denver Gas and Electric Company for making annual profits of $200,000 by charging residents nearly $1.00 per thousand cubic feet of gas more than the production cost. He felt that the utility had become lax in service and due to a lack of competition. Furthermore, the high rates the company charged for electricity given their monopolistic position was simply a case of "unmitigated hog."[18]

Patterson at first supported municipal ownership of the gas and electric business. When that idea did not appear to be popular, he advocated competition among two or more utilities. Either method would be, Patterson felt, effective in providing good service, reasonable rates and remuneration to the city.[19] Although many agreed with Patterson, his reputation as a reformer was later tarnished when it was discovered that he had a significant interest in one of several utility companies bidding for a new franchise to compete with Denver Gas and Electric.[20]

In 1900 the Lacombe Electric Company emerged to challenge the Denver Gas and Electric Company for the franchise, which was expiring in 1901, to light Denver's streets. Charles Lacombe submitted a proposal which offered the city much more than the existing Denver Gas and Electric contract. He proposed to furnish arc lights at the rate of $7.50 per 1,000 lamps per month for a period of ten years, where the Denver Gas and Electric Company had been supplying arc lamps at $10.00 per 1,000 lamps per month. Lacombe offered to sell its street lighting plant to the City of Denver over a ten-year period. The city would then own the street lighting system and all subsequent profits would go to its treasury.[21]

In addition to the street lighting plant, Lacombe offered to sell his commercial lighting plant to the city after either ten, fifteen, or twenty years, at Denver's option. The new company also agreed to pay the city three per cent of the annual gross revenue from that commercial plant, and finally Lacombe agreed that the company would never combine with any other existing lighting company.[22]

The Lacombe proposal was quite effective in shaking the Denver Gas and Electric Company out of its monopolistic complacency, creating fear that it could lose control of the profitable lighting business in Denver. Company managers quickly devised a four-pronged strategy to fight the upstart Lacombe. They secretly formed another electric company. They asked city Council for a law requiring that all wires be put underground. They slashed their own rates, and, finally, they tried to prove that the Lacombe proposal was invalid.[23]

The hastily-put-together organization, the Benett-Myers-Smith-O'Donnell Electric Light Company, submitted its proposal to city council as the Board of Supervisors was considering the Lacombe offer. (The council at that time was bicameral with five supervisors and seventeen aldermen.) In an effort to prevent passage of the Lacombe franchise the Bennett-Myers-Smith-O'Donnell Electric Light Company proposed to do everything that Lacombe had offered, and in addition offered to make a $100,000 lump sum payment upon the signing of a contract.[24] Many people including the *Times* saw through the scheme, realizing that the newly-created light company was controlled by friends of the Denver Gas and Electric Company. The amount of $100,000 was considered a small price to pay for control of Denver's lighting business.

The Board of Aldermen had already voted in favor of Lacombe, and so the decision was in the hands of the five Selectmen. M. H. Mitchell and Charles F. Wilson, who served on the light committee, were thought to be favorable to the Lacombe franchise. Supervisor H. Brown Cannon opposed it, and Thomas A. Uzzell and Jacob Fillius were undecided. Secret negotiations continued and many Denverites assumed that political deals were being made because discussions were not held in an open atmosphere.

As they sat in caucus, discussing the issue, another group was in secret session at a downtown hotel. Meeting together in a room at the Brown [Palace] Hotel were stock holders of the Denver Gas and Electric Company and some of the investors of the Bennett-Myers-Smith-O'Donnell Light Company. The second group asked the Supervisors to come over to join them for discussions.[25] Despite any cajoling the Selectmen voted to grant Lacombe a license to operate.[26]

When the Lacombe franchise bill was passed the Denver *Times* jubilantly reported the event as a setback to the Democratic bosses, and claimed that the "light trust" had been broken at last. In clear support of the new electric company the *Times* published a letter from Charles Lacombe:

> . . . I am a corporation man but I learned a long time ago that corporations must treat the people or they will not be allowed to live. There is no corporation so strong that it can defy the people. This had been illustrated in the case of the present gas and electric light company. Had they made concessions six months ago when members of the council went to them and pleaded with them to do it there would have never been a bill passed. Had they even reduced the cost of arc lights from $100 to $75 as they now propose to do legislation

would have been headed off.

> When we made our application for our franchise they thought we were a lot of boys and did not pay much attention to us. They did not believe for an instant that we stood the modest chance of getting a bill through council. While they were ignoring us we were not asleep and we caught them napping. 27

The Lacombe Company deposited $25,000 with the city to be refunded if it met the promised terms. Charles Lacombe noted that there were between seven and eight hundred miles of streets to be lighted in the sixty-square mile city of Denver, and laid out a detailed schedule for purchasing land, constructing the electric plant, erecting poles, and stringing wires. Lacombe estimated that these items would take a year to accomplish and cost $250,000.[28]

Denver Gas and Electric Company was not only caught napping, but in order to compete with Lacombe, had to spend $500,000 to modernize its electrical generating system. During the years since the Denver plant had been built new technology had been developed to reduce the power loss between the generation and delivery points. With a forty per cent loss the Denver Gas and Electric Company could not match the eight per cent loss which Lacombe would get with its improved equipment.[29]

The investors of the Denver Gas and Electric Company were a tenacious bunch who refused to give up. When their attempt to beat Lacombe by creating a new company failed they tried another scheme. In April, 1900 they asked for a court injunction to stop Lacombe from stringing wires, claiming that Denver, like other cities in the nation, should begin putting all wires underground. Alderman Kelly was persuaded to introduce an ordinance to the city council which would require that all wires be put underground. Five years would be granted to comply with the new ordinance, but the requirement would impose an insurmountable financial burden on Lacombe. Although it was a sound idea, in reality, it was a political ploy and a majority of the Council saw through the proposal and turned it down.[30]

The Denver Gas and Electric Company used price cutting as its third line of attack to fight Lacombe.[31] The *Rocky Mountain News* reported that Denver Gas and Electric had been quietly buying new equipment during the franchise hearings in order to reduce its cost of production. The company had also developed a new rate schedule with prices even lower than Lacombe. John H.

Poole, vice president and general manager of the company said:

> . . . people will see that we mean to stay in the field and do business at a price lower than any other company can or will quote. If the Lacombe people or anybody else goes ahead and names a rate we will cut it at once and get so much below them that another cut will mean free electricity . . . We will meet and cut any rate that can be made and will come out ahead, and if the other people hold out too long it will be a case of exact similarity to the water fight. 32

Poole's reference was to the 1891-92 price war between Citizens Water Company and the Denver Water Company. During the battle prices were slashed so much that customers were supplied with water free. Denver Water Company won the war, absorbing the other company, to become the Denver Union Water Company.[33]

The final effort against Lacombe came in early 1901 when Denver Gas and Electric tried to invalidate the Lacombe franchise on the theory that Denver Gas and Electric Company had submitted a lower bid for lighting Denver streets.[34] The actual suit to invalidate the franchise was brought against the city for wrongfully awarding the franchise to the Lacombe Company, and was won by the city in the court of appeals in May of 1902. During the period of litigation the Lacombe people had confidently built their plant and provided service to the city.[35]

While Lacombe had won these battles, Denver Gas and Electric Company eventually won the war in an interesting fashion. Denver Gas and Electric Company lowered its rates to 2 1/2 cents per kilowatt hour in a rate war and simply forced Lacombe out of business. However, Denver Gas and Electric Company could not survive by providing electricity at such a low rate. It failed to make payment on a $15,000 promissory note to Dennis Sullivan, a stockholder, and Sullivan sued for collection in Denver District Court. He chose a court 150 miles away, in Canon City, to assure a favorable decision. On 2 May 1902 Judge Morton S. Bailey put the Denver Gas and Electric Company into receivership, appointing Henry L. Doherty as receiver. Doherty had served as president since May, 1901 and acting president since October, 1900.[36] The Denver Chamber of Commerce among others protested against this legerdemain, but the decision was upheld. Therefore, a company capitalized and bonded for $11,310,000 went into voluntary receivership over a $15,000 promissory note, and continued doing business with the same staff almost as if nothing had happened.[37]

In June, 1902 the Lacombe Electric Light Company was purchased by the Denver Gas and Electric Company. During the long period of litigation regarding the validity of the Lacombe franchise, Emerson McMillin and other Denver Gas and Electric Company men were buying Lacombe stocks and bonds, and by the time the Court of Appeals ruled that the franchise was valid, McMillin and cohorts owned a controlling interest in Lacombe.[38] The Denver Gas and Electric Company guaranteed to pay the "interest and principal of the $900,000 outstanding Lacombe Company bonds, and to pay into the sinking fund the amount provided for in the Company mortgage."[39]

In theory the two companies had not combined, and Lacombe was to stay in business to supply lights to the city, while Denver Gas and Electric Company served businesses and residents.[40] In reality the Denver Gas and Electric Company controlled Lacombe and the very valuable lighting contract. The pressure of the ordeal was apparently too much for Charles Lacombe, and on 5 July 1902 he tried unsuccessfuly to commit suicide.[41]

Although stockholders of the Denver Gas and Electric Company had purchased a majority share of the Lacombe Company, Irving Butterworth, who had become president of Denver Gas and Electric Company in 1902 denied that one company owned the other. In a letter to the Denver *Times* on June 25, he said:

> In view of the erroneous impression that seems to prevail on the subject, will you kindly state to your readers that the Denver Gas and Electric company is not in any sense the purchaser of the Lacombe Electric company and that there is not now nor will there ever be in the future any consolidation between the two companies.
>
> We are informed that the purchase of the Lacombe Electric company had all the conditions and proceedings passed upon by Denver attorneys who assured them that the city's interests had been properly safeguarded and that otherwise they would not have purchased the stock.[42]

Irving Butterworth had come to Denver in 1901 to assume the position of general manager of the Denver Gas and Electric Company when Henry L. Doherty became president. Before coming to Denver Butterworth was president of the Ohio Gas Company and a stockholder of the Denver Gas and Electric Company and by the age of forty, had received national acclaim in the power industry as an engineer. Butterworth's words in his letter to the *Times* proved false, because later board minutes of the Denver Gas and Electric Company stated that the stockholders of the Denver Gas and Electric Company purchased all capital stock of the Lacombe Company.[43]

Denver Gas and Electric Company continued to make newspaper headlines in 1902. When a September Denver *Post* editorial accused the company of avoiding taxes. Company managers appeared in the District Court to answer charges that the company used the figure of nine million dollars to justify dividends, but paid taxes on only $800,000. Denver Gas and Electric Company, the editorial pronounced, was either robbing the public or robbing the stockholders:

> . . . the company has attempted to escape by far the larger part of its just taxation by direct misrepresentation as to its holdings.
>
> Either that, or it has attempted to secure from the district court an order for an unwarrantedly high schedule of rates to consumers by direct misrepresentation as to the amount of its liabilities. . . .
>
> It is the fact . . that the company is capitalized at $9 million while the value of its cash investment is, according to the sworn statements of its officers, only $800,000.
>
> In otherwords it claims the privilege of earning dividends upon $9,000,000 when only $800,000 in cash is invested. . . .
>
> Either it must cease to earn such dividends, and thus destroy the investments of its innocent stockholders, or it must continue to rob

the consuming public of Denver by rates out of all proportion to the legitimate cost of its service.

This is the great evil involving the whole trust question. 44

The company escaped prosecution because the lawyers claimed that the Arapahoe county assessor, under whose jurisdiction the company fell, asked them only about their land and physical property, and not about their extensive delivery system.[45]

In 1904 Denver voters approved a charter amendment making Denver a home rule city, and requiring that utility franchises be approved by a vote of the taxpaying electorate and be granted for no more than twenty years. Power of the electorate increased even more with a provision that whenever a petition was signed by twenty-five percent or more of the qualified electors, proceedings for the city to acquire any public utility could begin.[47] These amendments were the first step in breaking a cozy relationship between government and the gas/electric, tramway, and water utilities.

A part of the home rule charter made the corporate limits of the City of Denver and the County of Denver identical. In order to include new territories in the service areas gained as a result of that provision, the Denver Gas and Electric Company, had to submit a new franchise for the voter approval.[46] On 15 May 1906 by a very close vote, Denver voters approved the franchise expansion and the right of the company to acquire all the property, contracts and franchises of the Lacombe Electric Company.[48]

In fact, the election was so close that many people became suspicious and petition was filed asking the Grand Jury to investigate possible election fraud.[49] The complaints came from The League for Honest Elections, a nonpartisan, volunteer organization whose sole reason for being was to ensure honest elections. The plaintiffs were reformers who maintained that the District Attorney had been lax in enforcing the election laws.

Referring to the alleged stuffed ballot box as "the big mitt," the League argued that non-property owners had been given false tax receipts which allowed unqualified people to vote. The League also suspected that hundreds of votes had been cast irregularly by people given small amounts of land out on Colorado's eastern plains by the Denver Gas and Electric Company. Many of those accused of having fraudulent tax receipts were utility company employees.[50] The League further charged that the election judges had made errors in counting.[51]

In his book, *The Beast*, Judge Ben Lindsey, a vocal Denver Progressive who fought against political corruption, described the offenses of the 1906 election.[52] Writing about the Grand Jury investigation, Lindsey said that those called to the witness stand testified that they had bought the land through Frank Frueauff of the gas and electric company. A notebook in Frueauff's handwriting later corroborated the charges. Many called by the Grand Jury to testify refused, including Henry Doherty, president of Denver Gas and Electric. District Court Judge Frank T. Johnson, who was not cowed by the power magnate, sentenced him for contempt of court for refusing to testify.[53]

> Doherty made a triumphal descent of the Court House staircase, smiled at by the crowds in the halls, as if he were the hero of some huge practical joke that was admirable in its insolence; and he was taken by the sheriff to a neighboring hotel where he waited until Judge Gabbert directed his release under a writ of habeas corpus--a proceeding which the Supreme Court itself afterward repudiated as illegal. 54

An appeal to stop the case was sent to the state supreme court delaying the investigation of fraud on technical grounds. The case was eventually brought before Judge Lindsey who at that time presided over county court. Doherty's lawyers argued that the district court did not have the right to hear franchise matters, but Lindsey determined that according to the Denver City Charter the county court has a right to hear all election irregularities.[55] The lawyers accused Lindsey of prejudice and demanded a change of venue, a demand which Lindsey curtly denied.[56]

As the case continued many of those who might have testified against the electric corporation left town to avoid being put on the stand.[57] Others, who did not leave, came to Judge Lindsey's chambers begging for clemency for their previous perjury. Henry Doherty took the witness stand albeit in a belligerant mood, and when Doherty refused to answer questions about bribing election officials. Lindsey fined him $500 and ordered him sent to county jail. Doherty's attorneys asked that he be held in the sheriff's custody rather than in jail until they obtained writs to free him. Judge Lindsey denied the request, remarking that Doherty would be given the same treatment as any ordinary citizen.[58]

Apparently once behind bars by Lindsey's order Doherty's air of confidence deflated. Nevertheless, he was supposed to have stayed in jail for three days and two nights, but the newspapers reported that the sheriff gave him some privileges and even dined with him in an expensive restaurant. The Colorado Supreme Court was not in session, and so a lower court granted, although incorrectly, a writ of habeas corpus. A free man, Doherty promptly left town, and as he left by train Doherty was quoted as saying: "Denver has more sunshine and sons of bitches than any other town in the country."[59]

The district court never ruled on the election fraud case because the supreme court determined that the district court was not empowered to hear franchise cases. In response to the decision Judge Lindsey asked angrily:

> But do you realize what these facts mean? Do you realize that the citizens of Denver, robbed of millions of dollars by a franchise steal, found themselves in 1906 with no court under heaven to which they could appeal for redress? Do you realize that the robbers, caught in the act, were able to laugh at their victims and defy the law? Can you consider what an example of citizenship was set for those young men and women who were compelled to betray their city to perjure themselves on an oath before their God, and to see Doherty and his associates smile upon the treason and this perjury? Doherty--the millionaire

> president of a score of power companies, rich, honoured, admired! Freuauff, [sic] the manager of the Denver Gas Company, ex-treasurer of the Board of Deacons of the Central Presbyterian Church, an active religious worker, a most "respectable" man! 60

Despite the scandals of the 1906 election, the approved franchise benefited the city much more than the agreements which preceded it. For the first time the company would pay an annual fee of $50,000 to the city. More could have been required, but the city had at least taken the first step in generating income from the utilities.[61]

After Doherty became head of the Denver Gas and Electric company he started an aggressive advertising campaign. He was an able marketer who was conversant in the technology of the services and extremely creative in devising strategies to sell power. Doherty was a relatively early user of advertising, and may have been the first in the nation in 1901 to use letters outlined with lights for advertising.[62]

The wide use of advertising, particularly as a trade, did not come about until the late 1800s. Before that time people hung out a sign to bring in business and Europeans had used the written word to sell their wares, but a systematic approach to sway public opinion did not take place until the twentieth century. Advertising, although begun in other countries, was used most extensively in the United States. ". . .the advertising business seemed to fit best the enterprising and expansive American character."[63]

Doherty used advertising because it sold products and drew attention to his companies, particularly the Denver Gas and Electric Company. During the first few years of the twentieth century Denver Gas and Electric Company participated in local parades with colorful advertising, used the newspapers, and stamped its envelopes with the slogan "cook with gas." It also enticed people to come look at their wares by displaying them in prominent places at the company office or, on nice days, rolling them out onto the sidewalk.[64]

Doherty received national recognition for his many unusual and successful advertising ideas and other companies throughout the country eagerly emulated his approach. Acknowledgement of Denver Gas and Electric's enterprising advertising came frequently in national trade magazines such as *The Electrical Review*, which in July of 1906, reported that Doherty would try anything that might have some success in selling products. The same article pointed out that the citizens of Denver realized that gas and electric company advertising was earning a national reputation. Denver was known as the "City of Lights," and in the early part of the century Denver used a slogan: "Boost for the City of Lights" to encourage all businesses to use lighting to sustain the city's reputation.[65]

There are many examples of the gas and electric company's unusual advertising schemes, but a particularly uncommon one is described in a 1902 issue of *Progressive Age* by Irving Butterworth, president of the Denver Gas and Electric Company. The gas company ran an ad in the local paper asking to rent as many dogs as possible. Owners were to lend their dogs to the company for ten cents a day a dog for two days. Any dog (pedigree was not required) was welcome and was to be brought to the office by 10:00 on a particular Saturday morning. The ad, of course, caused much curiousity and talk about the company, and when the dogs were brought to the office, a sign that read: "Buy a Gas Stove" was tied around each of their necks.

If the dog was returned in two days with the sign still around its neck, the owner would collect the twenty-cent payment. Butterworth's comment was: "If this scheme does not sell gas stoves and popularise [sic] the company, then the community is simply too 'dog-goned' dignified to appreciate a good thing."[66]

Cleverly drawn caricatures of people who had made history in Colorado were one of the most popular advertisements. The cartoon message that if prominent people used gas appliances, common people should also. The demand was so great for reproductions of the carocatires that the gas and electric company printed a booklet of such cartoons in 1904 called "The City Beautiful."[67]

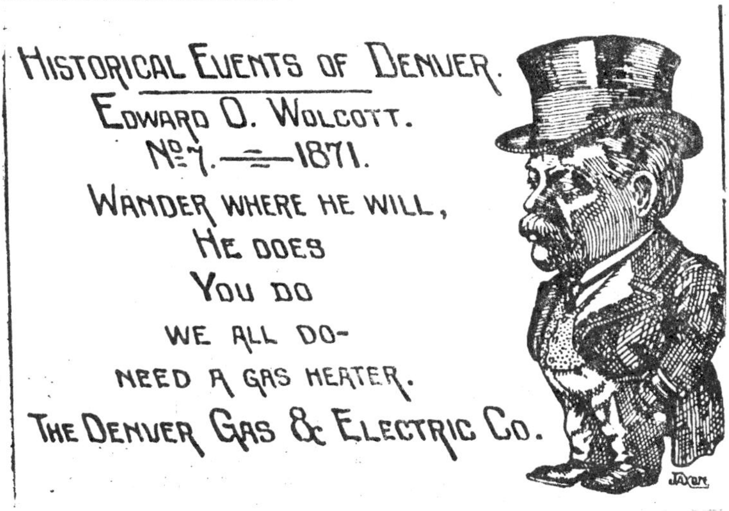

Caricatures from "The City Beautiful"

Caricatures from "The City Beautiful"

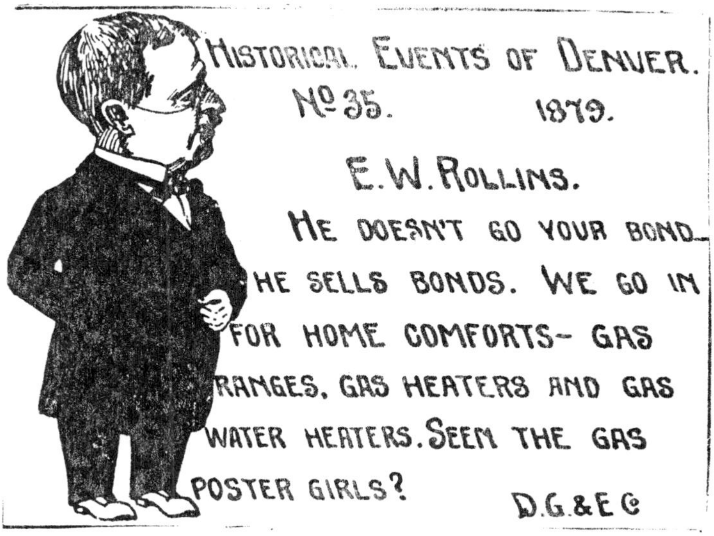

Caricatures from "The City Beautiful"68

In order to familiarize salesmen with the variety of products the Company supplied "solicitors" with a twenty-one page source book all the gas and electrical appliances catalogued by the places they could be used.[69] A decade later the company provided salesmen with portable models, and also outfitted an electric truck to carry gas and electric appliances, such as water heaters, different models of ranges, flatirons, waffle irons, toasters, fans, and percolators. The truck had a set schedule to visit different geographical areas of the city, and the company representatives demonstrated the appliances to as many as one hundred women in a day. The truck caught the attention of men too, although they were often more interested in examining the truck itself rather than the appliances on it.[70]

Denver Gas and Electric Company realized that it was important not only to market the product, but also to promote the company. With that in mind it made good use of Denver trolley cars: "Street car advertising is a means of advertising as much as to keep people in good humor with the advertiser as to sell his goods." The Denver Gas and Electric Company designed its cards to please the customer.[71] An early example of street card advertisement featured a series of four signs which were changed twice a week. The successive signs read:

IF

If you love

If you love your wife

If you love your wife, buy her

If you love your wife buy her a gas stove.[72]

Demonstrations and exhibits proved an effective way to sell appliances. The company instituted a variety of ways to let the customers examine its appliances. For example, at a weekly Denver Gas and Electric cooking school a butcher block was set up in the office to demonstrate the best cuts of meat to use when cooking with gas.[73] Cooking classes were also taken to churches, with Denver Gas and Electric Company furnishing the food and teacher and the church providing the kitchen and students. Both benefited because the church often charged an admissions fee and the gas company gained new customers and created good public relations.[74] Editors of *Progressive Age* explained that the cooking demonstrations were successful because the would-be customers were eager to use a modern convenience and the demonstrations simply gave them a graphic reason to switch.[75]

After canvassing various businesses, the gas and electric company decided to have an exhibition to demonstrate industrial appliances. It collected as many appliances as possible that had never been shown in Denver, including machines for metal workers, assayers, hotel and restaurant men, bakers and candy makers. The exhibit, held in 1903, was very well attended.[76]

Lighting displays were also a spectacular means of advertising. In 1906 the Denver Gas and Electric Company illuminated the welcoming arch constructed in front of Union Depot. Thirteen thousand dollars was raised in the community to pay for the lighting, and residents considered it a brilliant success.[77] While the Union Depot display was permanent, others were temporary, such as the one at the 1906 Elks's convention. Seventeenth street was canopied with multicolored lamps, including lamps in the Elks's color of purple. Every intersection was full of lights as were all blocks of Fifteen and

Sixteenth streets. At night the center of downtown Denver was reported to be as bright as day. Guests remarked that the enterprising efforts of Denver would make the city a favorite convention city of the country.[78]

Colorful commercial lighting was also promoted the company. One particularly unusual sign was erected for a dentist at Sixteenth and Curtis Streets, shaped like a lyre, with letters spelling out the dentist's name, on each string. As the letters flashed on and off, a variety of musical tunes were played. When the sign was new someone with a sense of humor arranged to have the tune, "How Dry I Am," and "I won't go home until morning" played late at night.[79] Late-night reveillers that evening must have cast a skeptical eye at the "singing" sign.

In a report to the stockholders 8 April 1905 Denver Gas and Electric Company's president pointed out that the company had made a determined effort to improve business through solicitation and advertising. Management's efforts had been successful in increasing gas sales and in electric lighting for signs. Its plans were to increase earnings by $100,000 each year and advertising was an essential part of the plan.[80]

A subtle indicator that gas appliances were becoming a standard rather than a luxury could be seen in the want ads. By 1913 gas had become important enough to be listed as one of the amenities of houses for rent, and[81] most of the listings in the classified ads included gas service. If gas were not considered important, people would not have spent the money or space to include it in their advertisement.

When Doherty and McMillin restructured a business or merged two companies they made improvements such as modernizing plants and reorganizing the staff so that the operation was more efficient. They were also able to manipulate the finances to have a sum for influence. They could ensure dominance of the lucrative contracts and control the rates the company charged. Although the chamber of commerce and other citizen groups protested the influence of utilities, the powerful businessmen and politicians were too strong to control. The franchise system seemed to offer little effective regulation and provided only a token amount to municipal income.[82] As it always seemed to be, Henry L. Doherty was a leading participant in the political maneuverings surrounding franchises and lighting contracts. He was also at the forefront of innovation and was one of the first utility leaders to use extensive advertising. He tested his advertising methods in Denver which, because of Doherty, gained the reputation of being the "City of Lights."

NOTES--CHAPTER 4

1
Ellis, *On the Oil Lands with Cities Service* (Tulsa, OK: Cities Service Company, 1983) p. 63.

2
Denver *Times*, 3 February 1899, p. 1.

3
Articles of Incorporation, Denver Gas and Electric Company Minute Book 35113X, 1899-1909 (Public Service of Colorado, Denver, Colorado). Despite the name of the Company, Denver Gas and Electric Company, it was incorporated to serve Arapaoe and Jefferson counties as well as Denver.

4
William Van Saun, Tobias B. Liverman, Sam W. Cantrell, Frank H. DuPrey, Guy Young, Robert C. Young, Angus W. Ward, William A. Burke, Elroy N. Clark, Herman H. Dunham, William W. Field, Charles W. Waterman and George Treadway Thompson. Certification of Incorporation, Colorado State Archives and minutes of Denver Gas and Electric Company 29 April 1899. Public Service Company, Denver, Colorado.)

5
Minutes of the Denver Gas and Electric Company, 29 april 1899 (Public Service Company, Denver, Colorado).

6
Clyde King, *The History of the Government of Denver with Special Reference to Its Relations with Public Service*, (Denver: The Fisher Book Co., 1911), pp. 207-08.

7
Denver *Times*, 8 June 1899, p. 1.

8
Denver *Times*, 8 June 1899, p. 1. Members of the new board of directors were: Emerson McMillin, chairman, James B. Grant, George W. Skinner, John C Mitchell, H. K. Devereaux, A. S. H}ghes, Harry C. James, John H. Poole, Charles W. Waterman, George T. Thompson and Edward W. Rollins. Two remaining members would be chosen at a later date.

9
Denver *Times*, 8 June 1899, p. 2.

10
Ibid.

[11] Denver *Times*, 1 August 1922, p. 7.

[12] Ibid.

[13] John W. Leonard, et al., eds. *Romance of American Petroleum and Gas* II (New York: J. J. Little & Ives Company, n.d.), p. 349.

[14] Denver *Times*, 1 August 1922, p. 7.

[15] Denver *Post*, *Empire Magazine*, 2 January 1983, p. 23.

[16] Roland L. DeLorme, "Turn-of-the-Century Denver: An Invitation to Reform," *Colorado Magazine*, XLV (Winter, 1968), 6-7.

[17] Will C. Ferril *Sketches of Colorado*, I (Denver: The Western Press Bureau Co., 1911), p. 111.

[18] DeLorme, *Colorado Magazine*, (May, 1968), p. 10.

[19] Robert E. Smith, "Senator T. M. Patterson, the Colorado Supreme Court and Freedom of the Press, *Colorado Magazine*, LIV (January, 1977), 58.

[20] Patterson's company was the Denver City Light and Power Company, an offshoot of Patterson's Denver, Boulder, and Northern Railroad. Delorme, *Colorado Magazine*, (May, 1968), 10.

[21] Clyde L. King, *The History of the Government of Denver, with special Reference to Its Relations with Public Service* (Denver: The Fisher Book Co., 1911), pp. 208-09.

[22] Ibid., p. 209.

[23] Denver *Times*, 23 March 1900, p. 1.

[24] Denver *Times*, 28 March 1900, p. 1.

[25] Denver *Times*, 29 March 1900, p. 1.

[26] Denver Ordinance No. 35, 1900, in Charles Varnum and J Frank Adams, *Franchises and Special*

Privileges of the City and county of Denver (Denver: Smith Brooks, 1907), p. 112.

[27] Denver *Times*, 30 March 1900, p. 1.

[28] Ibid.

[29] Denver Times, 2 April 1900, p. 1.

[30] Denver *Times*, 15 April 1900, p. 2.

[31] Denver Gas and Electric Company Minute Book 3511cX, p. 125 (Public Service Company of Colorado, Denver, Colorado).

[32] *Rocky Mountain News*, 22 April 1900, p. 1.

[33] Denver *Times*, 3 July 1900, p. 1.

[34] Denver *Times*, 3 February 1901, p. 7.

[35] Denver *Times*, 3 June 1902, p. 2.

[36] J. Warner Mills, "The Economic Struggle in Colorado," *Arena*, XXXIV (November, 1905), 490-91.

[37] Ibid., pp. 490-491.

[38] Denver *Times*, 19 June 1902, p. 2.

[39] Minutes of the Board of Directors of the Denver Gas and Electric Company, 7 May 1901 (Public Service Company of Colorado, Denver, Colorado).

[40] Denver *Times*, 19 June 1902, p. 2.

[41] Colorado Springs *Gazette*, 5 July 1902, p. 2.

[42] Denver *Times*, 25 June 1902, p. 12.

[43] Minutes of the Board of Directors of the Denver Gas and Electric Company, 2 September 1910, (Public Service Company of Colorado, Denver, Colorado), pp. 2-3 and *Moody's Manual of Railroads and Corporation Securities*, (New York: Moody's Publishing Company, 1910), p. 1617.

44 Denver *Post,* 20 September 1902, p. 1 and editorial, p. 4.

45 Denver *Post,* 20 September 1902, p. 1.

46 *Moody's Manual of Railroads and Corporation Securities* (New York: Moody Publishing Co., 1905), p. 1303.

47 Denver. Charter of the City and County of Denver, Article III, "Franchises," C3.1, C3.2, C3.3, March 29, 1904 and Article IX, "Public Utilities," p. 90 Section 257, 29 March 1904.

48 King, *History of the Government of Denver,* pp. 210-211.

49 *Commercial and Financial Chronicle* LXXII (26 May 1906), 1214. According to the 9 June 1907 *Commercial and Financial Chronicle* the vote was 8340 for and 7725 against.

50 Denver *Republican,* 27 May 1906, p. 1.

51 Ben B. Lindsey and Harvey J. O'Higgins *The Beast* (New York: Doubleday, Page and Company, 1910).

52 *Rocky Mountain News,* 12 August 1906, p. 1. In addition to the Denver Gas Company other utilities were accused of enjoying enormous profits and power. They were the telephone company, run by Edward F. Field,Jr., the water company, headed by Walter S. Cheesman, the tramway company, with William G. Evans as president, and various railroad enterprises controlled by David H. Moffat.

53 In 1907 Judge Ben Lindsey established the first juvenile court in the country; a system that was copied by many other justice systems.

54 Lindsey, *The Beast,* p. 241.

55 Ibid.

56 Ibid., p. 243.

57 Ibid., p. 244.

58 William G. Evans, president of the Denver Tramway Company also left town to avoid being subpoened. *Rocky Mountain News*, 9 August 1906, p. 1.

59 *Rocky Mountain News*, 11 April 1959, p. 6.c.

60 Lindsey, *The Beast*, pp. 250-51.

61 King, *The History of the Government of Denver*, p. 279.

62 *Lines*, August-September, 1950, p. 10.

63 Alex Groner, *American Heritage History of Business and Industry* (New York: American Heritage Publishing Co., Inc., 1972), p. 249.

64 *Progressive Age* XX (1 April 1902), 131 and *Progressive Age*, XX (15 August 1902), p. 234.

65 *Electrical Review*, No. 2 (14 July 1906), 61.

66 *Progressive Age*, XX (1 April 1902) 131.

67 "The City Beautiful", unpaged (Denver Public Library Western History Room, Denver, Colorado).

68 Ibid.

69 *Progressive Age* XXI (August 15, 1903). 176.

70 *Progressive Age*, XXX (August 15, 1912), 710.

71 *Progressive Age* XXI (1 May 1903), 221.

72 *Progressive Age* XX (1 April 1902), 131.

73 Ibid.

74 Ibid.

75 *Progressive Age* XXI (1 October 1903), 473.

76 *Progressive Age* XXX (15 November 1912), 989.

77
Electrical Review LXIX (14 July 1906), 61.

78
Progressive Age, XXIV (15 August 1906), 519.

79
The inventor of the sign, G. E. Williamson, worked for the Denver Gas and Electric Company. *Progressive Age*, XXVIII (10 April 1910), 295.

80
Denver Gas and Electric Company stockholders meeting --memo to stockholders 8 April 1905, p. 213 (Public Service Company, Denver, Colorado).

81
Progressive Age, XXI (15 August 1903), 176.

82
King, *The History of the Government of Denver*, p. 210.

CHAPTER 5

EARLY UTILITY REGULATION

During the period between 1890 and World War I America became less agrarian and decentralized and increasingly more integrated and urban. This transformation was aided by utilities as they supplied power for new industrialization and provided amenities that enticed people to move to the city. As more people flocked to urban areas, utilities likewise expanded and became an even more dominant political force than they had previously been. Many people objected to the power of the utilities, as well as to the urban political machines, often controlled by the same men. In response, a group of progressive reformers rose up to establish a regulatory body that could control utilities.

It was clear that neither competition from other utilities nor provisions of the franchise system would adequately regulate utilities. Ruthless competition actually proved detrimental to the consumers, and a franchise was not flexible enough to accommodate changing economic situations. Furthermore, people wished to remove the regulatory process from the politics of local government, and as a result, many states turned to the commission system to control utilities.

The state utility commissions had their antecendents in the Granger era when midwestern farmers opposed the excessive railroad and warehousing rates. The United States Supreme Court, in *Munn* v. *Illinois* (1877), affirmed the right of states to regulate businesses affected with public interest, and gave them the authority to fix rates--authority which was delegated to commissions.[1] However, in 1886 the Supreme Court repudiated some of this state control by ruling, in *Wabash, St. Louis and Pacific Railway Co.* v. *Illinois*, that it was the exclusive power of Congress to regulate interstate commerce.[2] The Wabash case had much less effect on gas and electric utilities than it did on transportation, because most energy utilities were intrastate operations.

Munn v. *Illinois* created problems for utilities because it did not set clear guidelines for setting rates and regulating businesses. In some states where the utilities had strong political influence, they were allowed to charge almost any rate they wished, while in others the rates were set so low that a utility could not provide adequate service. Because of the difficulties of determining fair returns for regulated businesses, it was clear that a standard for arriving at reasonable rates had to be delineated.

In 1898 the United States Supreme Court, in *Smyth.* v. *Ames,* set forth specific factors to determine the value of a company's property. Once the value was properly determined, the rates could be set, and the court was given the right to review the rates, if contested, (although it did not have the authority to set rates).[3] *Smyth* v *Ames* was decided more to insure private companies a fair return on their investments than to protect the public rights.[4] This landmark decision made it necessary for the states to create full-time utility commissions because city councils and state legislatures had neither the time nor the expertise to manage the regulatory process.[5]

Progressives designed the commission to carry out the day-to-day detail of the broad policies set forth by a state legislature.[6] The commission system provided for a permanent staff of non-political personnel that had the expertise, training, and time to make decisions according to well-defined rules. They were given some flexibility to tailor decisions in response to special situations, and the system was, therefore, much more flexible than franchise regulation.[7] The commissions also developed a system of uniform accounting, to eliminate discrimination between classes of consumers, and to establish standards of service.[8]

Wisconsin, New York, Massachusetts and California were the first states to implement the modern commission system. In 1907 Senator Robert M. La Follette of Wisconsin, an ardent progressive, led the way by advocating a strong commission in his state and Governor Charles Evans Hughes of New York followed suit soon thereafter. When the Wisconsin and New York commissions proved to be very effective, California and Massachusetts set up strong commission systems, and other states picked up the idea in the following years. Early on, most commissions acted more as a forum for hearing complaints than as a body to administer rates.[9]

In some states even utilities joined consumers in advocating regulation by a state commission. When Samuel Insull was president of the electric industry's trade association, the National Electric Light Association (NELA), he tried to convince member utilities to support legislation which would regulate rates and service. Utilities could, he argued, submit to control in exchange for an exclusive franchise, i.e., a guaranteed monopoly. He reminded industry members that competition had often resulted in an unstable price structure and had made investments riskier. Very few utility leaders agreed with Insull, but he aggressively promoted his ideas for many years.

In the early 1900s many municipalities threatened to acquire utilities as the only means of exercising authority over them. This alarmed the utility magnates, and Insull was able to put together a committee of NELA members, including Henry L. Doherty, a past president, to lobby for the commission system. Committee members, as well as many utility leaders, realized that the prices their companies charged were going to come under scrutiny in one way or another, and a commission system was much preferred over municipal ownership.[10]

Colorado's attempts to regulate utilities with a commission adhered to the national trend. In 1862, the territorial legislature passed a law to secure good service and maintenance of wagon trails and railroads. Fourteen years later when Colorado became a state its constitution included provisions for supervising the railroad rates and service and in 1885, the Colorado legislature established a one-member railroad commission and gave the comissioner power to act only in an advisory role. The legislature diminished the commission's powers when it discontinued funding in 1886, and in 1893 abolished it altogether.[11]

Although the transportation commission disappeared, the need for a regulatory body did not. As a result, in 1907, The Colorado legislature passed a new act creating a more comprehensive railroad commission. While it was more effective that its predecessor, it was hampered by lawsuits from three railroads challenging its constitutionality.[12]

The following year, when progressive John Franklin Shafroth was elected governor, in 1908 he asked the legislature for a new law which would establish the legality of the transportation commission. Shafroth believed that railroads were quasi-public corporations whose rates should be regulated to insure that they would be fair and nondiscriminatory.[13] In a fractious legislative session the law was turned down by a vote of nineteen to nine through the influences of the Democrat machine and conservative Republicans.[14]

Shafroth, an astute politician, waited until the public was so outraged by high rates that it could overcome the power of the Robert Speer political machine. In August, 1910 Shafroth called a special session of the Colorado General Assembly to again appeal for a public service commission.[15] The General Assembly passed a modified and weaker bill than that of 1907 and Shafroth reluctantly signed the bill on the premise that it was better than no law at all. The bill prohibited unreasonable charges, rebates and freight discrimination,[16] but it set no initial rates, nor did it abolish the free passes given to many businessmen and politicians to ride the railroads. Furthermore, the maximum fine that could be imposed was $1,000. A stronger entity, the Public Utilities Commission of Denver, which was a municipal railroad commission, was born from the new law, and existed from 1910 until 1918, when it was incorporated into the Colorado Public Utilities Commission.[17]

Denverites reelected Shafroth in 1910. He renewed his energies to fight for a more comprehensive public utilities commission. In his 1911 inaugural address he lashed out at the overly powerful transportation, communication, and energy utilities. He asked for a commission with broader power to protect both the investor and the consumer, but the Speer "machine" had the votes to defeat the bill.[18]

Shafroth's campaign for an effective commission was aided by Progressive George Creel, a *Rocky Mountain News* reporter who fought Denver's political machine. Speer, who was mayor from 1904 to 1912 and again from 1916 to 1918, gained most of his support from strong business elements, including the utilities although he appealed to both parties and all classes.[19] In order to diminish this power, Creel, presented arguments for removing the corruption from Denver's election process, and with the help of progressives, legislation was passed to adopt the direct primary and to regulate voter registration. In 1912 the state also adopted laws to allow for citizen initiative and referendum in an effort to make government more responsible to the electorate. In spite of the new reforms the influence of the power brokers continued, and utility men freely admitted that manipulating politics was part of their business.[20]

In 1913 a different bill for a strong utility commission was introduced in the General Assembly. This brought Thomas Patterson, another newspaperman and fighter against political corruption, into the fray. He argued that the proposed public utilities bill was well conceived and that it was the only way to end the corruption. Corruption for which the "public utility corporations were responsible in their desire to control towns and counties and to build up a vast political power."[21] Finally, on 1 January 1913 the legislature passed the bill, known as the Burris-VanTilberg Public Utility Act. Although it was not as strong as the laws in New York and Wisconsin, it was much more encompassing than the railroad commission. The Colorado Public Utilities Commission, with three commissioners appointed by the legislature began functioning in 1914.[22] It was given control over railroads and express companies, gas, electric power, water, telephone, and telegraph. The commissioners, empowered to determine fair rates and suspend rates during an investigation, were also responsible for overseeing service and maintenance.[23] The new law eliminated the free pass, which in the past had been liberally distributed to influence governmental decisions.

Denver's utilities escaped regulation by the new commission, nonetheless. The Colorado State Constitution specified that control of public utilities is a governmental power which can be carried out by the state or delegated to the municipalities, and in Colorado such jurisdiction given to home rule cities. Although this was questioned several times.[24] By a close decision the judges of the Colorado supreme court, in the Mountain State Telephone and Telegraph case of 1920, ruled that self government rested in the municipalities according to the recent adoption of the home rule article in the constitution. The court's decision brought problems to public utility regulation in Colorado, since it created a division of control over public utilities between the state and local governments resulting in unequal treatment. Residents in different parts of Colorado paid different rates for the same service, and a single utility operating in different areas had to obey diverse rules.[25]

The home rule cities like Denver had no workable procedure for determining valuations or investigating earnings and expenses in order to establish rates. Any decision by council vote was too subjective unless an outside consultant was hired for each case. It was also expensive for cities to research rate requests, and home rule cities, including Denver, Pueblo, Colorado Springs, Boulder and Grand Junction continually asked for help from the state commission. Although the commissioners were not compelled to do so, they were willing to give advice because they realized that they had many more resources available. Fortunately, with the exception of Denver, few home rule cities wanted the responsibility of regulating public utilities, and therefore lobbied for an amendment to the constitution restoring the Public

Utility Commission's jurisdiction in home rule cities.[26] In Denver the City Charter was not amended to accomplish this until 1953.

It was little wonder that a city council had difficulty determining fair and reasonable rates for utilities. Utility pricing was complex to begin with and was made more complicated by the regulation statutes. The public utilities commission did not actually set the rates, but instead approved a rate schedule based on the revenue requirements needed for a fair rate of return.[27]

Since the public utility commission system was first established, opinions have differed on how much profit a utility should be allowed to make. Between 1915 and 1929 rates were established to allow between seven- and eight-percent profit, because other businesses were earning at approximately that level. During the Great Depression and for thirty years thereafter, the rates hovered around the six percent profit range. After World War II, with rising inflation and interest rates, regulators raised the rate of return to eight percent, and since then it has continued to rise.[28]

The public utility commissions established a comprehensive system of gathering information, including extensive public hearings, to arrive at fair and reasonable rate schedules. Each time a rate proposal was submitted to the PUC, the commissioners had to determine the cost to produce the service, the amount of cash flow needed for the business to remain financially sound, the operational efficiency of the company, and the degree to which the rates were reasonable and non-discriminatory.[29] The commission and the utility were often in an adversarial position where the utility asked for more than it really needed just to get enough. The commission system of regulation has been preoccupied with the past, slow to adapt to change, and thus has been a detriment to the setting of future goals by the utility. Nevertheless, commissions seemed to be the best form of control since the utilities had proved that they could not regulate themselves.

Utilities are affected by federal regulation as well. Most federal legislation attempted to limit the unfair advantage of the monopoly position rather than to set rates. The history of federal regulation, like the commission system in the states, began with the railroads and evolved into regulation of other utilities and big businesses. In response to the Wabash decision insuring federal control over interstate commerce the Interstate Commerce Commission Act of 1887 was passed to control unfair trade practices. Although the ICC was authorized to investigate complaints and recommend reparations, it had little effect on the strong monopolies.[30] Therefore in 1890, Congress passed the Sherman Antitrust Act, the first law to limit monopolies in any meaningful way.[31] Rather than regulating rates, the Sherman Antitrust law forbade the concentration of economic power and challenged the corporations which tried to gobble up competitors and control an industry.[32] Any combination or form of trust that conspired to restrain trade was outlawed. In an effort to circumvent the new law, some trusts reorganized into giant corporations, while others resorted to a holding company to control subsidiaries through ownership of small amounts of stock.

President Theodore Roosevelt, annoyed at the gigantic national trusts which manipulated power companies and other industries, decided that the government had the legal right and ability to prosecute these quasi-monopolies. His first target was the Northern Securities Company which controlled several important railroads. Although opposed by the moguls of the railroad industry, the President in 1903 secured a federal court order to break up the Northern Securities company, and established the authority of the federal government to restrict the misuse of trusts. At his urging Congress passed the Hepburn Act in 1906 giving more teeth to the Interstate Congress Commission to regulate American industry.[33]

Progressive reformers continued to curb the ability of holding companies to eliminate competition and make enormous profits. Because there were so many complaints that the Sherman Act was too broad, President Woodrow Wilson proposed the Clayton Act which Congress passed in 1914, defining unfair practices with more specificity and outlawing interlocking directorates. The Federal Trade Commission was created the same year to enforce the Clayton Act in the same way that the Interstate Commerce Commission enforced laws relating to transportation. In their early years, however, the ICC and FTC proved more a friend to business than a regulator. In 1920 Congress passed the Federal Water Power Act and created the Federal Power Commission, giving it jurisdiction over all projects involved with the development, transmission and utilization of hydroelectric power on navigable waterways. When the generated electricity was used in interstate commerce the FPC was given the authority to regulate rates, service, and securities. At that time state commissions jealously guarded their right to regulate intrastate commerce.[34]

Although the progressives attempted to turn the railroad commissions of the Populist/Progressive era into a system that would control and clean up the utility business, they were not entirely successful. It was not until legislation was passed during the New Deal that state and federal regulation was adequate to control monopolies, protect the consumers, and provide a standard of reasonableness for utilities rates. The commission system was simply not strong enough to provide a substitute for competition and to put the regulated industries under the same restraints competition places non-regulated industries.[35]

NOTES--CHAPTER 5

1 John Bauer, *Updating Public Utility Regulation: Assuring fair Rates and Fair Returns* (Chicago Public Administrative Service, 1966), pp. v-vi.

2 Henry C Spurr, *Guiding Principles of Public Service Regulation*, I (Rochester, NY: Public Utilities Reports, Inc., 1924), pp. 5-6.

3 Bauer, *Updating Public Utility Regulation Public Utility Regulation*, p. 18.

4 Ibid., p. v.

5 Martin T. Farris and Roy J. Sampson, *Public Utilities: Regulation, Management, and Ownerhip* (Prospect Heights, IL: Waveland Press, Inc., 1973), p. 160.

6 Charles L. Phillips, Jr., *The Economics of Regulation, Theory and Practice in the Transportation and Public Utility Industries* (Homewood, Il: Richard D. Irwin, Inc., 1969), p. 85.

7 Farris and Sampson, *Public Utilities*, p. 66.

8 John Bauer, *Transforming Public Utility Regulation: A Definite Administrative Program* (New York: Harper and Brothers Publishers, 1950), pp. 27-29 and 55.

9 Farris and Sampson, *Public Utilities*, p. 270.

10 Douglas D. Anderson, *Regulatory Politics and Electric Utilities: A Case Study in Political Economy* (Boston, MA: Auburn House Publishing Company, 1981), pp. 34-37.

11 Wilbur Stone, *History of Colorado*, I (Chicago: the S. J. Clarke Publishing Company, 1918), p. 206.

12 *State Railroad Commission of Colorado, First Annual Report*, 1907-08 (Denver: 1908), pp. 7-11.

13 Colorado. *House Journal* 1909 (Denver: 1909), p. 75.

14 "John Franklin Shafroth, Reform Governor of Colorado, 1909-1913," *Colorado Magazine*, XXIX (January, 1952), 45.

15 Ibid.

16 Colorado: *Session Laws of Colorado* 1910 (Denver: 1910), p. 45-46.

17Denver *Post*, 31 May 1918, p. 20.

18 "John Franklin Shafroth," *Colorado Magazine*, p. 46.

18 Ibid., p. 71.

19 Carl Abbott, Stephen J. Leonard, David McComb *Colorado: History of the Centennial State*, revised edition, (Boulder, CO: Colorado Associated University Press, 1982), pp.246-47.

20 Ibid., pp. 249-50.

21 *Rocky Mountain News*, 6 March 1913, p. 7.

22There are now three commissioners appointed by the governor and approved by the legislature.

23 *Electrical Review and Western Electrician*, LXV (29 August 1914), 423.

24 Colorado Public Utilities Commission Decisions: *Castle Rock Mountain Railway and Park* v. *Denver Tramway Company Public Utility Reports* (Rochester, NY: The Lawyers Cooperative Publishing Company, 1915)p. 244; *East Denver Business and Property Association* v. *Denver Tramway Company Public Utilities Reports* (Rochester, NY: The Lawyers Cooperative Publishing Company, 1917) pp. 206-15; *City and County of Denver* v. *Mountain States Telephone and Telegraph Company, Public Utilities Reports* (Rochester, NY: Public Utilities Reports, Inc., 1920), p. 238.

[25] Henry C. Spurr, *Guiding Principles of Public Service Regulation*, I (Rochester, New York: Public Utilities Reports, Inc, 1924), p. 136.

[26] Ibid., pp. 138-39.

[27] Leonard S. Hyman, *America's Electric Utilities: Past, Present and Future* (Arlington, VA: Public Utilities Reports, Inc., 1983), p. 143.

[28] Ibid.

[29] Farris and Sampson, *Public Utilities*, p. 234.

[30] Paul W. McAvaoy, ed., *The Crisis of the Regulatory Commissions, an Introduction to a Current Issue of Public Policy* (New York: W. W. Norton & Co, Inc., 1970), p. 6.

[31] Martin G. Glaeser, *Public Utilities in American Capitalism* (New York: The MacMillan Company, 1957), p. 69.

[32] John M. Kohlmeier, Jr., *The Regulators: Watchdog Agencies and the Public Interest* (New York: Harper & Row Publishers, 1969), p. 21.

[33] Martin and Farris, *Public Utilities*, pp. 64-65.

[34] Phillips, *Economics of Regulation*, p. 115.

[35] Ibid., p. 125.

CHAPTER 6

DENVER GAS AND ELECTRIC LIGHT COMPANY

1909-1923

Henry L. Doherty decided to expand his utility operations by establishing the Denver Gas and Electric Light Company in 1909, and in the following year the Cities Service Company, a holding company which would eventually acquire two hundred electric and oil properties. The Denver company created a confusion of similarly titled companies because the old Denver Gas and Electric Company, (created in 1899 by combining the gas and electric companies), the nucleus of his new holding company, existed until 1911 when it was absorbed by the Denver Gas and Electric Light Company, which also became part of Cities Service Company. The Denver Gas and Electric Light Company existed until 1923 when it was absorbed by Doherty's Public Service Company of Colorado.

Articles of incorporation for the Denver Gas and Electric Light Company were filed on 29 November 1909, authorizing a capital of ten million dollars, or three times that of the predecessor Denver Gas and Electric Company. Henry L. Doherty was president of the new company, Franklin W. Frueauff was vice president and general manager, William J. Barker was second vice president and general superintendent, and Clare N. Stannard, was secretary.[1] In 1910 Doherty established the Cities Service Company and acquired the stock of Denver Gas and Electric Company through the exchange of 1.8 shares of preferred stock and .9 of a share of common stock of Cities Service for each share of Denver Gas and Electric. The transfer was made using the Henry L. Doherty Company and the acquisition was financed with the transfer of property and very little cash.[2]

The holding company was a growing trend in the early 1900s. The holding company was not an operating company. It merely owned common stock and other securities to control the policies of the operating companies in its system. The holding company usually exchanged its own capital stock for the capital stock it sought to control. The theory was that the consolidation of competing or scattered plants increased profits, eliminated competition, and avoided regulation. Prior to 1900 there were only five holding companies of any description in the United States; between 1900 and 1910 eleven new holding companies were established; seven appeared during the next decade;

and, between 1920 and 1930 forty-six holding companies were created.[3]

The early holding company operations were usually quite simple, where the primary company owned stock in its operating subsidiaries. Over the years, however, and particularly in the 1920s, the system became more complex with multiple levels of holding companies in one system. This was called pyramiding. The true parent company could control many more assets with less capital through pyramiding. Over the years the complexity of holding companies grew, and companies in separate systems began to buy the stock of other holding companies which produced a maze of intercompany ownership.[4]

The advantages of the holding companies were similar to the conglomerates of today. Large amounts of capital for building and improving public utilities could be more easily raised. Securities could be sold more readily than those of a smaller company with a narrower market. There was also a higher degree of stablility in earnings, because the poor business performance of a single company would have only a small effect on the large group. Finally, the holding company with its large financial accumulations could afford to diversify more easily than the smaller companies.[5]

The holding companies serviced their subsidiary businesses by providing sophisticated management and capital. These services were not provided free of charge, however, because large management fees were assessed. Unscrupulous managers at the top of the pyramid would often arrange for engineering, management, and financial services at a premium price for their "family members."[6] Never missing a chance for earnings, holding companies also borrowed money from the operating companies at an unreasonably low rate of interest. The money was then lent to other companies within the system at much higher interest rates.[7]

The highly organized and unified utilities worried critics who were concerned about the increased concentration of ownership. A few utility barons seemingly controlled the industry for their own self interests, and it was not clear whether people who depended on gas and electricity would be able to regulate them.[8] Gifford Pinchot, Governor of Pennsylvania and father of the conservation movement said, ". . . shall we and our decendants be free men, masters of our destinies and our own souls, or we shall be the helpless servants of the most widespread, far-reaching, and penetrating monopoly ever known."[9] Expressing the opinion of many he stated that, "Either we must control electric power, or its masters and owners will control us."[10] Until the Public Utility Holding Company Act of 1935 the trusts did, in fact, control the industry.

In 1911 the Denver Gas and Electric Light Company consolidated its holdings by adding the property and franchises of Denver Gas and Electric Company, the Lacombe Electric Company, Denver Highlands Company, and various coal fields throughout the state.[11] The Denver Gas and Electric Light Company served all of Denver, as well as Golden, Englewood, Littleton, Aurora, Edgewater, Petersburg, Arvada, Sheridan and Ft.Logan. The population involved in this area was 215,000.[12]

One of the companies acquired in 1911 was the Denver City Steam Heating Company.[13] The steam heating operation was begun by hotel man John W. Smith, who built the city's first flour mill, and in 1869, Denver's first modern hotel. His hotel, the American House, located at Sixteenth and Blake Streets, was so popular that Smith could not afford to use valuable space for boilers to heat his establishment. Therefore, he looked for a suitable location for the steam heating equipment, which he found at Nineteenth and New Haven Streets near the railroad tracks and a coal supply. After building the steam plant he constructed pipes underground for six blocks to convey the steam to the American House.[14] The plant grew and demand from other businesses increased at such a rate that on 12 December 1879 he organized the Denver City Steam Heating Company to supply his hotel and other businesses.[15] By the time the Denver Gas and Electric Light Company acquired the Denver City Steam Heating plant in 1910, it was owned by Henry M. Porter and served much of the business section of the city. The new company added to its capacity and upgraded its facility.[16]

While Doherty was engaged in putting together a financial empire, he was also constructing a new building for Denver Gas and Electric Light Company, because the business had grown too large for its old headquarters. The Gas and Electric Building at Fifteenth and Champa streets was designed to be a showpiece. The interior was decorated with white stucco ceilings appointed with elegant fixtures. The building contained an auditorium which could also double as a theater. Lights literally covered the outside. One hundred thousand people attended the dedication to see the spectacle of the lighted building. It officially opened on 12 November 1910. At 8:00 p.m. when Mayor Robert Speer mounted a platform with General Manager Frank W. Frueauff and pushed a button to turn on the 13,000 exterior lights. The headquarters was touted as the most impressive of any power company in the country.[17]

In 1913 there was a slight shift in management for Denver Gas and Electric Light. Doherty was elected chairman of the board, a new position. Frank Frueauff stepped up to the office of president. William J. Barker became vice president and general manager, and Clare Stannard was reelected secretary. *Moody's Manual on Utility Investments* described the company that year as:

> . . . the only company furnishing electricity and gas for light, power and heating purposes in the city of Denver, Colorado. It is known to gas and electric men everywhere as one of the model properties in the United States. Its steady growth and success have been secured by the establishment of harmonious and cordial relations with the public, by furnishing the highest quality of service, by stimulating the growth of business through the vigorous use of approved modern and progressive methods, and by voluntarily lowering rate charged for service, both gas and electric, until now they are proportionally lower than in any other city of the United States. 18

Denver Gas and Electric Light Company encouraged people to use as much electricity as possible by introducing energy-consuming appliances to housewives. An employee during those days described one of their sales techniques:

> We used high-pressure (but wholly legitimate) methods to place irons in Denver homes. Every two salesmen were assigned a driver for a horse-drawn wagon, piled high with electric flatirons. We drove down each street, with one salesman covering each side of the street. We would ring the bell, shove a flatiron into the hands of the housewife, explain that this was a free one-week trial of the iron and that we would be back within a day or two, to show her how to operate it.
>
> We would then dash back to the slowly moving wagon and disregard the housewife's usual protests that she didn't want a flatiron, that she already had a perfectly satisfactory sad iron, and that she did not care to try it. Our reply--thrown over the shoulder, as we hurried away--was that she was under no obligation, and that we would be back in a day or two. The return call was made upon a bicycle so that it was obvious that we could not transport the flatiron back to the office.
>
> Sometimes on our return call the flatiron would still be on the front porch, sometimes just inside the door, and sometimes back in the kitchen. We persuaded the housewife to permit the flatiron to remain for the week's trial or to do some ironing with it. When we returned with the horse-drawn wagon at the end of the week--sometimes it was ten days or two weeks later--an occasional sale would be made.19

During it twenty-four year existence Denver Gas and Electric Light Company was involved in several notable disputes. When the company absorbed Denver Gas and Electric Company in 1911 it acquired the latter's

1906 franchise, which stipulated that all receipts the company collected in excess of 75 cents per 1,000 cubic feet of gas and six cents per kilowatt hour of electricity would be paid to the city treasury.[20] The Denver Gas and Electric Light Company decided to test the franchise clause by not paying the city the excess amount.[21]

Soon after that, in 1919, the Colorado Supreme Court announced its *Denver v. Mountain States Telephone and Telegraph Company* decision which gave home rule cities, rather than public utility commissions, jurisdiction over utilities.[22] Because of the ruling the city of Denver ordered an audit of Denver Gas and Electric Light Company books for the year 1918 to determine the mount owed the city. As a result, the city brought suit in district court against the company for $88,134.24. In December 1920 Judge Greeley W. Whitford ruled that Denver should collect the excess amount owed for 1918, and that the company would be required to abide by the 1906 franchise agreement in future years.[23] The utility appealed the case to the Colorado Supreme Court. While the case was being decided the company continued to withold the extra payment due the city and in retaliation, the city refused to pay its bills for street lighting.[24]

The disagreement went on for years, but it was finally settled out of court. General Manager Clare Stannard reported to the board of directors in 1923 that an agreement had been reached with the city of Denver which required the company to pay the receipts for the sale of gas in excess of 75 cents per 1000 cubic feet. In return the city would allow the company to subtract its uncollectable receivables from that amount, and the city would forego interest charges for the period in question, and pay Denver Gas and Electric the money it had withheld for street lighting.[25] In May, 1925 the successor company, Public Service Company made a final payment to the city of $74,843.70 and the same day city auditor Begole wrote a check to the company for $537,000 owed for street lighting.[26]

A second dispute was a disagreement with labor. In May, 1920, members of three unions, the Electrical Workers Union Number 111, the Gas Stoker Union Number 357, the Gas Fitters and Stenographers Union all voted to strike the Denver Gas and Electric Light Company.[27] Union members were protesting low wages, as well as an unfavorable ruling from the State Industrial Commission with regard to these wages. The strike continued into the summer, and the Denver Trades and Labor Assembly put the Denver Gas and Electric Light Company on its "unfair list."[28] Company official Wiliam J. Barker took a hard line when he said: "We don't care whether they put us on the unfair list or not. We might just as well be there as any place." He went on to declare that there would be no settlement made with the strikers.[29] The newspapers made no mention of the strike, but it is probable that, with the State Industrial Commission and the company against the unions, the strikers were forced to give up.

World War I demands for electricity put extreme pressure on utility operations. Many large generating stations were built and the war department encouraged extensive interconnection in order to meet anticipated needs.[30] Interconnection, the joining of small electrical systems, was more efficient than larger plants working in isolation. Despite the progress many military people felt that, had a serious shortage existed, the interconnection would have been insufficient to avoid a crisis. Some went so far as to say that it was fortunate that the war ended when it did because there was never a well-developed plan that would have allowed an overloaded system to take advantage of the surplus of a neighboring utility.

Although the government did not support an effort to promote a regional system of electric service after the war, there were those who did.[31] Proponents tried to garner support by writing in journals and speaking to trade organizations. This movement, although not embraced by all, probably contributed to the growth of monopolies and holding companies in the 1920s.

Another interesting aspect of the war also had an effect on the utility business in the 1920s. Samuel Insull, Chicago's utility entrepreneur, organized a publicity campaign to rouse the American people after his native England had gone to war in 1914. Insull was the epitome of the self-made man. Born in England, his father was a poor clergyman, and in order to earn badly needed money young Insull went to work for a newspaper. When he learned that the newspaper was owned by one of his heroes, Thomas Edison, he worked extra hard in his job as stenographer. His efforts were rewarded when Edison sent for Insull to be his secretary.[32] Working long hours Insull rose rapidly in the management ranks to become president of the Chicago Edison Company when he was in his thirties. By 1907 all of Chicago's electricity was provided by Insull through the Commonwealth Edison Company. He accumulated enough money to begin acquiring property of his own, and over the years put together a complex holding company system called Utility Investments, Incorporated.[33]

Because of his patriotism, Insull was named chairman of the State Council of Defense in Illinois. He was a master at organizing speakers bureaus, neighborhoods, committees, newspapers, ministers, labor and fraternal organizations in support of the war effort. When the United States entered the war Insull expanded his efforts by forming a coalition of thirteen state defense councils and served as its chairman. At the end of the war the President, several foreign countries, numerous governors, and the press commended his successful efforts in aiding the country.[34]

The Rocky Mountain Committee on Public Utilities, a group consisting of the thirty leading utility men in Colorado, New Mexico and Wyoming, publicized the wartime contributions of utilities which included high employment and low energy prices.[35] Denverities, however, did not necessarily agree, and at the end of the war complained that large corporations, including the utilities had taken advantage of the war to raise prices. The Denver Gas and Electric Light Company had been given a six percent increase in domestic and industrial rates in the winter of 1918, and by the fall of 1919 the company was asking for higher price. The public utilities commission investigated the rate schedule but did grant the rate hike.

The end of World War I marked the end of a phase in United States industry. Business historian Thomas Cochran points out that both electricity and the gasoline engine changed business, the economy, and society beginning in the 1890s. Between 1900 and 1930 public utilities of every description added fuel to the economy by demanding and using new capital.[36] At the end of the war the steam engine was being replaced by electric motors which were supplied with electricity from power plants and high-voltage lines. The use of electricity continued to change the lives of people and businesses. Factories could now be built smaller, cleaner and more efficiently with the use of electricity.[37] Furthermore, the automobile and truck, which was increasingly available to people, altered transportation patterns and living arrangements.

After World War I people became increasingly resentful of the exploitation and arrogance of the monopolistic holding companies which took advantage of the absence of competition by charging rates that were not commensurate with operating costs. The public distrusted all large corporations, including utilities.[38] Their abuse brought an outcry for stronger regulation to restrain these seemingly uncontrollable monsters. To change the negative image of the utilities, Samuel Insull came to the rescue, mobilizing the same public relations tools he had used during the war effort. The publicity campaign of the 1920s was a study in marketing expertise,[39] but one so intense that it would eventually backfire. Henry L. Doherty put Colorado in the middle of the effort to change public opinion.

Doherty had a great stake in creating favorable public opinion because he did not want consumer resentment to escalate into regulation that would harm his business. He had spent the years between 1909 and 1923 creating new companies and merging others under his powerful holding company, Cities Service. Each maneuver was calculated to enrich his empire and although he made a profit from each acquisition, he also improved the companies he created or acquired. One of his more successful venture would be to create the Public Service Company of Colorado.

NOTES--CHAPTER 6

1 Articles of Incorporation of the Denver Gas and Electric Light Company, November 29, 1905 (Colorado State Archives, Denver, Colorado). Incorporators were Willis V. Elliott, Rodney J. Bardwell, and Charles A. Frueauff. Board of Director were Willis V. Elliott, R. J. Bardwell, Charles A. Frueauff, Roy C. Hecox, H. H. Scott, Paul R. Jones, Harry T. Hughes, J. M. Mulvhill, Thomas F. Kennedy, Edgar McComb, George W. Bickler, W. C. Sterne and A. F. Traver.

2 U.S. Congress, Senate, *Report of the Federal Trade Commission*, S. Doc. 92, 70th Cong., 1st sess. 1934, pt. 35.

3 U.S., Congress, House, Committee on Interstate and Foreign Commerce, *Public Utilities Holding Companies*, before a subcommittee on the Committee on Interstate and Foreign Commerce, House of Representatives, on H.R. 5423, 74th Cong. 1st sess., 1935, part III, p. 2191.

4 Eli Winston Clemens, *Economics and Public Utilities* (New York: Appleton-Century-Crofts, Inc., 1950), pp. 494-95.

5 Thomas Cochran, *America Business in the Twentieth Century*, p. 42.

6 Eliot Jones and Truman C. Bigham, *Principles of Public Utilities* (New York: The MacMillan Company, 1931), pp. 591-94.

7 Martin T. Farris and Roy J. Sampson, *Public Utilities: Regulation, Management, and Ownership* (Prospect Heights, IL: Waveland Press, inc., 1973), p. 144.

8 Thomas P. Hughes, *Networks of Power, Electrification in Western Society, 1880-1930* (Baltimore: (Prospect Heights, IL:" Waveland Press, Inc., 1973), p. 144.

9"Gifford Pinchot," *Cyclopaedia of American Biography* XXVI (New York: James T White and Co., 1936), p. 28.

Hughes, *Networks of Power*, p. 305.
10
Minutes of Lacombe Electric Company, 24 May
11
1911 and 11 July 1911. (Public Service Company of Colorado, Denver, Colorado).
Moody's Manual of Railroads and Corporation
12
Securities (New York: Moody Manual Company Publishers, 1913), p. 3126.
13
Minutes of Denver Gas and Electric Light Company 13 July 1911 (Public Service Company of Colorado, Denver, Colorado).
Rocky Mountain News, 17 May 1951, p. 61.
14
"History of Company Steam System" (Public
15
Service Company of Colorado, Denver, Colorado: n.d.), p. 1.
Denver *Republican*, 18 March 1911, p. 1.
16
Progressive Age XXVIII (15 December 1910),
17
1103-04.
Moody's Manual of Investments 1913, p 3122.
18
Public Service Company of Colorado:
19
Providing Energy for More than a Century, (Denver: Public Service Company, 1976), pp. 6-7.
20
Denver Municipal Facts, City and County of Denver, July, 1919, II p. 10 and *Rocky Mountain News*, 19 November 1913, p. 14.
21
Rocky Mountain News, 5 December 1920, p. 4.
Denver *Times* 14 January 1919, pp. 1 and 9.
22
Rocky Mountain News 5 December 1920, p. 4.
23
Rocky Mountain News, 2 July 1922, p. 5.
24
Denver Gas and Electric Light minutes, 26
25
June 1923, (Public Service Company, Denver, Colorado), p. 2.
Denver *Post*, 6 May 1925, p. 31.
26
Denver *Times*, 17 May 1920, p. 1.
27

Denver *Times*, 7 June 1920, p. 8.

28
Ibid.

29
Hughes, *Networks of Power*, p. 291.

30
Philip J. Funginello, *Toward a National Power*
31
Policy: The New Deal and the Electric utility Industry, 1933-1941 (Washington, DC: The American Enterprise Institute for Public Policy Research, 1936) p. 227.

Alex Groner, *The American Heritage History of*
32
American Business and Industry (New York: American Heritage Publishing Co., Inc., 1972), p. 283.

Ibid.
33

Lee Metcalf and Vic Reinemer, *Overcharge*,
34
(New York: David McKay Co., Inc., 1967), p. 93.

Rocky Mountain Committee on Public Utilities,
35
Bulletin, No. I (15 November 1920), no pagination. (Denver: 302 Gas and Electric Building).

Thomas C. Cochran, *American Business in the*
36
Twentieth Century (Cambridge, MA: Harvard University Press, 1972), p. 20.

Ibid.
37

Martin and Farris, *Public Utilities*, pp. 144-
38
45.

William E. Keily, ed., *Public Utilities in*
39
Modern Life: Selected Speeches (1914-1923) by Samuel Insull (Chicago: privately printed, 1924), pp. v-vii.

CHAPTER 7

PUBLIC SERVICE COMPANY 1-2-3

When Henry L. Doherty left Colorado the state's largest utility was no longer closely associated with his flamboyant personality. In fact, as utilities expanded they were much less identified with their top executive who took on the role of manager rather than entrepreneur. As public opinion grew more negative during the 1920s, many utility executives intentionally avoided publicity. Doherty moved to New York and was able to stay out of the local press, but he continued to play an active part in developing Colorado utilities during the 1920s and 1930s.

Colorado politics in the 1920s was primarily an adherence to the status quo. For Coloradans, and the rest of the nation, the spirit of youth and the drive to improve society weakened, and people appeared to be more interested in their own well being than in reform. In the absence of progressive thinking, reactionary groups like the Ku Klux Klan moved in, winning support of many in a confused decade. The KKK blamed labor, and especially the foreign born and so-called radicals for the ills of society. The Klan contributed to successful political candidates, and for a while wielded significant influence in the governmental process. Although the Klan's power began to decline in the mid-twenties, Colorado voters continued to elect conservative leaders who were opposed to progressivism.[1]

Colorado's growth slowed after World War I, bringing low prices and hard times to the grain and livestock business. Mining also suffered when the end of hostilities brought a dramatic decrease in the demand for industrial metals. The decline in mining and agriculture led to a slump in manufacturing enterprises that processed foodstuff and minerals.[2] In spite of some "sick" industries, the post-war years were a time of prosperity for the nation as per capita income rose by twenty-three percent.[3]

A new wave of business mergers came in the 1920s with an increase from 368 in 1920 to 1,245 in 1924. For manufacturers, particularly, acquiring new companies allowed them to apply large-scale technology and organizational methods to their operations. In addition, more capital was available to finance the research and development of new products.[4] The expanding economy created increased demand for electricity and gas which spurred further development of utilities. They too joined in the merger cycle and gained larger service territories and the concomitant areas of control, and even greater ability to set prices and exploit their markets.[5] Colorado would follow the national trend with the merging of several energy utilities in the 1920s.

The Denver Gas and Electric Light Company had difficulty meeting the rapidly increasing post-war demand for electricity. The firm had to purchase hydroelectric power from sources other than its own, but was not sure that this extra supply would be available for a long period of time. Because of the scarcity of power Henry L. Doherty decided to expand and form a new utility in Colorado. Formation of the new company took more than a year, and developed in three stages, referred to as Public Service Company numbers one, two, and three.

Cities Service filed articles of incorporation for its new subsidiary, Public Service Company (one) on 2 August 1923. The authorized capital was $100,000.[6] Two months later, on 3 October 1923, the stockholders of three other companies voted to merge with Public Service Company (one) to form Public Service Company (two). Consolidating were the Denver Gas and Electric Light

Company, the Western Light and Power Company and the Lakeside Construction Company. The latter was another Cities Service subsidiary established to build a steam generating plant.

PSC (two) was capitalized with forty million dollars and the articles of incorporation listed Charles A. Frueauff as president and John E. Loiseau as secretary. Very shortly after incorporation there was a change. A seventeen-man board of directors was elected with Henry L. Doherty as president of the company and Clare N. Stannard as vice-president and general manager. Although the important policy decisions for PSC (two) were made in New York where Doherty's Cities Service Company was based, most of the employees and directors were Colorado people. For example, fourteen of the seventeen board members were local men.[7] Stannard announced that the new firm would provide an ample source of power to supply the industries of the state, to attract new business, and to allow smaller communities to grow. He said that, "An infallible rule in the economic development of our country is that communities develop just as their public utilities expand."[8]

During 1924 PSC (two) began accumulating stock of Colorado Power Company and its subsidiary in Wyoming, Cheyenne Light and Power Company.[9] On 3 September 1924

Public Service Company (three), the last in the series, was created through the merger of the Colorado Power Company and (two).[10] The third merger, with a capitalization of fifty million dollars, gave Public Service Company a broader territory for Colorado Power's Shoshone Hydroelectric plant served Leadville, Salida and most of the San Luis Valley. The water power plant near Glenwood Springs was connected to Denver with 160 miles of high tension transmission lines.[11]

The emergence of PSC appeared to be the result of amiable agreements that helped all entities involved rather than being an attempt to curtail competition. Western Power and Light Company had been having trouble meeting the growing demand for electricity in northern Colorado. By combining with Denver Gas and Electric Light Company and forming (two) it was financially feasible to build a larger power plant and, as one unit, to have a better load factor and diversity of earnings.[12] The increased earnings would protect the investors and attract new capital. The creation of PSC (three) enabled the Colorado Power Company to provide a backup source of power for the Glenwood Light Company during times when it could not meet demand. Before consolidation managers of the smaller company had modernized the hydroelectric plant, and Public Service Company added even more improvements to increase productivity.[13]

PSC (three) was consistent with the national trend toward interconnection of electric properties to serve a large area with a central system.[14] However, the mergers also made good business sense, and helped Henry L. Doherty and Cities Service to make a great deal of money. Some of Doherty's profits were the result of unusual accounting techniques. This was later revealed through investigations of utilities by the Federal Trade Commission and Securities and Exchange Commission. For example, in 1910 when Doherty and a group of his associates created Cities Service, they traded Cities Service stock certificates for Denver Gas and Electric Company stock at par value even though Cities Service stock was valued at least two million dollars less than par.[15]

In 1911 Doherty merged several utilities into the Denver Gas and Electric Light Company by inflating the property account by $3,500,000. This write up which is an increase in the book value of an asset in excess of its actual cost, enabled the issuance by the new company of two shares of its own $100 par value common stock for each share of Denver Gas and Electric Company's $100 par value stock. In 1913 the property account was again inflated by $2,998,700 to balance an issuance of common stock for a stock dividend. In the October 1923 merger the property was increased once more by the amount of $2,500,000 for another common stock issue. Prior to these transactions the par value of the common stock of the Denver Gas and Electric Company was $3,500,000 and after the three transactions the common stock liability was $12,498,700.[16]

In April 1923 the Cities Service Company organized the Lakeside Construction Company, which in the following month began building the Valmont steam plant with funds supplied by Cities Service Company. On 23 October 1923 Public Service Company (one) issued to Cities Service Company, via Lakeside Construction Company, over ten million dollars worth of PSC (one) securities. The Valmont property was recorded in the property account of PSC (one) at $10,125,000, while actual cost was only $4,484,671.45. Cities Service's paper profit, therefore, was $5,640,328.55. A large part of the funds required for the construction were obtained through the public sale of securities of Public Service Company (one).[17] Ultimately, the stockholders of PSC (one) were the ones who suffered the dilution from these unconventional accounting maneuvers.

When Public Service (two) took over the steam generating plant from Public Service (one) in 1923 PSC (two) paid PSC (one) $2,666,608.50 more for Valmont than the inflated cost which had been paid by PSC (one). In other words, PSC (one) stockholders reaped the benefits of this quasi pyramid scheme by passing on an inflated asset to the next company. Cities Service completed the merger of PSC (one) and the Western Light and Power Company to form PSC (two) in a similar fashion by exchanging preferred and common stock among the parent and subsidiary companies.

In 1924 Cities Service Company bought more than eighty percent of the common stock of Colorado Power Company for $3,194,188.64 in cash. The cash was obtained through the sale of securities of Public Service (two). Cities Service immediately sold the stock of Colorado Power Company to Public Service (two) for $3,681,240 in cash and $5,500,000 PSC (two's) common stock. The total profit, computing the Public Service common stock value at par was $5,987,051.26. Profit was made without risking a dollar of its own capital because Public Service Company (two) issued the securities while Cities Service took the profit. Public Service Company (two) recorded the Colorado Power Company stock at the price paid Cities Service. $9,181,240 which included the profit to Cities Service Company of $5,987,051.36. On 3 September 1924, when Public Service (two) and the Colorado Power Company were consolidated to make Public Service (three) the plant and property account included the $9,181,240 price paid to Cities Service Company by Public Service (two) for the common stock of the Colorado Power Company.[18]

Cities Service continued to make profits in Colorado through acquisition and merger. In 1926 it acquired six small utility companies (Suburban Light and Power Company, Brighton Ice, Light and Power Company, the Federal Gas Company, the Poudre Valley Gas Company, the Grand Junction Electric Gas and Manufacturing Company, and the Rifle Light, Heat and Power Company) for $2,190,242.97 which was $818,949.27 more than the book value of those companies. A few months later Cities Service sold these six companies to Public Service Company for $2,785,000, thereby making a profit of $594,757.3.[19] In 1931 Cities sold the Colorado-Wyoming Gas Company (organized in 1925) to Public Service Company for a profit of $1,029,505.99, a 68.57 percent return on its six-year investment. By selling its fifteen percent share of Colorado Interstate gas to PSC in 1931 Cities Service made an additional profit of $1,852,000.[20] One of the SEC commissioners, commenting in a 1935 opinion, made an understatement about the financial transactions when he said: "I do not believe that this impressive earnings record is necessarily indicative of a sound financial structure."[21]

Before Public Service Company of Colorado was created Cities Service planned its new Valmont generating plant. Engineers decided to use steam power because there were no streams close to the Denver market with an abundant flow of water to generate adequate hydroelectric power. Water in arid eastern Colorado was so scarce that even finding a sufficient amount for condenser cooling presented a problem, and the engineers created an artificial lake. Since much of the Company's service area was in northern Colorado, a generating plant north of Denver was considered most practical.[22] A site for the plant was chosen 25 miles north of Denver near the confluence of the Middle Boulder and South Boulder creeks where water for the lake could be provided through small canals. A 2,000 acre-foot reservoir was constructed to hold water that would be continually recirculated.[23]

Valmont was close to the Union Pacific and

Colorado and Southern stopping points, and was easily supplied with coal from northern Colorado's lignite which was softer and of lower heat content than the coal found in the East. The grade of fuel was known as slack which was a relatively fine and dusty by-product of the mining of domestic lump coal. It was a definite advantage to the coal mining industry to dispose of great quantities of this coal. Because of its moderate ash content, it had to be treated carefully, unless sprayed periodically the dust would explode spontaneously.[26] Transmission lines were strung twenty-eight miles to carry electricity to the main Denver system. Valmont also interconnected to supply power to the Boulder Canyon and Shoshone hydroelectric plants. An additional 125-mile transmission loop furnished power to nine substations in northern Colorado.

The Valmont steam plant produced electricity for the first time in November, 1924. It was the largest plant west of the Missouri Valley to use pulverized coal as fuel, and the largest steam plant in the country to utilize an artificial body of water for condensing. In addition, Valmont was unique in employing a hydraulic structure near the water source to control stream flow and insure that there was enough water for the plant's condensation purposes.[26]

Valmont in several ways represented entrepreneur Doherty's business ethic. He was willing to employ innovative solutions to problems created by conditions in the arid West and, in fact, he seemed to thrive on attempting something new and the attendant publicity. The innovations which were introduced under his management were used to improve the utility industry throughout the nation. One the other hand he used his subsidiaries to make inordinate profits for his major holding company.

Shortly after Valmont went into operation with four turbines and a capacity of 117,000 kilowatts, Public Service Company announced that it would spend two million dollars to double the size of the new plant and to construct several dams to enlarge the reservoir. Anticipated domestic and industrial demand was the chief reason for making the decision to expand the capacity of Valmont so soon. Shortly after the second unit was completed PSC announced plans to enlarge the plant again in 1928.[27]

After establishing a new company and building the Valmont plant, the Public Service executives in 1925 decided to apply for a renewal of the 1906 franchise with Denver even though it did not expire until 1926. The utility wanted to submit a ballot question for the regular city election to be held on May 1925 in order to save the $80,000 cost of a special election. PSC was anxious to insert a new clause into the franchise allowing the company to raise rates during the next franchise period. Company officials realized that twenty-years was too long a period to commit to a single fixed rate and wanted the ability to increase rates based on the price level of other commodities.[26]

Since the previous franchise renewal in 1906 gas rates had decreased as follows.

1906-1910	$1.00 per 1,000 cubic feet
1910	.90
1912	.85
1914-1918	.80
1918	.85 and .95 29

During World War I the government had limited the production of gas for domestic use and the company had lost money on that part of its business. Since the end of the war, however, Public Service had engaged in an active advertising campaign enabling it to make a three percent profit on gas sales to go along with the profitable electrical sales.

The new franchise proposal established a reduction in gas prices of ten percent and five percent for electricity. These reductions may have been for the purpose of pacifying the public which might not have looked favorably on the clause allowing the company to raise rates without a vote by the electorate.[30] Public Service Company also agreed to supply a new commodity, natural gas, to its customers. In fact, the public demand was so ardent that the company agreed to include a clause in the franchise proposal which called for penalties up to $50,000 a year for failure to bring natural gas to Colorado.[31] The 1906 franchise required a $50,000 a year payment to the city along with the amount collected over 75 cents per 1,000 cubic feet for gas and six cents per kilowatt hour for electricity, and this provision was continued. The company would also continue to be assessed approximately $450,000 annually in taxes.[32]

Public Service submitted its franchise proposal to the city council in March 1925. The law required a thirty-day period between the time a bill was presented to the council and the time it could be voted on. When the bill was advertised the required seven times in the press[33] it was not long before the critics spoke up. Arguments against the early franchise renewal were several. Wilbur F. Denious, a member of the Denver Chamber of Commerce and crusading attorney who would serve as president of both the Denver and the Colorado Bar Association, stated that the company was trying to rush the proposal through before adequate study could be done.[34] The Denver *Post*, considered the response of the chamber of commerce too mild.

Henry E. May, the Denver city attorney joined Denious and the chamber in criticizing the proposed franchise. May objected to: allowing Public Service Company to change rates during the franchise period; fixing the same average charge as the last franchise even though profits had increased; confining the time of auditing to a thirty day period; agreeing to automatic change in rates; failing to provide proper provisions for standards of service;[35] failing to eliminate the continuing claim of a perpetual franchise which the company had agreed to drop earlier.[36]

Mayor Benjamin Stapleton appointed a special committee to review the merits of the new franchise. The Denver Grand Jury, as an inquisitional body, also made an extensive investigation into the proposed franchise renewal and reported many concerns, including cases of rate discrimination among Public Service customers. It recommended that there be a thorough study of rates and valuation of the company, and that the proposal not be referred to the voters until these and other questions had been answered.[37]

An additional criticism came from the Bureau

AND HE MEANS BUSINESS

39
"And He Means Business"

manufactured was only 400 British Thermal Units, which the Bureau considered well under standard. As far as the Bureau could ascertain, Denver was the only large city supplied with such a low-rated gas.[40] The Bureau had investigated Public Service Company after receiving complaints from manufacturers about the difficulty in making appliances work with Denver gas. In manufacturing artificial gas, the Bureau recommended a relationship of twenty-five percent water gas and seventy-five percent coal gas, whereas Public Service Company used sixty percent water gas and forty percent coal gas, lowering the heat output.[41]

Opposition to the franchise alarmed PSC. Hearsay had it that the company was so desperate for support that it made a deal with the Ku Klux Klan. Newspaper headlines read "GAS COMPANY BEGS SUPPORT OF KLAN FOR FRANCHISE, RUMORS ASSERT." The Post reported that the company was, at first, unwilling to pay the Klan's price, but later agreed to it. The Klan's price for endorsement was unknown.[42]

Despite the wide-based opposition to the proposal the franchise was scheduled to appear on the 10 May ballot. In the pre-election press coverage the scandalous 1906 franchise election was reviewed along with reports that current city officials were being paid for "campaign work." District Attorney Foster

HELP WANTED

Help Wanted

Cline warned that "Bribe takers and bribe givers in connection with the gas and electric franchise will be relentlessly prosecuted."[44] A week before the election the Denver Post conjectured that Public Service Company had decided to present a franchise proposal a year earlier than scheduled, knowing that if they lost they could submit another franchise before their current contract expired. The newspaper urged the voters to turn down the proposal until there was more public input on the franchise.[45]

As the antagonism built during the weeks before the election people compared the prices of electricity in Denver with other cities. Denver's rate of 7.2 cents per kilowatt hour for electricity was much higher than some other cities, for example, Lincoln, Nebraska at 3.8 cents per kilowatt hour, Springfield, Illinois at 3.9 cents, Cleveland, Ohio at 3 cents, Omaha, Nebraska, at 5.5 cents, Seattle, Washington at 3.4 cents (water power), Tacoma, Washington at 3 cents, and Los Angeles, California, 3.2 cents.[46] Even Doherty's utility in Kansas City, Kansas charged only 2.8 cents per kilowatt hour for its steam generated electricity.

On 19 May 1925 the people had their say, turning down the franchise proposal 31,028 to 15,765.[47]

THE THINKER

48
The Thinker

PSC leaders were forced to produce a new proposal. And as they did, disgruntled Denver City Council members passed new ordinances so that the city would not be rushed into a premature vote again. They first required that any utility seeking a franchise give the mayor an application six months before the election date, (although this rule was later judged unconstitutional). The application also had to be accompanied by a financial statement and a utility inventory.[49]

Public Service Company prepared a new draft that was submitted to the city council's five-man public utility committee in March, 1926. At the same time councilman George P. Steele wrote Secretary of Commerce, Herbert Hoover to obtain recommendations for a national expert to make a thorough study of the new proposal. Soon after the city council announced that two nationally-known engineers would work with Herbert B. Dwight, Colorado Public Utilities Commission electrical engineer, to oversee an investigation of the franchise. City council would pay the engineers $200 a day, and estimated that the total cost would be in the range of $30,000 to $50,000.[50]

The Denver Chamber of Commerce studied the franchise as it had the year before to insure that an equitable proposal was being offered to the people. President of the chamber, L. Ward Bannister, questioned the ability of citizens to determine fair rates, and recommended that the public utilities commission be given the responsibility of setting rates. At that time the Colorado PUC had little to do with franchises and rate setting. Since Denver was a home rule city, the electorate was empowered to determine utility rates.[51]

While the engineers were evaluating the proposed franchise, the old franchise expired on 15 May 1926. The city instructed the PSC to proceed under the terms of the old franchise, and even requested that it submit the $50,000 franchise tax and gas collection taxes.[52] An election was promised soon, but time stretched on as the experts continued to appraise the utility.[53] Initially the election was to be held on 7 September 1926, a week before the primary elections.[55] However, the primary elections came and went and the experts were still haggling over details of their review.

In November, 1926 after the engineers released their report, Denver City Council scheduled a public hearing. The engineers had determined that the proposed electric rates were too high, yielding an eight percent net return. Since the gas department was only earning

3.97 percent, the engineers recommended that it be reorganized to be more efficient. The engineers valued the company property at $21,174,772, much lower than Public Service valuation of $27,762,179. The utility valued its gas facilities at $11,753,267, while the engineers judged it to be worth only $9,829,995. PSC's total valuation was $39,515,446 as opposed to the engineer's valuation of $30,995,767.[55] Engineer Dwight and his team asserted that even after allowing eight percent on the company's valuation there was an excess income of $675,000 per year. Clare Stannard, PSC general manager, was disturbed about the $8,519,679 difference claiming that the engineers overlooked valuable property in their appraisal.[57]

Even though the company did not agree with the engineers' report, management felt that it had no other choice but to submit a new proposal. On 1 December 1926 the Public Service Company agreed to reduce its gas rates five percent and electrical rates twelve and one-half percent. Electricity for domestic use would cost seven cents per kilowatt hour for the first fifteen hours, six cents a kilowatt for the next thirty hours, and five cents a kilowatt hour thereafter. The company lowered gas prices from ninety-five cents per 1000 cubic feet to ninety cents.[57]

The revised franchise proposal was modified to allow the city to use Public Service Company utility poles free of charge for the municipal alarm system. The company also agreed to spend $100,000 to put some of its wires underground, and to take over the responsibility of maintaining the street lighting system. The city negotiated a reduced rate for street lighting, and required that the gas quality be no lower than 400 BTUs. The franchise fee was raised to $60,000 and the Manager of Parks and Improvement was to enforce the franchise and could examine Public Service Company books at any time. The claim of a perpetual franchise was also dropped.[58]

Officials set the day of the election for 8 February 1927, almost a year after the franchise had expired. By that time the mayor, city attorney, chamber of commerce, major newspapers and most civic groups had endorsed the new franchise proposal, and Denverites cast their votes in favor of a new twenty-year franchise, 19,354 to 7,963.[59]

Since its establishment in 1924 Public Service Company continued to grow until, by the end of the decade, it was the largest public utility in Colorado. In 1926 it had purchased six small electrical companies.[60] It controlled utility systems in Longmont, Loveland, Greeley and Rifle. After purchasing controlling interest in Rifle County Light and Power where there was a large vanadium mine, PSC extended power lines forty miles from the Shoshone reservoir at Glenwood Springs to Rifle at a cost of $85,000. The line had a capacity of 44,000 volts.[61]

As the decade closed General Manager Clare Stannard announced that the budget for 1930 would be the largest in the company's history, with more than $4,500,000 allocated for refurbishing its plants and equipment.[62] The beginning of the 1930s saw Public Service Company of Colorado growing rapidly with the use of electricity for the first five months of 1930 exceeding any other five-month period by nine million kilowatt hours. According to the National Electric Light Association Colorado's utilities were in stronger financial shape than most utilities in the rest of the country.[63] The net profit of Public Service Company and its subsidiaries for 1920 was $2,731,624.[64]

Public Service Company's strong financial position was an advantage to Cities Service, and Doherty made it clear that every subsidiary should make a contribution to the parent company. In the fall of 1930 Cities Service sent a letter instructing Public Service employees to conduct a customer ownership campaign by selling Cities Service preferred and common stock. The sale, said the letter, would help promote the business of the subsidiary as well as aid in distributing the securities of the holding company.[65] One can imagine that when this communication was sent to subsidiaries with lower profits across the country, those employees might be unwilling or resentful about investing.[66]

Public Service Company continued new construction, improvements, and replacements despite the fact that during the depression years of the 1930s Colorado's economic problems persisted. Net income decreased in 1932 and 1933 because of higher taxes, increased operating costs, and lower gross revenues.[67] However, beginning in 1934 income gained each year.[68] Mining activity, tourism and business conditions all improved bringing Public Service Company gains ahead of national figures.[69] One sign of the growing business was the expansion of the generating capacity of the Valmont Steam plant in the late 1930s.[70] By the end of the decade PSC felt satisfied that it had weathered the worst of the depression. Doherty still considered Public Service Company of Colorado a well-managed company to which other Cities Service managers were sent for training.

During the 1930s, at the time of the nation's worst economic collapse, Colorado became more conservative in a political sense. Professing a belief in self-help solutions to their problems, Coloradans for the most part, rejected Franklin Roosevelt's New Deal philosophy and elected Republicans or conservative Democrats.[71] Despite this individualism the West needed help from Washington. The West in fact, benefited from the New Deal programs on a per capita basis more than any other section of the country between 1930 and 1939. For example, by 1935 the government had granted $48,500,000 to the region for relief.[72]

Colorado, like the rest of the nation encountered hardships during the 1930s. Mining and agriculture continued to suffer from a deepening depression that had begun in the early 1930s. On top of the desperate economic problems, there were years of droughts which dried the topsoil for erosion by prairie winds.[73] Colorado's industrial plants also suffered a shortage of orders causing them to release workers. Both the Colorado Fuel and Iron Company at Pueblo and the Denver and Rio Grande Railroad were in receivership in the mid-thirties.[74]

In the 1930s Henry Doherty made a decisions for the Public Service Company of Colorado from his

Manhattan office, but in Denver Guy William Faller, vice president and general manager, oversaw the day-to-day business for much of the decade. Faller had come to Denver in 1905 to be engineer and superintendent of gas distribution for the Denver Gas and Electric Company. He remained with the company for eight years before leaving to work for another utility in Amarillo, Texas. In 1923 he returned to Denver to join the new Public Service Company of Colorado as vice president, serving in that capacity until 1930 when Henry L. Doherty asked him to manage the securities department of the Denver branch of Henry L. Doherty and Company. In 1934 he returned to PSC as vice president, general manager and director. He was elected president of the Company in 1940, at the same time retaining the positions of general manager and director.[75]

Faller's place of birth was North Freedom, Wisconsin. He was born 16 April 1878 to William and Georgina Faller and after completing high school in the rural Wisconsin public school system, he entered the United States Naval Academy. He graduated from the Academy in 1898 and served in the Spanish-American War in Cuba, in the Philippines, and in China during the Boxer rebellion.[76] In 1902 he retired from the navy and three years later married Celia Astle after several years of courtship.[77]

Faller enjoyed telling people that his first utility job was with the Madison (Wisconsin) Gas and Electric Company where he was paid fifty dollars a month.[79] When he moved to Denver he was director of the Doherty Training Course and one of his primary interests at Public Service Company was management training and employee relations. Guy Faller fit into a consistent mold of forward thinking and effective managers that has spanned the twentieth century of PSC presidents.

CHAPTER 7 FOOTNOTES

1
Carl Abbott, Stephen J. Leonard, and David McComb, *Colorado: A History of the Centennial State*, revised edition (Boulder, Co: Colorado Associated University Press, 1982), pp. 267-72.

2
Ibid., p. 262

3
W. Elliot Brownlee, Dynamics of Ascent: A History of the American Economy, (New York: Alfred A. Knopf 1974), PP. 264-65.

4
Ibid, p. 271.

5
Ralph I. Nelson Merger Movements in American Industry 1890-1956, (Princeton, NJ: Princeton University Press, 1959), P. 106.

6
The Public Service Company Minute Books date filing as 31 July 1923, Articles of Incorporation Book 223, (Public Service Company of Colorado, Denver, Colorado), pp. 429-434. Board of directors members were Rodney J. Bardwell, Roy C. Hecox, and Edgar McComb joined to create the new company with a five-member board of directors: E. H. Johnson, William P. Lehrer, Charles B. Wedun, Thomas P. Lyon, and E. E. Weger.

7
Certificate of Incorporation, Book 225, (Public Service Company of Colorado, Denver, Colorado), pp. 182-197 (pp. 1-16 of the document) listed Charles A. Frueauff as president and John E. Loiseau as secretary of the new company. The company elected new officers and directors, apparently the same day, at the stockholders meeting. Henry L. Doherty, president, C. N. Stannard, general manager and vice president of the Denver Gas and Electric Light Company, Rodney J. Bardwell, James C. Burger, Joseph H. Davis, Henry L. Doherty, Charles A. Frueauff, Harry T. Hughes, Paul R. Jones, Thomas F. Kennedy, Paul W. Lee, Walter B. Lowry, John M. McMillin, Godfrey Schirmer, Charles A. Semrad, Frank E. Shepard, Clare N. Stannard, Thomas B. Stearns, and Charles S. Thomas.

8
Journal of Electricity LI (1 September 1923), 186.

9 Public Service Company Minute Book No. 1 31 March 1924, (Public Service Company of Colorado, Denver, Colorado).

10*Public Service Compendium*, I, No. 2, (2 November 1928), 80. The records list Charles A. Frueauff as president and John Loiseau as secretary with a new board: Paul R. Jones, Charles A. Frueauff, Frank B. Shepard Walter B. Lowry, Thomas B. Stearns, Harry C. James, James C. Burger, Godfrey Shirmer, John C. Mitchell, Joseph A. Davis, Clare Stannard, Paul W. Lee, Harry T. Hughes, Charles A. Semrad, Robert Haddock, John Connell, D. Edgar Wilson, Edward H. Coe, Norman Read, Guy Faller, John C. Loisseau. According to p. 31 of Minute Book Number 2 on 4 September 1923 Charles A. Frueauff was replaced by Henry L. Doherty as president and chairman of the board. Six board members also resigned: Paul Jones, Robert Haddock, John Connell, Edward H. Coe, D. Edgar Wilson, and Guy W. Faller who were replaced by Rodney Barnwell, Charles S. Thomas, Thomas I Carter, E. W. Rollins, V. L. Board, and W. V. Hodges.

11 Public Service Company minute book No. 1, 31 March 1924, (Public Service Company of Colorado, Denver, Colorado).

12 Denver *Post*, 20 August 1923, p. 14.

13 Lena M. Urguhart, *Glenwood Springs: Shoshone Spa in the Mountains*, (Boulder Co: Pruett Press, 1970), P. 133.

14 *Journal of Electricity* LI (1 September 1923), 186.

15 *Security and Exchange Commission Decisions and Reports*, V Appendix 3, 1 June 1939 to 30 September 1939, (1941), pp. 837-38.

16 Ibid., p. 839.

17 *U.S., Congress, Senate, Report of the Federal Trade Commission.* Corporations, S. Doc. 92, 70th Cong., 1st sess., 1934, pt. 55, p. 274.

18 *Security and Exchange Commission Decisions and Reports*, V. Appendix 3, 1 June 1939 to 30 September 1939, (1941), pp. 841-45.

19Ibid., p. 847.

20 *Security and Exchange Commission*, V Appendix 3, pp. 847-48.

21 Ibid., p. 850.

22 *Journal of Electricity* LV, (1 September 1925), p. 161.

23 Ibid., and "The Valmont Plant," (Denver: Public Service Company, revised September, 1947), unpaged. It was close to the 1,000 acre-foot reservoir of the Boulder hydroelectric project also owned by the company.

24 *Journal of Electricity* LV, (September, 1925), 162.

25 "The Valmont Plant," unpaged.

26 *Journal of Electricity* LV, (September, 1925), 161.

27 Denver *Post*, 25 January 1925, p. 1.

28 *Rocky Mountain News*, 12 March 1925, p. 8.

29 Ibid.

30 Denver. City Council Proceedings, 22 August 1927, Book 7, (25 July 1927 to 28 April 1930), p. 27.

31 Ibid.

32 Denver *Post*, 23 March 1925, p. 1, *Rocky Mountain News*, 24 March 1925, p. 2, and "Report to the Board of Directors of the Denver Chamber of Commerce," Denver Chamber of Commerce Proceedings of the Board of Directors, 1 November 1924 to 1 May 1925, (Denver Public Library Western History Department, Denver, Colorado), pp. 252-54.

33 Denver *Post* 25 March 1925, p. 1.

34 "Dissenting Report by Wilbur Denious to the Board of Directors of the Denver Chamber of Commerce," Denver Chamber of Commerce, Proceedings of the Board of Directors, 1 November 1924 to 1 May 1925, (Denver Public Library Western History Room, Denver, Colorado, pp. 291-314. Information about Wilbur Denious was

obtained from an interview by the author with William P. Denious, III, 13 May 1985.

35 "Report of the City Attorney on proposed franchise to the Denver City Council." Denver. City Council Proceedings, 27 March 1925, (City and County Building, Denver, Colorado), p. 1.

36 Since 1869 the company had claimed that it had been given a perpetual franchise--a frachise forever--even though records did not substantiate its claim.

37 Denver Chamber of Commerce, Proceedings of the Board of Directors, 1 November 1924 to 1 May 1925, (Denver Public Library Western History Room, Denver, Colorado), p. 253.

38 Denver *Post* 28 April 1925, p. 2.

39 Denver *Post* 12 May 1925, p. 1.

40 S. Doc 92 70th Cong., 1st Session, No. 81. "Utility Corporation" letter from the acting chairman of the Federal Trade Commission (Washington, DC: U. S. Government Printing Office, 1936), p. 90.

41 Denver *Post*, 7 May 1925, p. 3 and 14 May 1925, p. 1.

42 Denver*Post*, 10 May 1925, p. 5.

43 Denver *Post*, 11 May 1925, p. 1.

44 Ibid.

45 Ibid.

46 Denver *Post*, 13 May 1925, p. 1.

47 Denver *Post*, 20 May 1925, p. 1.

48 Denver *Post*, 14 May 1925, p. 1.

49 *Rocky Mountain News*, 23 March 1926, p. 1.

50 Denver *Post*, 11 March 1926, p. 1, 16 March 1926, p. 16, 23 March 1926, p. 11, and 27 March 1926, p. 3.

51 "Report on the Public Service Company of Colorado in Connection with the Proposed Franchise for the Supplying of Electricity and Gas to the City and County of Denver," 3 November 1926, Denver Chamber of Commerce, Proceedings of the Board of Directors, 1 November 1926 to 1 May 1927 (Denver Public Library Western History Room), p. 105b.

52 Denver *Post*, 19 May 1926, p. 14.

53 Denver *Post*, 2 July 1926, p. 17.

54 Denver *Post*, 7 July 1926, p. 1.

55 Denver *Post*, 4 November 1926, p. 1.

56 Ibid.

57 Denver *Post*, 29 November 1926, p. 1 and 1 December 192, pp[. 1 and 5.

58 Denver *Post*, 1 December 1926, p. 1.

59 Denver *Post*, 9 February 1927, p. 1.

60 *Securities and Exchange Commission Report, p. 801.*

61 *Rocky Mountain News*, 22 May 1926, p. 15.

62 Denver *Post*, 31 October 1929, p. 1.

63 Denver *Post*, 24 June 1930, p. 24.

64 Denver *Post*, 26 March 1931, p. 26.

65 Public Service Company of Colorado Minute Book No. 2, Exhibit A, (Public Service Company, Denver, Colorado), p. 207.

66 *Journal of Electricity* LIII (15 July 1924), 70.

67 *Moody's Manual of Investments*, (New York: Moody's Investors Service, 1937), 1727.

68 *Public Utility Compendium*, xii (New York: 31 October 1939), 7

69Denver *Post*, 17 April 1935, p. 22, 19 April

1935, p. 45, and 23 April 1940, p. 25.

70 *Rocky Mountain News*, 9 July 1939, pp. 1-2.

73 Abbott, *Colorado*, p. 277.

74 Carl Ubbelohde, MaxineBenson, Duane A. Smith, *A Colorado History, Revised Centennial Edition*, (Boulder: Pruett Publishing Company, 1976), p. 208.

Richard Lowett, in his book *The New Deal and the West* (Bloomington, IN: Indiana University, 1984) takes a firmer stand regarding the West vis a vis New Deal programs than Ubbelohde, *et al.* In his preface (p. xi) he says:

Except for a few large cities the economy of the West was closely tied to farming and mining--two industries especially hard hit by falling prices and vanishing markets. Most Westerners accepted only one idea of prosperity: it was based on the rapid exploitation of natural resources, whether this meant opening new farm lands through reclamation or finding new oil wells for an already glutted market. Little wonder the westerners looked to Washington for a way out of the Great Depression and the hardships that characterized their undercapitalized society.

73 Ibid., pp. 305-06.

74 Ibid., p. 307.

75 *"Guy Faller," The National Cyclopaedia of American Biography: Being a History of the United States*, G 1943-46 (New York: James T. Whyte and Co., 1946), p. 234.

76 Ibid and Denver *Post*, 10 July 1940, p. 28.

77 *Lines*, (October, 1942), 3.

78 *The National Cyclopaedia*, G., p. 234 and *Rock Mountain News*, pictorial section, 13 November 1927, p. 2.

CHAPTER 8

NATURAL GAS DEVELOPMENT

After the 1927 franchise election Public Service Company began work on bringing natural gas to Colorado. In fact, early in 1926, while negotiations for the franchise renewal were taking place, Henry L. Doherty arranged to have a pipeline built from the Texas Panhandle natural gas fields to Denver.[1] Natural gas had not been widely used before the 1920s because there was not a functional pipeline system to transport the gas over long distances. In 1925 developments in electrical welding and the use of high-carbon steel led to the design of a seamless pipe which made long distance transmission practical.[2]

Coloradans wanted a supply of natural gas for several reasons. The energy content was approximately twice as great per cubic foot than the manufactured gas and, therefore, excellent for cooking and heating. It was clean, contained no carbon monoxide, and required no storage.[3] Businessmen also realized that the low cost of natural gas would make building and operating factories and warehouses much more practical than with manufactured gas or coal.[4]

Colorado pioneers had noticed natural gas seeps near the future Canon City. Natural gas is commonly trapped in rock formations above oil deposits. In 1887 residents around Florence were the first Coloradans known to take advantage of natural gas from oil wells,[5] and beginning around 1892 the Florence Oil Company supplied a few homes with gas from its well.[6] In the same decade wells drilled in the towns of Garcia and Las Animas produced enough natural gas to supply several ranches.[7] Gas was also discovered east of Boulder sometime around the turn of the century, and for a short time the Federal Gas Company distributed natural gas until 1910 when a flood destroyed its well and make-shift transmission line.[8]

The first major gas discovery in Colorado came in 1923 when Union Oil of California drilled for oil in the Wellington Field northeast of Fort Collins and hit natural gas. Union continued drilling for oil, but the natural gas flow was so great that they ceased operations after two days. One employee reported "rocks, hurled up from deep in the earth by the gas-pressure crashed against the wood derick with bullet-like velocity, causing it to crumble." The crew gave up, withdrew and it was several days before the well could be capped.[9]

Although Union Oil considered the well a failure Cities Service Company was delighted with the strike. The latter formed the Colorado-Wyoming Gas Company on 1 December 1925 to use the natural gas to supply the cities of Fort Collins and Cheyenne.[10] Despite the serendipitous find company officials knew that a much larger supply would be necessary to fulfill potential demand in other areas of the state. For that reason PSC announced plans in the spring of 1927 to transport natural gas to Colorado from other states.

Colorado Interstate Gas's history began in the same year when several enterprises joined forces to supply natural gas to Colorado. The first, Standard Oil of New Jersey, brought capital and pipeline construction experience to the venture. The second firm, Prairie Oil and Gas Company, (under control of Southwestern Development Company) owned 300,000 acres of oil and natural gas leases in the enormous Amarillo Field of the Texas Panhandle. (The area eventually produced one billion cubic feet of gas per day.) Southwestern Development Company organized a third firm, Canadian River Gas Company, to tap natural gas in the Amarillo field and transport it to Clayton, New Mexico. Standard Oil completed the loop by incorporating, Colorado Interstate Gas Company (CIG), on 8 June 1927 in (Delaware) in order to construct and operate 149 miles of 22-inch pipeline and 105 miles of 20-inch line from Clayton, New Mexico to Denver. The actual construction work was done by Ford, Bacon and Davis, Incorporated.[11]

CIG had a unique problem. It had an over-abundance of natural gas with no definite markets. As a result it moved aggressively to convince cities and large businesses in Colorado to switch from manufactured to natural gas.[12] CIG had previously contracted to supply natural gas to the Colorado Fuel and Iron Company's steel mills in Pueblo. The excess gas went to Denver in an extended pipeline, and CIG also sought to develop markets in towns along the route of the pipeline.[13]

In anticipation of using natural gas the Denver City Council worked out a contract to establish natural gas prices in 1927. According to the agreement CIG would supply natural gas to Public Service Company, which could earn as much as eight percent annually per year for a period of twenty years. PSC stated that it would not make any profit the first several years because of the high costs involved in bringing natural gas to Colorado. In Denver, for example, during the first year, the company spent $750,000 on new installation, $175,000 to adjust appliances, $450,000 for an intermediate pipeline, and $100,000 for expanding old mains to handle 100 thousand cubic feet of gas per day instead of 13 thousand cubic feet of artificial gas.[14]

PSC proposed charging $1.50 for the first 200 cubic feet, $.75 per 1000 cubic feet for the next 2800 cubic feet, $.06 per 1000 cubic feet for the next 7,000 cubic feet and $.05 per 1000 cubic feet for all amounts over 10,000 cubic feet. The company explained that natural gas had a heating value of 875 BTUs or 2.65 times that of manufactured gas, and that there would be savings despite the much lower price of $.90 per 1000 cubic feet for manufactured gas.[15] An available supply of natural gas meant that the average homeowner, who previously used 5,000 cubic feet of coal gas a month for $4.50, would use less than 2,000 cubic feet of natural gas at a cost of $2.85.[16]

Not everyone supported the change to natural gas, one Denver newspaper reported: "Coal barons, girding on their armor and grasping stastical swords, are rushing onto the field to repel the invasion of the titans of the oil and gas industry."[17] The coal men were joined by the railroad workers who carried coal to distribution points, the United Mine Workers union, and also by truckers who delivered it to consumers. One of their arguments was the difference in price Colorado Interstate Gas intended to charge the Pueblo steel mills, i.e. twenty cents per 1000 cubic feet, and the forty cents rate for Denver residents. Public Service Company reminded critics of the large amount of natural gas C F and I would use, making the demand more reliable. Furthermore, in order to supply natural gas to Denver, PSC would have to install hundreds of meters to measure individual use.[18] The coal men also argued that coal industry profits in Colorado would be wiped out, and that the natural gas profits would go to the coffers of the East, particularly Standard Oil Company.[19]

An emotional letter addressed to the PSC appeared in the Denver Post column entitled "So the People May Know" on 14 June 1927:

> Isn't it true that you have made a contract with the Colorado Fuel and Iron at Pueblo to sell them natural gas at one fifth the price you propose to charge the domestic consumers in Denver.
>
> ISNT IT TRUE THAT EVERY LARGE CORPORATION ALONG YOUR PROPOSED GAS LINE IS TO GET GAS FROM YOU AT PRACTICALLY 1/5 WHAT YOU WILL CHARGE DOMESTIC CONSUMERS . . . The people of Denver want to know if this is true -- and the Post alleges that it is -- why Denver must continue to be the goat . . .
>
> Must Denver always be regarded by such public utilities as merely a frontier town to be exploited and robbed increasingly by every corporation doing business here.

> Denver will be charged much more than Dallas, Ft. Worth, Oklahoma City, Wichita, Kansas City, Missouri, Topeka and Kansas City, Kansas.
>
> JUST REFRESH YOUR MINDS. YOU CAME TO THE PEOPLE A YEAR OR SO AGO FOR A FRANCHISE THAT WOULD CONTINUE YOUR STRANGLEHOLD AND OUTRAGEOUS PRICES ON THE PEOPLE OF DENVER AND YOU GOT THE LICKING OF YOUR LIFE. THE PEOPLE TURNED DOWN YOUR PROPOSAL WITH A VENGEANCE.
>
> NOW DON'T GET GAY AT THIS TIME JUST BECAUSE THE PEOPLE GAVE YOU A FRANCHISE RECENTLY. DON'T TRY TO RAM DOWN THE PEOPLES' THROATS THESE ROBBER RATES THAT YOU SUGGEST FOR NATURAL GAS.
>
> Don't forget also that in proposing to bring us natural gas from Texas you expect Colorado to practically destroy her local coal industry, in which not less than 75,000 of our people are engaged. And you propose to take the money these people have been getting and give it to the foreign corporations of New York City. . . . Do you expect the people of Denver to stand for such insolence from you or any other corporation? 20

In June 1927 a special committee of the Denver Chamber of Commerce verified that the rates proposed for Denver were higher than those in other cities.[21] Clare Stannard, the vice president and general manager for Public Service, answered critics by saying his company was willing to bring natural gas to Denver for any reasonable price the the city council set. The manager also said that the company would consent to a contract provision to forfeit $50,000 if natural gas were not brought to Denver within a two-year period.[22]

Opponents of the natural gas rates were particularly outraged when they learned that Henry L.

HOW COME?

"How Come"

AS USUAL!

24
As Usual

I SAID, "LAY THOSE CARDS ON THE TABLE!!!"

I Said Lay Those Cards on the Table

THE NATURAL GAS BAG.

The Natural Gas Bag

Doherty owned one of the three companies bidding to furnish industrial gas to Kansas City, Missouri at a much lower price than that proposed for Denver. The Denver *Post* publicized the fact that the three companies in Missouri could build a 410-mile pipeline to Kansas City and supply natural gas to industrial consumers for between seventeen and thirty cents a thousand cubic feet compared to between fifty cents and $7.50 a thousand cubic feet for domestic gas from a 350-mile pipe line to Denver.[27]

A. C. King, an engineering expert hired by the city confirmed in August, 1927 that proposed rates were too high and recommended a rate not higher than $.90 per thousand cubic feet. PSC responded by saying the the British Thermal Unit value of natural gas was greater than the heat unit of coal gas and, therefore the price actually lower than manufactured gas. Opponents in turn claimed that the company wanted to keep domestic rates high so they could offer industrial customers a lower rate.[28]

In mid-August city and company officials sat down to talk about a rate schedule at a secret meeting.[29] The rates agreed on were the following:

cubic feet, per month	price
first 400	$.90/100 cubic feet
next 600	.15/100 cubic feet
next 1,000	.12/100 cubic feet
next 1,000	.075/100 cubic feet
next 7,000	.06/100 cubic feet
over 10,000	.05/100 cubic feet [30]

These prices were considerably lower than those originally requested by the PSC and were subsequently approved by a six to three vote of the city council.[31] While prices were set, the arrival of natural gas in Denver was still almost a year away.

Pipeline construction was hastened by a threatened coal strike in late 1927. At the same time company employees were scouring the Midwest for coal, in case the International Workers of the World (IWW, or Wobblies) struck before natural gas could be brought to Colorado.[32] Coal miners demanded better working conditions and higher wages. They were particularly desperate after two salary cuts in 1925, resulting from diminished use of coal by the railroads.[33] Public Service Company estimated that the use of natural gas would save the Company 15,000 tons of coal a month.[34]

The Wobblies did strike in 1927, leading to a series of clashes, the most violent of which were at the Rocky Mountain Fuel Company's mines near Lafayette, northwest of Denver. Six men were killed in a skirmish

35
Another Good Reason

in November. In early 1928 Governor Adams declared martial law and the strike was broken.[36] Many believed that Governor Adams was responding to a general fear of the IWW by most Coloradans but reformers felt that Adams' attitude toward the union was not unexpected. Ben Lindsey, (the reform judge involved in the 1906 franchise fight) had described Adams as "a skilled opponent of any reform measure that threatens the 'plum tree' of corporations."[37]

By 4 February 1928, a quarter of the pipeline had been laid,[38] and crews were making rapid progress. The next month, in fact, the workers set a one-day record by laying about two miles of twenty-inch steel pipe, doubling the daily average.[39] While pipes were being laid hundreds of other men were modifying the city's distribution system and adjusting various appliances.[40]

The long-awaited switchover day came on 21 June 1928 although actual service did not begin until two days later. Residents within a half a mile of the main plant were startled to hear the rumbling noise of air being pushed out of the pipes as natural gas flowed for the first time.[41] Flames shot ten to fifteen feet into the nighttime sky as the last manufactured gas was burned off in three north Denver

THE NEW PIONEERING

The New Pioneering

locations. Two months later another coal gas flame was extinguished.[43] The fire, lighted in 1888, had burned continuously for forty years at the coke plant at Seventh and Wewatta streets. That plant was subsequently closed, but kept in good repair for use during emergencies.[44]

By 1931 Public Service Company had been making excellent profits on natural gas for three years and consumers felt that the clause in the 1927 franchise about reducing rates to preclude windfall earnings should be followed. The franchise provided that rates could be reduced at any time with the mutual consent of the company and the city's manager of improvements. For that reason, the city in 1931 announced an investigation into Public Service Company rates and profits on both gas and electricity.[45] The investigation began early in November under the direction of Herbert S. Sands, a well-respected engineer and president of the Denver Chamber of Commerce.[46] Negotiations continued between the company and city officials for several months, and were at an impasse in February, 1932.

Clare Stannard, a vice president of Public Service Company, was unhappy with Herbert Sands's valuation of the company. The engineer had appraised the electric plant nineteen percent lower than the company's book value ($25,050,522 versus $30,915,830) and the gas plant twenty percent below what PSC thought it was worth ($11,359,216 versus $14,290,646).[47] The utility wanted plants valued as high as possible in order to maximize cash profits with a fixed rate of return. On the city's valuation PSC earned 9.9 percent on electric sales, but its profit on gas was merely .855 percent.[48]

PSC customers complained that their gas rates were too high because Colorado Interstate's charge of forty cents per thousand cubic feet was excessive. Sixty-five percent of PSC's natural gas operating budget went to CIG for Denver delivery.[49] PSC refused to change its gas rates, but to avoid costly litigation the company acquisced to the city and lowered electric rates for its 90,000 domestic and commercial users, creating a total reduction of almost $500,000. The domestic rate for electricity was reduced from $1.95 a kilowatt hour to $1.80. Despite the reduction, PSC never agreed with the city's valuation of the electric facilities.[50]

Both the city and public utilities commission felt that Public Service Company was charging too much for natural gas, but because of the Company's low percentage of profit, there was not much that could be done, at least until the United States Supreme Court ruling of 29 February 1932. Although the case itself concerned a Kansas firm, (the Western Distributing Company), the ruling established the principle that a utility "can't compel consumers to pay excessive rates merely because it is paying an excessive price"[51] for gas at the city gate.

Two weeks after the Supreme Court ruling the Colorado Public Utilities Commission assigned one of its engineers to begin an investigation into wholesale rates charged PSC. The fact that Public Service Company owned fifteen percent of Colorado Interstate Gas Company's stock was part of the issue. In other words, PSC had some control over its supplier and benefited from ownership interest. The CIG brought gas to Denver, but also controlled the Canadian River Gas Company which owned the Texas gas wells. As the Denver Post stated in March, 1932, interstate transportation of gas and local distribution were in reality one integrated operation not two.[52]

The Colorado Public Utilities Commission decided to put pressure directly on the Colorado Interstate Gas Company. It gave the company twenty days to change its contract with PSC and reduce the wholesale rate, or else face the possibility of the PUC breaking the Public Service Company, Colorado Interstate Gas contract.[53] CIG fought the commission's demands by arguing that it could not be governed by the rules for a public utility because it was not one. The PUC replied that CIG distributed gas directly to seven industries and four distributing companies, as well as to the municipal system of Colorado Springs,[54] and therefore fell within the definition of a public utility.

The Colorado Public Utilities Commission commenced a rate hearing on natural gas on Tuesday 20 September 1932 to determine whether CIG was being discriminatory in charging Colorado Fuel and Iron seventeen cents a thousand cubic feet and other customers forty cents. The decision of the three commissioners would affect the rates PSC could charge its customers. During the hearing irate customers accused CIG of charging whatever the traffic would bear.[55] Colorado Interstate Gas, in turn, vehemently denied the legality of the PUC's jurisdiction over its transactions.

The fall and winter of 1933 went by without a decision being made. Finally in March, 1933, to the chagrin of the natural gas consumers, the PUC decided not to take jurisdiction in the case, and ruled only on the rates CIG charged industrial customers through local distribution systems (intrastate operations). Such sales were only a small part of CIG business. This meant that CIG would be under PUC jurisdiction to the extent that it served industrial customers and towns with municipal systems. Home-rule cities including Denver, would not be affected, and would be regulated through city governments.[56]

At a special conference Mayor George D. Begole, Milton Smith, Jr. (CIG's attorney), George H. Shaw (PSC's attorney), Assistant City Attorney Frederick P. Cranston, V.L. Board, vice president and general superindendent of PSC and six of nine Denver City Councilmen gathered to discuss the high gas rates. For three hours city officials demanded answers from the PSC and CIG representatives, who, for the most part, artfully avoided saying anything of susbstance.[57] "I think the pipeline company is politely telling us to go to hell,"[58] snapped city attorney Parriott.

"We have tried to be fair in weighing the facts," declared Parriott. "The developments of today's meeting are not conducive to good feelings," he continued. "It reflects on our good intelligence to assume that the company doesn't know what is going on every minute in Denver." When Mayor Begole asked Smith to "lay his cards on the table," Smith replied weakly. "I'll be glad to write the company regarding the situation. I cannot promise what their answer will be, however."[59]

Mayor Begole had called the conference in an effort to lower prices and also to avoid a costly valuation of the Public Service Company. (The last investigation had cost the city $12,000.) The councilmen were irritated and made it clear to CIG and PSC that, unless essential information was given, they would use their legislative powers to fix rates.[60]

The city's threat was not an idle one, and when the conference failed to produce results, Denver City Council, ordered an investigation of the gas rates on 10 July 1933. The Manager of Improvements and Parks, who was the city official in charge of utilities, began retaining engineers, accountants and other experts to make the study. With some resentment the council transferred $5,000 to its "war chest" to pay these experts.[61] Mayor Begole also wrote to President Roosevelt to determine whether provisions of the National Industrial Recovery Act pertained to regulation of pipelines.

City Attorney Parriott wrote[62] to Dr. Francis Walker, chief economist of the Federal Trade Commission, concerning the recently completed investigation of holding companies. Parriott wanted to show that the relationship between Public Service Company and Colorado Interstate Gas was one of interlocking ownerships. The city knew that if the alliance could be untangled it would lead to a savings of thousands of dollars for Denver. The city hoped that the FTC could help uncover facts that would reveal inappropriate ownership connections.[63] Part of the letter to Mr. Walker read:

> Denver is supplied with gas by Public Service Co., a Doherty concern. The Public Service Co. in turn buys our gas at the city gate from the Colorado Interstate Gas Co. at 40 cents for 1,000 cubic feet.
>
> The Doherty interests claim they own but 15 per cent of the stock of the Interstate Co., but I am inclined to believe they have more than 15 per cent influence in shaping its policy.
>
> Our problem involves the procuring of information that would justify the city council in passing an ordinance readjusting the rates charged by the Public Service Co.
>
> . . . Can you help us obtain these facts? . . .[64]

Colorado Interstate Gas argued that the city council could not lower gas rates because the 1912 amendment to the City Charter specified that "all power to regulate the charges for service by public utility corporations is hereby reserved to the people."[66] Council, therefore, did not have authority to revise the rates voted approved by the electorate in the 1927 franchise renewal,[66] and could only retaliate by hinting that the city might consider municipal ownership of the gas plant. It was an empty threat, however, and was quickly dropped.[67]

Another of the mayor's strategies to remove the forty cent rate also failed. The 1927 franchise agreement left the rate for natural gas open, stating that a fair rate would be established when the costs of natural gas were determined. The mayor proposed to the council on 18 September 1933 a rate decrease from $1.80 to $1.25 per thousand cubic feet. The council hesitated to participate in this maneuver and declined to vote on the rate schedule under the "fair rate" clause because it believed the voters had exclusive authority to lower rates. Furthermore, the council assumed that Public Service Company would ignore the new rates, forcing an expensive court fight.[68] After these defeats, the city council, the mayor and other city officials and residents temporarily gave up on the campaign to lower gas prices.

The consumers and the weather accomplished what city officials were unable to do. Because of high

WHO SAID IT COULDN'T BE DONE?

Who Said it Couldn't Be Done?

gas rates many people switched from natural gas back to coal. For those who stayed with gas, consumption was down because of a mild winter in 1933-34. In order to regain lost business and to increase the use of gas, PSC agreed to negotiate with its supplier to lower the price for some consumers. Both CIG and PSC expected that increased volume, especially for heating, would offset the losses from reducing rates.[70] The utility submitted a proposal to city council to reduce charges for customers who used more than 3000 cubic feet of gas a month. The council approved the change, but vowed to continue fighting for a reduction of prices for the small user.[71]

Four years later in 1937 the issue of lower rates for natural gas was again front page news. The mayor of Denver, Benjamin Stapleton, had called for another survey of gas rates in other states. PSC cooperated with the survey, but at the same time explained that increased material and labor costs made it difficult to lower rates. The city's case was bolstered by a Federal Power Commission survey which showed that 126 cities throughout the country had reduced their prices during the depression years, while Denver's rates had remained stationary.[72] This constant rate may have resulted from the fact that

Colorado's economy was stronger than other states' during those years.

In January, 1939 the vice president of the Lower Gas and Light Bill League of Denver published the figures comparing various cities' rates to those of Denver which were estimated to be $4.80 per month.[73]

Fort Morgan (M)[municipal plant]	$2.70
Colorado Springs (M)	3.46
Tacoma, Wash. (M)	2.12
Los Angeles (M)	3.04
Seattle, Wash. (M)	3.20
Kansas City, Kans. (M)	2.80
Cleveland, Ohio (M)	3.13
San Francisco, Calif.	3.09
Portland, Oregon	3.39

The same month the *Post* published a rate survey which indicated that Denver's rates were higher than those of eighty-five cities in the United States[74]

In March, 1939 PSC agreed to reduce rates for electric service by about seventeen percent for 75,000 domestic customers, but natural gas rates remained the same. The city subsequently launched yet another study, and also filed a request for an investigation by the Federal Power Commission.[75] After the city petitioned the FPC, Colorado Interstate Gas Company lost some of its confidence and asked to return to the conference table. The council, however, was tired of negotiating and believed it would have better results with a ruling by a national regulatory agency.[76] The complaint to the Federal Power Commission requested an investigation of the relationship of Colorado Interstate Gas Company and Canadian River Gas Company with the Cities Service Power and Light Company on the theory that they were controlled by the same group of people.[77]

The day after Mayor Stapleton and City Attorney Malcolm Lindsey signed the complaint, the Colorado Interstate and the Canadian River Gas Companies filed a suit in federal court asking "that the Federal Power Commission be restrained from entering a finding."[78] Interstate Gas and its supplier, the Canadian River Gas Company, argued that the FPC investigation be stopped because the companies were not public utilities as defined by the federal Natural Gas Act of 1938 and, therefore, were not under the authority of the Federal Power Commission.[79] The 1938 Natural Gas Act granted the Federal Power Commission authority to regulate interstate sales of natural gas for resale to distribution companies. However, only the tariffs for transporting gas were regulated; the wellhead price (or production price) of natural gas was not included. Direct sales to end users, such as Colorado Fuel and Iron company, via interstate pipelines were also excluded.[80] CIG claimed exemption under these provisions, and also argued that the Federal Power Commission had no authority in any case because the contracts were made before the Natural Gas Act was passed.

The city plaintiffs asked the Tenth Circuit Court of Appeals to determine whether the pipeline companies were indeed utilities, asked for a ruling to decide if contracts made before the creation of the FPC could be regulated by the public utilities commission. The court ruled for the plaintiffs, and in 1940 the United States Supreme Court affirmed that decision. An investigation into the the rates charged Public Service Company by Colorado Interstate Gas Company began soon after.[81]

A cast of attorneys, company representatives and city officials was present when the Denver hearing opened in courtroom A of the City and County Building on 28 October 1940.[82] The hearings dealt with the disparity between low rates charged the Colorado Fuel and Iron Corporation in Pueblo and rates levied to Public Service Company and the City of Denver. During the hearing exchanges were often bitter:

"You are practically giving gas away to this customer and the people of Denver are footing the bill," Case March, attorney for the Federal Power

Commission declared as William A. Dougherty of New York city, attorney for the pipelines companies, the Colorado Interstate Gas company and the Canadian River Gas company, objected to the line of questioning.

"Oh, don't be a demagog," Dougherty interrupted.

"I'm not a Democrat, I mean a demagog", March shouted in reply. "I am a Democrat," he added.[83]

Case March believed that Colorado Interstate Gas sold C F and I gas at an extremely low rate, because the Rockefeller interests controlled the steel company.

> "You appeared before them representing the Standard Oil interests and millions of dollars were spent in trying to defeat the act."
>
> "You know that is an unmitigated lie." Dougherty shouted, shaking his finger at March.
>
> The government attorney leaped up and started around the counsel table toward Dougherty, but was grabbed by his colleague, . .
>
> "At least, I'm not a tool of Standard Oil," March yelled, as Lange continued to restrain him. "I demand that you take back that statement."[84]

Dougherty refused and examiner Gray restored order. George E. Rhodes, speaking for CIG, explained that Colorado Fuel and Iron's rate had been arrived at through lengthy negotiation, and that no special considerations were given. The lower rate was based on the fact that the steel company consumed a large quantity of gas.[85]

Other utility companies were awaiting the verdict of the Denver case because it was one of the first to deal with jurisdiction over natural gas suppliers--pipeline companies--since passage of the Natural Gas Act. The counsel for the Federal Power Commission filed a brief in Washington, D.C. stating that the combined profit for Colorado Interstate Gas Company and Canadian River Gas Company was at least fifteen percent. The commissioners determined that a fair rate to be earned was six and one-half percent, and the FPC attorneys recommended that CIG's rates be cut to that level.[86]

In March, 1942 the Federal Power Commission ruled that the natural gas rates charged Public Service Company should be cut to 16 1/2 cents per thousand cubic feet with the savings passed on to consumers.[87] The Colorado Interstate Gas Company and its supplier the Canadian River Company would be allowed to earn a return of six and one-half percent profit.[88] The rate of profit would be figured by a method called the "prudent investment" method of arriving at a rate base, i.e. a rate of return on equity commensurate with returns on investments in other enterprises with corresponding risks. Previously the rate base was figured by original cost method.[89] The Commission had struggled in using the old fair value and fair rate of return method, and decided that the system of "prudent investment" was an easier and more equitable method of determining a rate base.

The United States Supreme Court upheld this method of determining rate bases in the landmark *Federal Power Commission* v. *Hope Natural Gas Company* in 1944. The Hope Natural Gas Case further strengthened state commissions by asserting that the highest court of the land would no longer review cases that were appealed from a state commissions decision simply because the commission failed to follow a specific valuation formula. The Supreme Court in the Hope case also indicated that a rate base should be determined in a way that produced reasonable and nonconfiscatory rates rather than tying regulatory agencies to a specific method of determining rate base valuation. The Hope case moved decision making away from the court system.[90]

The Federal Power Commission decision was reviewed and upheld by the United States Circuit Court of Appeals in May, 1944.[91] By that time the case was over five years old, but Colorado Interstate Gas petitioned the United States Supreme Court for review of the ruling.[92] On 18 August 1944, the Supreme Court upheld the two million dollar rate reduction for Denver and other cities in Colorado and Wyoming.[93] Several months later the Federal Power Commission ordered a new gas rate schedule in effect, along with a refund of $8.5 million. Of that portion Public Service Company would return $4,320,000 to its customers. The Colorado Interstate Gas rate for natural gas in Denver would be twenty cents per 1000 cubic feet.[94] A plan to distribute the refund money was submitted to Judge John F. Mueller of the tenth United States circuit court of appeals for approval in March, 1946.[95] Checks were finally sent to the customers 2 May 1949.[96]

NOTES--CHAPTER 8

1

Denver *Post*, 11 May 1926, p. 22.

2

Alfred M. Leeston, John A. Chricton, and John C. Jacobs, *The Dynamic Natural Gas Industry* (Norman, OK: University of Oklahom Press,1963), p. 10.

Cities Service Company had played an integral part in the natural gas industry by developing a new kind of pipe to transport gas. Previously engineers had believed that long-distance transportation would require thick-walled steel pipes that would be too expensive to use over long distances. Henry L. Doherty felt that the problem was not insurmountable. He proposed a pipeline from Amarillo to Chicago. When experts came up with a 24-inch diameter pipe made of high-tensile steel that could withstand high pressure his project was assured success. Doherty was rarely daunted. W. Alton Jones, *"The Cities Service Story," Cities Service Company, A Case History of American Enterprise* (New York: Newcomen Society in North America, 1955), p. 16.

3

Martin G. Glaeser, *Public Utilities in American Capitalism* (New York: The MacMillan Company, 1957), p. 101.

4

Denver *Post*, 8 April 1927, p. 1.

5

Wilson B. Emery, "Natural Gas in the Rocky Mountain Areas," *Oil and Gas Journal* G XXVI (16 June 1927), 185.

6

Clark F. Barb, "The Oil and Gas Industry in Colorado," *Colorado School of Mines Quarterly* XXXVII (April, 1942), 109.

7

Colorado State Planning Commission,Colorado Yearbook 1945-57, p. 273.

8

"Natural Gas Industry Celebrates its 150th Anniversary this Year," *Lines* (June, 1966), 2.

9

Ibid., pp. 2 and 3.

10

Ibid., p. 3.

11 *Gasser* XXXV (February, 1978), 2.

12 Ibid., p. 6.

13 Denver *Post*, 28 May 1927, p. 4.

14 Ibid., and *Gasser*, XXXV (February, 1978), p. 6.

15 Denver *Post*, 10 June 1927, p. 9.

16 Denver *Post*, 13 June 1927, p. 1.

17 Denver *Post*, 13 June 1927, p. 1 and 23 July 1927, p. 12.

18 Denver *Post*, 22 July 1927, p. 15.

19 Denver *Post*, 13 June 1927, p. 1.

20 Denver *Post*, 14 June 1927, pp. 1-2.

21 Minutes of Meeting of Committee on Natural Gas Franchise, 27 June 1927, Denver Chamber of Commerce (1 May--1 November 1927), p. 350.

22 Denver *Post*, 22 September 1927, p. 4. The same provision was included in the 1927 franchise.

23 Denver *Post*, 16 June, 1927, p. 1.

24 Denver *Post*, 15 June 1927, p. 1.

25 Denver *Post*, 17 June 1927, p. 1.

26 Denver *Post*, 18 June 1927, p. 1.

27 Denver *Post*, 16 June 1927, p. 1.

28 Denver *Post*, 11 August 1927, p. 1.

29 Denver *Post*, 17 August 1927, p. 1.

30 Denver *Post*, 7 September 1927, p. 1.

31 *Denver Post*, 6 September 1927, p. 1 and *Rocky Mountain News*, 14 September 1927, p. 1.

32 Denver *Post*, 28 October 1927, p. 1.

33 Carl Ubbelohde, Maxine Benson, and Duane A. Smith, *A Colorado History*, Revised Centennial Edition, (Boulder: Pruett Publishing Company, 1976), pp. 302-303.

34 Denver *Post*, 2 November 1927, p. 10.

35 *Rocky Mountain News*, 28 October 1927, p. 1.

36 Carl Abbott, Stephen J. Leonard, David McComb, *Colorado: A History of the Centennial State* (Boulder: Colorado Associated University Press, 1982), p. 272.

37 Ben B. Lindsey and Harvey J. O'Higgins, *The Beast* (New York: Doubleday, Page & Company, 1910), p. 233.

38 Denver *Post*, 4 February 1928, p. 2.

39 Denver *Post*, 4 March 1928, p. 5.

40 *Rocky Mountain News*, 5 May 1928, p. 5.

41 Denver *Post*, 24 June 1928, p.1.

42 Denver *Post* 22 September 1927, p. 1.

43 Denver *Post*, 15 July 1928, p. 1. The three flames were at 38th and Kalamath streets, 48th and Clay streets, and 26th and Yale Ave.

44 Denver *Post*, 15 July 1928, p. 2.

45 Denver *Post*, 22 October 1931, p. 1.

46 *Denver Post*, 31 October 1931, p. 5 and 7 November 1931, pp. 1 and 5.

47 Denver *Post*, 13 February 1932, p. 1.

48 Denver *Post*, 20 February 1932, p. 1.

49 Denver *Post*, 19 February 1932, p. 1.

50 Denver *Post*, 20 February 1932, p. 1 and 23 February 1932, p. 3.

51 Denver *Post*, 9 March 1932, p. 7.

52 Denver *Post*, 9 March 1932, p. 7 and 17 March

1932, p. 16.

53 Denver *Post*, 25 May 1932, p. 3 and 15 June 1932, p. 16.

54 Denver *Post*, 13 June 1932, p. 1.

56 Denver 5*Post*, 20 September 1932, p. 2.

56 Denver *Post*, 5 March 1933, p. 1.

57 *Rocky Mountain News*, 23 June 1933, p. 2.

58 Ibid.

59 Ibid.

60 Ibid., p. 22.

61 Denver *Post*, 17 July 1933, p. 2.

62 The letter was actually written by Timothy A. Pedley a Denver broker who was connected with the Federal Trade Commission. *Rocky Mountain News*, 20 July 1933, p. 2.

63 Ibid.

64 Ibid.

65 *Post*, 23 July 1933, p. 10.

66 *Rocky Mountain News*, 7 September 1933, p. 1.

67 Denver *Post*, 30 July 1933, p. 3.

68 *Rocky Mountain News*, 6 September 1933, p. 22.

69Denver *Post* 22 September 1927, p. 1.

70 Denver *Post*, 11 August 1934, pp. 11 and 4.

71 Denver *Post*, 21 August 1934, p. 7.

72 *Rocky Mountain News*, 29 June 1937, p. 1.

73 *Denver Democrat*, 7 January 1939, p. 1.

74 Denver *Post*, 23 January 1939, p. 4.

75 Denver *Post*, 27 February 1939, p. 1 and 6, and the *Denver Democrat*, 25 February 1939, p. 1.

76 Denver *Post*, 7 July 1939, p. 1.

77 Ibid.

78 Denver *Post* 10 July 1939, p. 5.

79 In 1938 Congress passed the Natural Gas Act without a dissenting vote in either house to prevent the exploitation of the consumer at the hands of the natural gas companies. The Natural Gas Act said that no corporation may export or import natural gas in interstate commerce without the approval of the Federal Power Commission, such approval to be granted unless such exportation or importation will not be consistent with public interest. In 1954 the Supreme Court reversed the decision in the Phillips case (referred to in Chapter 13 of this paper) and held that the Natural Gas Act applies to sales of natural gas in interstate commerce which are made during the producing and gathering phases of the production for resale (before exempt) because the purpose of the Natural Gas Act was consumer protection. *FPC* v. *Hope Natural Gas Co.* 320 U.S. 591 (1944).

United States Supreme Court Confirmed the Federal Power Commission's right to change the method of establishing a rate base in the 1944 Hope Case.

80 Laurence Kumins, "Natural Gas Regulations: Problems and Options," in Werner Sichel, ed., *Utility Rate Making in an Energy Conscious Environment* (Boulder: Westview Press, 1979), pp. 41-47.

81 Denver *Post*, 28 October 1940, p. 6.

82 *Rocky Mountain News* 29 October 1940, p. 6.

83 Denver *Post*, 13 November 1940, p. 10.

84 Ibid.

85 Denver *Post*, 14 November 1940, p. 8.

86 Denver *Post*, 16 March 1941, p. 32 and 30 July 1941, p. 1.

87 Denver *Post*, 26 March 1942, p. 1.

88 *Rocky Mountain News*, 27 March 1942, p. 1.

89 Ibid.

90 *Martin T. Farris and Roy J. Sampson, Public Utilities: Regulation, Management, and Ownership* (Prospect Heights, IL: Waveland Press, 1973), p. 149.

91 *Denver Post*, 16 May 1944, p. 3. and *Rocky Mountain News*, 17 May 1944, p. 7.

92 Denver *Post*, 9 July 1944, p. 11. The companies ordered to reduce rates were Colorado Interstate Gas, Canadian River Gas Company and Colorado-Wyoming Gas Company.

93 Denver *Post*, 18 August 1944, p. 26.

94 Denver *Post*, 4 October 1945, p. 1 and 7.

95 Denver *Post*, 1 March 1946. p. 1.

96 The author would especially like to thank Edward Kelly, retired vice president of Public Service Company for reading and improving this chapter.

CHAPTER 9

PUBLIC OPINION AND GOVERNMENT REGULATION

The decades of the 1920s and 1930s were contrasting periods for public utilities. The earlier ten-year span was one of expansion and promotion in which energy technology, particularly electricity, substantially increased the American standard of living. The utilities were the beneficiaries of new demand for articles of mass consumption. Although people appreciated the improved material comforts, they nevertheless railed against the utilities for what they considered to be oxhorbitant prices, overblown advertising, and monopolistic practices. This was the era when President Calvin Coolidge proclaimed that the business of America was business, and utilities and other corporations were enjoying widespread public approval due to the prosperity of the country.

The 1930s were juxtaopposed to the previous decade. The Great Depression devastated the country. Business was discredited by government investigations exposing the misconduct of leading businessmen and bankers, as well as the excesses of holding companies. This prompted Congress to pass legislation that would restrict and change utilities. Congress had created the

Federal Trade Commission in 1914 to restrain the unlawful supression of competition, but the pro-business interpretation of the law led to ineffective regulation. In 1920, Congress passed the Water Power Act giving the Federal Power Commission authority to license the construction and operation of dams and hydroelectric plants. Once again, however, this legislation was ineffective, and people sought new, stronger regulation.[1]

Early in the 1920s public utilities mounted a national public relations effort to expand their markets, and also to create positive public opinion about the industry. Advertising and marketing had become a popular vehicle for businesses to sell their products, but utilities indulged in aggressive methods of indoctrination. Much of their efforts were modeled after the propaganda during World War I.[2]

Examples of public relations efforts were contained in a report to the United States Senate by the Federal Trade Commission. The report included a list of exhibits which help create a picture of what the utilities were doing in the 1920s. The utility industry was putting a new emphasis on public relations to improve its image. For example, the National Electric Light Association (the NELA), originally a technical association, changed its focus to public relations.[3] Utilities attempted to sway the opinion of everyone, from children to employees, to improve the industry's reputation. The FTC exhibits are no longer extant but following sample headings illustrate the scope of public relations efforts:

> Children teach elders aims of utility
>
> Employees have high place in public-relations program
>
> Employees recruited on basis of number of friends they can make, not as stenographers, etc.
>
> Entertainment of newspaper men
>
> School important link in public relations work . . .
>
> Utility courses in colleges, etc., exerting a most important effect on public thought
>
> Women employees trained to talk public ownership, regulation, etc., to friends, neighbors at church meetings, clubs, etc.[4]

Other entries demonstrate that adverse publicity had affected the way utilities did business:

> Good public relations when utilities come clean and discard watered stock, etc.
>
> Sloan says how to gain and hold elusive public good will--serious problem of every utility manager[5]

There appeared to be the feeling on the part of utility men that the public relations had accomplished positive results as indicated by other FTC exhibits:

> Before customer ownership utilities

constantly on defensive, now take case to own stockholders

Public ownership would have been 100 percent ahead without public relations work

Radio effects better public relations and increases understanding of utility industry

State Committees changed economic and political thought

Private utilities organized and employed associations and committees in nation-wide activities v. public ownership6

Colorado followed this public relations trend, and in some aspects led the way. Examples from the Federal Trade Commission subheadings provide a rough sketch of promotional work in the Colorado and indicate an emphasis on education of young people:

Ablest utility men employed in work in universities, etc.

Course put in Colorado and other schools through men higher up in educational circles--appeared that request came from schools

Every college and university in Colorado using utility speakers

High-school students mostly Denver, . . . heard utility message

Larger eastern educational institutions adopt Colorado plan

Pamphlets, etc. furnished school debating teams opposing Government ownership

Publicity secured in newspapers

Romance of power, lecture, Denver Boy Scouts

State committee aided universities financially

Utilities accomplish the impossible in Colorado

Work in universities and colleges changing, unfavorable public opinion 7

Historian Arthur Schlesinger, Jr. has given an account of the publicity effort. He said that the National Electric Light Association distributed its propaganda to educational institutions and community groups in great profusion to put utilities in a most favorable light. The National Electric Light Association also lobbied public officials to get favorable rulings for utility bills. Utility men went as far as having negative economic facts about utilities purged from textbooks, and also campaigned against public ownership which would cut into their profit. Schlesinger said that, "Rarely in American history has business organized so powerful a propaganda offensive."[8] He also pointed out the irony of the public's paying for the publicity campaign through utility bills.[9]

Colorado was apparently a leader in promoting public utilities. John Loiseau of Public Service Company said in 1924 that in Colorado ". . .every university and college has been systematically conducting lecture courses for two years is still leading the nation in utility study."[10] Loiseau said that other universities, including Harvard, were developing public service courses.[11]

Newspaperman Ernest Gruening from Alaska who became governor of the state and later a United States Senator, wrote a book called *The Public Pays*, in which he offered Colorado as a prime example of utility publicity. Gruening quoted George E. Lewis, Director of the Public Utility Information Committee of the Rocky Mountain Division of the National Electric Light Association, expressing delight with the inroads his organization had made with Colorado colleges and universities in the mid-1920s. Lewis had just put together an educational committee with a representative from each college in the state to oversee the introduction of utility subjects into the classroom, as well as in debating societies. Lewis told the group about a three-pronged effort to educate the college instructors, the students and the public through debates.[12]

At a committee meeting in 1924 the president J. G. Crabbe, of the State Teachers College in Greeley, Colorado reported enthusiastically that his college intended to give credit for courses on the public utility industry. Students who desired credit were required to listen to lectures as well as outside speakers. Dr. Crabbe recommended regular courses on public utilities rather than the hit or miss effort that had been attempted in the past.[13]

Later in 1924 Dr. Charles A. Lory, of the Colorado Agricultural College reconfirmed academic support at a meeting between utility executives and representatives from the University of Colorado, Denver University, Colorado State Teachers' College, Colorado College, Colorado Agricultural College, and the Colorado School of Mines. "I thought I'd never live to see the day when the utilities would be providing educational material for our universities," Dr. Lory commented enthusiastically. "Plainly a new day for the utility industry has arrived. I am certainly impressed with the progress you are making."[14] He encouraged the utilities to tell the educators even more of utility problems and ambitions. Lory's statements and the acknowledgement of the truth and sincerity of the utility representatives seemed to express the sentiments of the academicians gathered at the meeting.

In 1926 George Lewis wrote to the national chairman of the NELA Committee on Cooperation with Educational Institutions reporting that there were, at that time, twenty-four public utility executives teaching courses at the University of Colorado.[15] The Rocky Mountain Division of the National Electric Light Association decided to endow a fellowship at the University of Colorado to give more prestige and authority to its university program. The Association paid half the cost of the fellowship, amounting to $1,000 for the first year and increasing one hundred dollars in each successive year.[16]

The lengths to which The Rocky Mountain Committee of the National Electric Light Association was willing to go to educate students is shown by a paper written by George Lewis entitled, "Utilities Create Good Will by Advertising University Course." The paper revealed a plan to promote a course on public utility economics at the University of Colorado. In 1927 a poster was designed to advertise the course by listing numerous achievements of the industry, and implying that utilities would hire good students from the college course. The poster was sent to local newspapers to be run as a news story at the same time distributed in a three-state area. Although the poster appeared to be from the university, the utility actually created it and paid the costs. Students might have signed up for the courses expecting a job in the utility industry after graduation, but the intent of the courses seemed more to give young people a positive opinion of the industry rather than training future employees.[17]

GO TO COLLEGE BUT STAY AT HOME

> The Nation's street railway, electric, telephone, and gas companies are on the alert to recruit young men of ability.
>
> The University of Colorado now offers a non-technical course of study of the utility business by mail.
>
> In becoming identified with the public utility business, students will enjoy being part of an industry of tremendous achievements, among which is the feat of holding down the cost of its service to the same levels that prevailed a dozen years ago. This has required--and will continue to require--the utmost in skill and in training, such as this course affords.
>
> Each course (for which a year is allowed) contains from 12 to 18 lessons, at a cost of but 50 cents a lesson.
>
> University of Colorado, Extension Division
> Boulder, Colorado 18

These posters were sent to every utility company in Colorado, New Mexico, and Wyoming in December, 1927. Lewis encouraged utility managers to distribute them among consumers. The accompanying letter encouraged the managers to remind their customers of the low rates for utility service which were also shown in the poster. Plates and mats were sent with the letter so that the newspapers could reproduce the poster and all the information contained on it. As Lewis wrote, "Such a statement, made over the signature of the University of Colorado, naturally bears more weight than if it appeared in one of our own advertisements."[19] Although their methods were neither dishonest nor illegal they certainly raised some questions of business ethics, as well as university ethics.

George Lewis was eager to publicize utilities in every way he could. In addition to providing information through the educational system, he asked employees to speak out in their communities about utilities. Lewis said that he realized that representatives from utility companies were only human beings who were often inexperienced and reluctant to speak in public. He remembered that at the beginning of his program speakers from the company stood up in front of a group and shuffled their feet while trying to find something to do with their hands. They seemed to be so uncomfortable that their message was lost.

To solve the problem the Rocky Mountain Committee on Public Utilities Information organized a college to teach public speaking. The courses always had a large enrollment, including people from towns outside Denver. Graduates went on to speak at universities, high schools and community organizations, and a positive account of the public utilities was eloquently and frequently told.[20]

Lewis also cultivated the friendship of newspapers, remarking that it took several years to develop a good relationship. He and his colleagues frequently contacted newspaper editors, even holding a theater party and yearly breakfast for publishers. The friendly relationship was designed to bring about positive articles about the utility.[21]

Similar examples of public relations work were taking place in other locations. An article in the *New Republic* portrayed the effort in New York, where each year utilities spent between $28,000 and $38,000 for newspaper advertising. As the *New Republic* pointed out, there was nothing illegal about that sum, but dollars in that amount might influence the editorial policies of a paper in the utilities' favor. The reporter asked whether the money was being used to influence reporters to write positive stories about utilities in order to sway public opinion as well as to sell electricity and gas. Utility men themseveles wrote two high school textbooks and introduced them into 491 schools. The books emphasized the positive aspects of private ownership, giving the privately-owned utilities' biased opinions of public ownership.[22]

According to the *New Republic* a million dollars or more had been spent by utility corporations to influence college professors throughout the country. Those who agreed to teach a positive version of public utilities were rewarded with assistance in getting books published. Some were also paid handsome retainer fees, although payment was usually kept secret.[23] Utilities, of course, had the right to express their views and attempt to persuade others to agree with them. "The difficulty comes when they attempt, not to participate in a fair debate, but to smother all arguments in opposition to their own," stated the *New Republic* "By using the sheer weight of wealth, they have . . . attempted to conceal and distort the truth in order to make sure that a given point of view shall prevail."[24]

The large-scale public relations programs which were undertaken to defend the holding company structure and to maintain large profits in the 1920s ended with almost the opposite effect in the 1930s. The effort that was designed to shape public opinion, ironically resulted in the public's reshaping utilities. During the 1930s businesses, of necessity, became less aggressive in advertising methods, and also had to change their attitudes toward the consumer. New Deal legislation changed the financial structure of holding companies and also created programs whereby the federal government competed with private utilities.

Through efforts to shape public opinion, public relations became an important part of utility operations. Public relations departments had a broad range of responsibilities. Since there was eventually a negative response to the advertising methods of the twenties, however, utilities have tempered their approach and have built up public relations departments that, in subtle ways, market their companies to the public and their own employees.[25] Successful utilities have learned that the best-run company in the world will not succeed without good communication. A public statement that is not well thought out can be misunderstood and do great damage to a program that is otherwise sound. A creative, effective public relations department is essential and in most utilities is well developed, staffed and funded.

Since the twenties big businesses have not only had to change their advertising approach but their attitude toward the public as well. No longer are there robber barons who can ignore consumers, suppliers, employees and the public at large. The company philosophy has become as important as its product. The public expects company leaders to be honest, good citizens, as well as astute businessmen. A new philosophy of "public service" is often incorporated into company policy to appeal to the populace. Management is responsible for protraying an image of corporate fairness and responsibility to the public in addition to accomplishing company business and making a profit.

The utilities had, and still have, various "publics." They must serve their stockholders, consumers, employees, regulators, and the community as a whole, and to each they must market the company differently. Stockholders want utilities to make money, while consumers insist on low rates. Leaders spent much of their time bringing about the excellent performance that consumers and investors demanded, and then communicating that performance to the public.[26] Despite the monopolistic character of the industry utilities were expected to perform efficiently and with the most effective business profits.

Growth of the utility industry exploded during 1920s. Throughout the nation there was great enthusiasm for the benefits of electricity, but that enthusiasm was marred by the monopolistic power brought about by mergers and questionable financial arrangements of the holding companies. Holding companies were not confined to state borders, and, therefore, people feared that neither local nor federal regulation could control the exploitive giants. As the dependence increased on a way of life based on electric and gas appliances and machinery progressed, people felt they were at the mercy of these holding companies.[27]

It was the public outcry over this economic control and the system of holding companies that led the Federal Trade Commission (in 1928) to begin an investigation in 1928 into their financial structure and management. The inquiry lasted for nearly nine years culminating in a 96-volume report published in its entirety in 1937. As a result of information gathered during the investigation Congress passed a series of laws that finally established a federal regulatory structure which curbed big business.

One of these laws was the 1933 Securities Act which created the Securities and Exchange Commission to regulate interstate transactions of corporate securities and stock exchanges. The SEC was given significant power in 1935 to regulate the securities of interstate gas and electric companies with specific authority to approve all securities issued. The SEC used the law to force the restructuring of utility systems leading to the creation of companies to serve only a single state, or sometimes a region. State public utility commissions, therefore, acquired more control over power companies inasmuch as they served only one state.[28]

The Public Utilities Holding Company Act (known also as the Wheeler-Rayburn Act) was one of the most significant pieces of legislation. It required that all holding companies doing business in more than one state had to register with the Securities and Exchange Commission. The law defined a holding company to be one that owned ten percent or more of the voting securities of either a gas or electric utility.

The second part of the Holding Company Act contained the "death sentence clause" limiting holding companies to two layers of financial ownership, and compelling the companies to divest themselves of any intermediate companies or properties.[29] The Act also established a uniform system of accounts that all utilities were to use when reporting to the SEC. Loans from subsidiaries to the parent company were outlawed, and the SEC carefully monitored loans from the holding company to subsidiaries. President Franklin D. Roosevelt was a great supporter of the Holding Company Act, believing it to be the only way to rescue the industry from its own sins.[30]

The utilities rose up in arms against the Holding Company Act. Public Service Company of Colorado, Cities Service Company and Cities Service Power and Light Company were among those who challenged the act as unconstitutional, filing suit in United States District Court in November, 1935.[31] At the same time the board of directors of PSC resolved to fight the Act until it was rescinded.[32] For almost a decade Cities Service battled to avoid being dismembered. In the end, however, the government was successful, and Public Service Company of Colorado became an independent company in 1943.

The excesses of the 1920s and 1930s and the resulting regulation have shaped present-day utilities. Today, power companies are restricted to political boundaries, generally a single state even though geographical boundaries might be more efficient. The financial management is now conservative with a more realistic balance between long-term debt, preferred stock, and equity.[33] Although these changes forced utilities to be fairer to the consumer, the negative public opinion engendered by the abuses of earlier periods did not disappear altogether.

Public watchfulness and a desire for low rates were reflected in rather restrictive regulatory policies of state commissions and federal agencies. The regulations often restrained operations and profits to a level where, when problems arose, the companies went from one crisis to another, rather than implementing long-range plans to solve problems. One must ask whether the regulations developed half a century ago have created reactive businesses that cannot confront problems over a long period of time. The question of whether, in an era of cooperation and interconnection, these regulations make utilities perform better has not been decisively answered.

An indirect effect of New Deal legislation was a rise of public power systems which eventually competed with investor-owned utilities. As in other states the early history of electrification in Colorado occurred mostly in urban centers and mining towns. The development of electricity nationwide was an urban movement with only experimental rural lines before the 1920s. Bringing electricity to rural areas was hampered by low populations and the expense of stringing wires over long distances. As more people settled in urban areas and enjoyed material well-being, rural life was considered almost second class, especially without the amenities of energy technology.[34] To solve the problems of rural America, Congress established the Rural Electrification Administration in 1935 to spread electricity to the less populated areas of the country. To do this, the REA lent money to local cooperatives at a low rate of interest to build power plants and transmission facilities.

In the 1930s three major hydroelectric projects were built by the government. The first, Boulder Dam, was conceived during the Hoover administration, completed in 1936, and eventually named after him in 1947. Located at the Arizona-Nevada border, the dam had a capacity of 1,354,000 kilowatts using the Colorado River as its source of energy. The second was the Bonneville Dam, the beginning of a multipurpose development of the Columbia River in the Northwest. The project evolved to control floods, increase water for domestic and industrial use, and provide additional hydroelectric generation. The dam was forty-two miles upstream from Portland, Oregon where the Columbia River cuts a deep canyon through the Cascade Mountains.[35] The third, the Tennessee Valley Authority, was probably the most successful of

Roosevelt's New Deal undertakings. Located in a poverty-stricken valley of the Tennessee River, the TVA put people to work building dams and powerhouses while others channeled the river which flowed through parts of eight states. In fact, all three of the projects provided employment, flood control, and area development for the regions in which they were located.

Private power companies objected to the low rates REAs could charge as a result of the government subsidies, i.e., the two-percent loans and the preference clause. That clause dated back to the 1902 Reclamation Act, and gave public power systems a preference or first right to electric power derived from federal water resource development. The preference provision had been created to encourage the development of public power systems, and also to guarantee customers maximum benefit from federally-developed projects.[36] The fact that rural electric cooperatives did not have to pay income tax, if no less than eighty-five percent of their operating revenues came from members, was another factor to which private utilities strongly objected. All of these REA advantages made it difficult for the private companies to compete with the federally subsidized cooperatives.[37]

The benefits given to the REA and its cooperatives varied with the political party in power. The Republicans were inclined to diminish the advantage, while the Democratic administrations supported the idea. During the political battles waged for decades over public power, it was clear that the lobbying power for public power was large and strong. The utility lobbies were at the same time an active force that wielded power, particularly with Republicans.[38]

Private utilties waged a battle against public-supported power referring to it as "creeping socialism." However, whatever takeover there was by the government did not go nearly as far as its adversaries feared. In fact, across the nation only twenty-five percent of the power produced today is from publicly-owned facilities.[39]

Another form of public ownership was the municipal utility, which was a trend from the mid 1880s to the 1920s when it peaked at about three thousand municipal systems. By 1969 that number had been reduced to two thousand, and only half of those produced their own electricity. Municipal ownership accounts for only five percent of the country's electrical generation. State ownership also gained popularity in the 1920s.

New York, South Carolina, Texas, Oklahoma, and Nebraska all established some sort of state ownership. Nebraska had the most complete program, buying up private facilities and owning all electric power distribution in the state by 1946.[40] Just how much any governmental agency should infringe upon the private enterprise system is a matter of opinion. Private versus public ownership is a topic that will be continually debated and will remain a tremendous concern to investor-owned utilities.

During the 1930s Henry L. Doherty knew he was fighting a losing battle in resisting the wave of the New Deal. His peer, utility mogul Samuel Insull, had run short of cash and his empire had fallen down around him. But at the depths of the Depression in 1933 two thirds of the offices in Doherty's Sixty Wall Towers were leased, and in the same year the earnings of his company were only down two percent. In 1935, when Congress passed the Holding Company Act Doherty felt that the government was destroying the utility business. Some said that America was simply looking for someone to blame for the Depression and Insull and other utility tycoons were the scapegoats. One of Doherty's top executives, W. A. Jones, said "The government found a mouse in industry's pantry. To find it, they're tearing down the house."[41]

Not only was Doherty fighting the government, but he was battling poor health. Frequently in the hospital with arthritis and neuritis, he entered under a fictitious name to escape the press. Perhaps it was just as well that he died before the full brunt of federal regulation fell upon his empire. The day after Christmas in 1939 he succumbed to bronchial pneumonia at the age of 69.[42] He had polarized people--some admiring him, others vilifying him. Whatever one's sentiments, it is accepted by almost everyone that he contributed as much to the utility industry as any man in history.

NOTES--CHAPTER 9

1

John M. Blum, Edmund S. Morgan, Willie Lee Rose, Arthur M. Schlesinger, Jr., Kenneth M. Stampp, C. Vann Woodward, *The National Experience: A History of the United States since 1865* fourth edition (New York: Harcourt Brace Jovanovich, Inc., 1977), pp. 545 and 578.

2

Lee Metcalf and Vic Rainemer, *Overcharge* (New York: David McKay Co., Inc., 1967), p. 93. The authors said that by 1923 the agencies were turning out volumes of publicity that almost matched the volumes of publicity that was much like the propaganda during World War II. Lee Metcalf was a United States Senator from Montana who carried on a long, hostile battle against privately-owned utilities. Although he seemed to hold a personal grudge against investor owned utilities the information he disseminated did have supporting information.

3

U.S., Senate, Report of the Federal Trade Commission, S. Doc. 92, 70th Cong., 1st sess. 1935, pt. 71-B, pp. 334-339.

4

Ibid.

5

Ibid.

6

Ibid.

7

Ibid, pp. 339-40.

8

Arthur M. Schlesinger, Jr., *Crisis of the Old Order, 1919-1937* (Boston: Houghton Mifflin Company of Boston, 1957), pp. 121.

9

Ibid., pp. 118-124.

10

Public Service Bulletin, II (2 June 1924), 1.

11

Ibid.

12

Ernest Gruening, *The Public Pays: A Study of Power Propaganda* (New York: Vanguard Press, 1964), p. 42. His original book was published in 1931.

13 Ibid., p. 40.

14 Ibid., p. 38.

15 Ibid., pp. 43-44.

16 Ibid., p. 44 and Exhibits 1788, 1794 of Senate Document 92, part 84-D indicate that a professor from the University of Colorado received $1,692.33 from the Rocky Mountain Committee for a report on municipal plants which he wrote during summer vacations.

17 Gruening, *The Public Pays*, pp. 46-47.

18 Ibid., pp. 47-48.

19 Ibid., p. 48.

20 Ibid., pp. 135-36.

21 Ibid., p. 162.

22 "Public Utilities and Public Opinion," *New Republic*, 27 June 1928, pp. 135-36.

23 Ibid., p. 135.

24 Ibid.

25 Martin Farris and Roy Sampson wrote that every public relations program is based on the six Ps of public relations: philosophy, policy, performance, publics, planning, and publicity. Martin T. Farris and Roy J. Sampson, *Public Utilities: Regulation, Management, and Ownership* (Prospect Heights, IL: Waveland Press, Inc., 1973), pp. 240-45.

26 Ibid., pp. 241-43.

27 Merryle Stanley Rukeyser, "Is There a Power Trust?," *Nation* CIIVIII, 6 March 1929, p. 281-83.

28 Farris and Sampson, *Public Utilities*, p. 149.

29 Leonard S. Hyman, *America's Electric Utilities: Past, Present and Future*, (Arlington, VA: Public Utilities Reports, Inc., 1983), pp. 87-88 and Farris and Sampson, *Public Utilities*, pp. 146-47.

30 Philip J. Funigiello, *Toward a National Power*

Policy: The New Deal and the Electric Utility Industry, 1933-1941 (Pittsburgh: University of Pittsburgh Press, 1973), p. 98.

[31] Denver *Post*, 29 November 1935, p. 1.

[32] Public Service Company 1935 Minute Book, (Public Service Company, Denver, Colorado), p. 48.

[33] Farris and Sampson, *Public Utilities*, p. 149.

[34] Funigiello, *Toward a National Power Policy*, p. 13.

[35] Hyman, *America's Electric Utilities*, p. 86.

[36] Jack Doyle, *Lines Across the Land: Rural Electrification Cooperatives, The Changing Politics of Energy in Rural America*, (Washington, DC: The Rural Land and Energy Project Environmental Policy Institute, 1979), p.1.

[37] Ibid., p. 19.

[38] Ibid., pp. 8-12.

[39] Farris and Sampson, *Public Utilities*, p. 265.

[40] Ibid., p. 271.

[41] William D. Ellis, *On the Oil Lands with Cities Service Company*, (Tulsa, OK: Cities Service Corporation, 1983), p. 166.

[42] "Henry L. Doherty" Robert L. Schuyler and Edward T. James, eds., *Dictionary of American Biography*, XXII Supplement Two (New York: Charles Scribner's Sons, 1958), p. 155.

PART III

AN INDEPENDENT PUBLIC SERVICE COMPANY OF COLORADO

1943-1969

CHAPTER 10

WAR AND POST WAR YEARS

The war years and those following brought significant changes for Public Service Company of Colorado. In 1943 the Holding Company Act caused Cities Service Company to divest itself of its Colorado subsidiaries. As a result an independent PSC set up its own financing, formed a new board of directors and went on to a period of unprecedented growth. Company leaders worried that the postwar years would be a time of economic slowdown, but instead it became a period of prosperity.

In the late 1930s and early 1940s Cities Service Company was preocuppied with warding off the effects of the 1935 Holding Company Act. Of particular concern was Section II, known as the "death sentence" clause. It required the Securities and Exchange Commission to limit the layers of corporations to two and that no holding company be more than two entities removed from an operating company. The holding companies were also ordered to dispose of all properties that did not fit into one integrated power system.

The holding Company Act broke up Doherty's empire and tore apart his concept of a central holding company system. In the 1920s, when utilities were beset with management problems and in financial disarray, Doherty believed that a parent company organized to supply capital, research, engineering and management to various subsidiaries would bring order to the industry. Had it not been for the gross misuse of subsidiaries the holding company idea might have been praised rather than the object of government regulation.

To fight the effects of the "death sentence" clause Cities Service lawyers argued , in several suits filed against the federal government, that the act was unconstitutional. Litigation lasted for approximately three years until the United States Supreme Court, in 1938, ruled the Public Utility Act of 1935 is constitutional. As a final effort Cities Service Company filed for an exemption to the Act, claiming that it was an operating rather than a holding company because most of its business was in oil and gas production. Petitions for exemptions were heard before the Securities and Exchange Commission which, after reviewing the case, disallowed the request.[1]

When divestiture appeared inevitable, Public Service Company submitted a refinancing plan to the Securities and Exchange Commission early in 1939. After reviewing the plan for eight months the SEC approved it, albeit with some reluctance, in August 1939.[2] The commission complimented the company on its impressive financial wellbeing, remarking that the Public Service of Colorado had one of the soundest records of any utility during the Depression. However they insisted that the company's financial figures had been consistently inflated since its organization in 1924.[3]

One of the SEC commissioners, Robert E. Healey, wrote a long dissenting opinion. Healey had been the chief counsel for the Federal Trade Commission during hearings on public utilities in which Public Service Company of Colorado and Cities Service Company had been used as examples of wrongdoing. Healey criticized the company for overpricing its construction projects. He also disapproved of a new refinancing plan to pour five million additional dollars of investors' money into the company. The money he said, would not be used for the properties or facilities, nor for the corporation's capital, but would merely continue the fourteen-year trend of benefiting the owners of the common stock, who had already received $27 million. Finally, he objected to the fact that control of the company was vested in a small minority of common stock owners.[4]

Even the majority opinion censured the company for financial abuses revealed in the FTC hearings. However, the SEC commissioners said that their role was not to judge what happened in the past, but to rule on the present proposal, one which they deemed reasonable and not adding to any further excesses in the company's financial dealings.[5] According to the approved refinancing program, $2,190,000 of common stock would be given to Cities Service Power and Light Company to retire the Public Service Company debt. In addition, $12,500,000 of four percent sinking fund debentures and $40,000,000 of 3 1/2 percent first mortgage bonds would be issued in 1949, due in 1964.[6]

Cities Service Company continued to resist the divestiture until 1943. Fifteen days prior to the legal deadline, the company finally made a choice deciding to devote its energies to the oil business and to a single utility permitted under the SEC decision. Cities Service proposed to keep all its utility properties in Colorado, Wyoming, New Mexico, claiming that it fit under the definition of one geographic area. The Securities and Exchange Commission, however, ruled that its restriction to "localized management" did not refer to properties spread over 900 miles and four states.[9]

In August, 1943 the Securities and Exchange Commission directed the public sale and distribution of the Cities Service Power and Light Company's common stock holdings in Public Service Company of Colorado. Cities Service Power and Light Company had been created in 1924 as a holding company and owned all the common stock of Public Service Company of Colorado.[10] The 875,000 shares of $20 par value of stock were offered to the public at $25 a share. Thereafter, the Public Service Company of Colorado became an independent and autonomous entity. The official divestiture took place on 29 November 1943. At that time PSC's assets exceeded liabilities by $2,184,397.[11] The "death sentence" clause of the 1935 Holding Company Act removed the heart of the late Henry L. Doherty's public utility system.

Under the provisions of the law, Public Service Company had to sell its tar and ice businesses. The company was allowed to keep the East Boulder Ditch Company, the Hillcrest Ditch and Reservoir Company, and the Eastern Colorado Power and Irrigation Company. The

SEC did not rule on the status of Boulder's bus system.[12] and it remained under Public Service Company ownership.

At the time of divestiture, Public Service Company supplied eighty percent of Colorado's gas and electricity. The city of Denver was the company's biggest market, although the Public Service Company also provided electricity to 138 other communities, including Boulder, Grand Junction, Aurora, Brighton, Sterling, Alamosa, Salida, Leadville, Idaho Springs, and smaller towns. In addition the company sold electricity wholesale to 109 communities for distribution by other utilities. PSC, buying from Colorado Interstate Gas Company, supplied many of these same cities with natural gas. Through its subsidiary, the Colorado-Wyoming Gas Company, it supplied gas to the Cheyenne Light, Fuel and Power Company (also owned by Public Service Company) for service to Wyoming's capital city.[13]

When Public Service Company of Colorado became independent, John E. Louiseau, who had been secretary, became the new president and general manager, and Guy Faller was named chairman of the board.[14] In his first presidential message in the 1943 Annual report, Loiseau explained the divestiture:

> The year 1943 witnessed one of the most important developments in the long history of your company.
>
> On November 29 1943, pursuant to an order of the Securities and Exchange Commission, Cities Service Power and Light Co., a subsidiary of Cities Service Co., which had held the entire common stock ownership of your company, diversified itself of the ownership through the sale of its common stock holdings to some 8,300 investors. As a result of this the number of stockholders, both preferred and common, at the end of 1943 numbered approximately 12,500 and your company in its 74th year of operation, entered upon a new era of individual ownership, locally directed and managed and operated by the same experienced personnel as in the past. 15

When the company's stock was offered for sale, some Coloradans were eager to have the state buy the utility with the hope of lowering rates. Some Public Service Company managers were also interested in pursuing state ownership, but for different reasons. These executives feared that if private investors could not be found that the utility would be broken into small units. The company believed that keeping the consolidated utility would be more efficient and profitable; interconnected electric and gas system would conserve natural resources and better provide low cost energy for mineral, industrial, and agricultural development.[16]

Some people suggested establishing a Colorado Power Authority to purchase PSC property. The proposed authority would have been a non-profit organization created by legislative decree and financed by revenue or income bonds. The profits would have gone to communities where the authority owned property.[17] There was little support, however, for state ownership and neither house of the state legislature acted on the question when it was proposed in the spring of 1943. As a final attempt at government ownership, the city of Denver considered buying part of the utility, but again there was not enough support to purchase the utility[18] In the end private investors bought the stock.

World War II revived Colorado's economy. The federal government built facilities such as Lowry Field, Fitzsimons Army Medical Center, Fort Carson, and Peterson Field. The war also brought into existence the Rocky Mountain Arsenal and the Denver Ordnance Plant. Camp Hale was built in 1942 to train American forces for mountain campaigning. Manufacturing firms prospered from increased orders and agriculture responded to the new demand for food products.

War-related activities had brought many people to Colorado who had never come before. At the end of the war many had become so fond of the climate and beautiful vistas that they decided to move to the state permanently. Houses sprouted up in great numbers to accommodate Denver's new residents. Many of the housing developments were unimaginative affairs. From the air one could see a grid of treeless tracts on the edge of the plains. It would take water and hard work to make them green, inviting communities.

For a decade Colorado politics had been controlled by the "old guard" who, for the most part, were conservative men uninterested in change. However, in 1947 Denverites ousted powerful long-time politicians. For example, Quigg Newton replaced Benjamin Stapleton who had held office for most of twenty-five years. With new leadership Denver was ready to encourage development and recruit industries to the city and state. Investors looked at the opportunities in Colorado with favor and many financed expansion of existing businesses while others built new enterprises in the state.[18]

To meet the increasing demands for energy Public Service Company of Colorado completed a four million dollar expansion plan, which had been approved in the early 1940s. One major project increased the capacity of the Valmont steam plant by twenty-five percent to 90,000 kilowatts. It was already the largest steam plant in the Rocky Mountain region, but additional capacity was needed because of civil defense activities and anticipated post-war growth. The company quickly placed orders for turbines, generators and boiler equipment. It foresaw that manufacturers might have such heavy demands from the European war effort that equipment might not be available at a later date.[20]

The Public Service Company of Colorado implemented a reduction in rates in 1940. Customers had been paying five cents each for the first forty kilowatts, four cents each for the next seventy, and 2 1/2 cents for additional kilowatts. Beginning in 1941, rates were changed for the 241,419 customers to 5 cents for the first forty kilowatts, 3 1/2 cents for the next forty, and two cents for additional kilowatts. Because of the reduced rates consumers collectively saved about $288,960 annually. Gas rates were also lowered with an estimated savings of $10,600 a year.[21]

Reductions in prices, labor costs and taxes cut Public Service Company's profits 28.08 percent in 1941. Net income was $2,980,035 compared with $4,143,688 in 1940.[22] In August, 1942 the company reported that over one third of the electricity produced was going to industries involved in the manufacture of war products. The war industry sales brought the net income to $3,738,409 in 1942. As new plants came on line during the next several years the war segment of the company's business dropped to twenty-five percent.[23]

Unlike many utilities in other parts of the country the company was able to meet the needs of all its customers. The company complied with the War Productions Board order prohibiting the use of natural gas for heating in new buildings after 15 September 1942. The WPB also forbade any consumer to switch from another fuel they were using to natural gas for any reason. The order was issued because suppliers could not obtain materials for the construction of pipelines to enlarge their operations.[24]

The company contributed to the war effort. For example, before the bombing of Pearl Harbor, the company began collecting scrap for war material. It dismantled its 1891 power plant at Sixth and Curtis streets and from the refuse donated 1,500 tons of iron, steel and other metal scrap for war production.[25] In 1944 the company was recognized for having collected seven and one half million tons of scrap.[26]

Many Public Service Company employees left to serve in the armed forces. In March 1943, shortly before retiring, president Guy Faller wrote in the employee magazine that "395 of our men have left the company to answer the call of Uncle Sam."[27] He went on to explain that women willingly came to the work to replace the men and fill vital positions.

> This month, for the first time in our history, women are reading electric and gas meters. . . . [they] will be doing a fine job of filling men's shoes too, for they know that the battle on the home front must be won to keep men on the fighting front supplied with the guns, planes, tanks, and and bullets . . . 28

Employees also participated in war-time activities such as bond sales.

According to the 1943 annual report the company made three new system improvements during that year. PSC rebuilt the turbo-generator at Valmont Steam Generating Plant; added thirty-four miles of 100,000 volt transmission line with a spur to the Rocky Mountain Arsenal; and added a dam and lake was added near Boulder for condensing water. The company planned more construction but cut plans back because of wartime restrictions. The PSC also signed a contract with the United States government in 1943 to buy nearly all the power generated by the Bureau of Reclamation project near the mountain town of Dillon.

While cost of most consumer items was rapidly increasing, energy continued to be a bargain. The annual report included statistics showing that food prices were up 67 percent, house furnishings up 38 percent, clothing up 32 percent, rent 17 percent, but the cost of electricity and gas was down 33.8 and 11.5 percent, respectively.[29]

In 1945 the federal government asked businesses to turn off outdoor advertising and display lighting. As a conservation effort the company in 1943 extinguished the 13,000 exterior lights on their downtown office building. Public Service Company president John Loiseau estimated that the "brown out" would cost the company between $300,000 and $400,000 in lost revenues per year,[30] but after several months of restrictions, the company realized that it was not losing as much revenue as anticipated. It had been a Denver tradition for people to go downtown at night and look at all the beautiful retail displays. Now, with the lights off, people consumed more electricity at home.[31]

Keeping up with the demands of the war industries was difficult for the men and machines at the Public Service company, but PSC executives realized that the end of hostilities would bring just as many challenges. Before the war ended plans were made to adjust to post-war demands which were assumed to be a lower demand of energy. Peacetime conversion brought a pleasant surprise, however, having a minimal amount of effect on the company.[32] Because people had a pent up desire for products which could not be manufactured during the war, a slump in the demand for electricity did not come about.

People eagerly bought new refrigerators, stoves and small appliances as well as other manufactured products. The power it took to produce and operate these items added to utility profits. Mines, which had been closed to conserve energy, were opened once again. Housing construction boomed. The heating business soared. People were willing to use more natural gas, in part because Colorado Interstate Gas had reduced its price again in 1945.[33]

While demand was high, supply of gas and electricity was not. President John Loiseau discovered that post-war shortages of construction materials were as acute as those experienced during the war. Construction of vitally needed electric transmission lines and substations was substantially delayed.[34] In fact, PSC was forced to operate without a reserve in 1946, despite the fact that the company and its subsidiaries had spent $3,970,000 on extensions to its gas and electric distribution systems. The same year the board of directors authorized $15,750,000 for construction in selected areas. Not included in this funding were the Cheyenne Light Fuel and Power Company, the Pueblo Gas and Fuel Company, and the Colorado Wyoming Gas Company, all PSC subsidiaries, which were confronted with problems of insufficient capacity.[35]

To pay for the largest construction project in its history, Public Service Company of Colorado initiated a refinancing plan in 1947 to raise nine million dollars, and in 1948 another sixteen million dollars. These funds were partially earmarked for a new generating plant to be built in two phases; one 44,000 unit to be in place in 1950, and another in 1951. Anticipated cost was $14,300,000 for the new structure to be named the Arapahoe Plant located in southeast Denver.[36]

Since the divestiture from Cities Service Company, PSC had considerably improved its capital structure. In 1943 the capital structure was represented by 66 percent long-term debt, 8.3 percent preferred stock and 25.7 percent common stock and surplus. Five years later the capital structure was represented by 50 percent long-term debt, 21.2 percent preferred stock and 28.8 percent common stock and surplus. This was a reduction of sixteen percent in the ratio of long-term indebtedness to total capitalization with a corresponding percentage increase in equity securities and surplus over the five-year period.

In 1948 the company also completed the refinancing of two subsidiaries, the Cheyenne Light Fuel and Power Company and the Pueblo Gas and Fuel Company. Refinancing raised enough proceeds to retire all outstanding indebtedness of these companies, and provided necessary funds for their construction requirements for the subsequent two years.[37]

Public Service Company construction projects were extensive throughout the state. They included a 35,000 kilowatt generating unit for the Lacombe steam plant in Denver, a 5,000 kilowatt generating plant in Grand Junction, 5,000 kilowatt generating unit in Alamosa, reconditioning of the Barker Dam near Boulder, supplying water to the Boulder Canyon Hydro Plant, the South Denver high voltage substation, and a 110,000 volt substation loop from the Valmont Plant. Gas facilities were also expanded with the addition of a new line to Layton, Kansas, a 1,200 horse power compressor station, eight district gas regulating stations, 123 miles of gas main, and 131 miles of service lines to connect 9,339 new gas customers. The Colorado-Wyoming Gas Company also completed an eight-inch natural pipeline from Denver to Cheyenne, Wyoming in 1948.[38]

In 1947 Public Service Company applied to Denver for a renewal of its twenty-year franchise. Everyone had assumed that the company would ask for a new franchise, but through the spring and summer of 1946, PSC was silent. Some thought the company was working behind closed doors with city officials to negotiate an acceptable agreement. It was clear that the company wanted to avoid having the franchise rejected, as had been the case two decades before. The company finally announced on 10 November 1946 that it would file a franchise renewal proposal with the Denver City Council at its 2 December meeting.[39] The council was bound by law to wait thirty days from the submission date to rule on the proposal.[40]

The citizens were eager to learn what the company would offer in exchange for a new twenty-year franchise, and when the franchise proposal was released, it did, indeed, contain a number of changes over the previous franchise. The company agreed to lower electric rates an average of thirteen percent; to pay the city an annual franchise tax of $375,000 ($60,000 previously); to modernize and increase the number of street lights; to reduce the street lighting fee by ten percent; to allow the Denver

City Council to lower rates after an extensive arbitration procedure; and to buy any hydroelectric power generated by the city and by the proposed Colorado-Big Thompson project. (Big Thompson was a United States Bureau of Reclamation project to divert water from the Colorado River for flood control, agriculture and generating of small amounts of electricity). The company also agreed to pay the city a sum of $1,200,00 over the twenty-year period in addition to the franchise tax. The proposal offered no reductions in natural gas rates because the company had reduced rates by 26.35 percent in October, 1945.[41]

These changes in the franchise were made in exchange for concessions from the city. For example, the street lighting portion of the franchise agreement would guarantee the company a minimum of $5.5 million; the city would not be allowed to buy electricity for its lighting from other sources; and a complicated arbitration system that would make lowering rates virtually impossible.[42]

The Denver City Council chambers were packed for a hearing on the franchise on 17 December 1946. The most vocal speaker that night was Eugene Cervi, Democratic state chairman, who accused the city administration of making a secret deal with the Public

Service Company. The large crowd cheered in response to his accusation. Loiseau and city officials sat quietly while Cervi fulminated:

> It is an affront to the people of this community to ask them to attend these hearings after a secret deal has been consummated between city officials and officers of the company.
>
> This matter--the fixing of electric and gas rates at a time when metropolitan Denver is emerging as an exciting Western civic development--should have been given the most careful and exhaustive public scrutiny.
>
> It is unfair and unwise to impose hastily on this community a 20-year proposal which may easily retard its economic and industrial potentialities. It is impossible to learn between now and the February 11 (the date of the franchise election) whether this is a good or bad offer.
>
> The people of the community are completely at the mercy of the representations of the company. 43

President John Loiseau did not respond directly to Cervi's charges, but promised that full details of the negotiations with the city would be revealed. At the hearing he reviewed the company's plans for construction and described how it planned to meet gas and electrical needs for Colorado over the franchise period.

During the technical discussions of the franchise, Cervi and others raised concerns about the qualifications of the city's representative, the Manager of Improvements and Parks, who had the authority to enforce the provisions of the franchise; when a customer complained about service, the manager determined whether the standards of the franchise had been met.[44] It was important for the manager to understand the technicalities of the law and the technology of gas and electricity. The people in attendance at the hearing wanted to question him to determine his knowledge of the complicated economic matters of private utility financing, but he was not present that evening.[45] It was conjectured that he wanted to avoid embarrassing himself.

Various groups busied themselves working for or against the franchise proposal. Some unions were for it, while others were against. The Denver Trades and Labor Assembly of the American Federation of Labor voiced objections to the franchise renewal. Members believed that the company should operate without a franchise which they considered to be a twenty-year monopoly. The members adopted a resolution in January, 1947 objecting to the fact that PSC had not made available original cost studies necessary to justify to proposed rates. Apparently, the company was conducting a valuation study that would not be complete until March, a month after the election.

The resolution also indicated that union

members had no confidence in the Manager of Improvements and Parks's credentials and abilities to recommend rate changes. The resolution asked for even further reduced rates. Union members believed PSC could decrease the price charged consumers because the federal excess profits tax had been removed in 1945. They also suggested that the company could reduce interest on its "watered stock" (stock priced higher than its assets warranted). Finally, the Trades and Labor Assembly wanted PSC to commit to lowering rates by using the less-expensive power from Big Thompson.[46]

The International Brotherhood of Electrical Workers, also of the American Federation of Labor, spoke in favor of the franchise at the hearings. Local 111, which included the bulk of PSC workers believed that consumers would best be served if the company operated with a franchise to give the business some stability. Local 111 members set up a speakers' bureau to support the franchise renewal. Members went to numerous groups to educate other workers about the franchise. The union was willing to support the franchise proposal because the Public Service Company had cooperated with the unions. The Electrical Workers added significantly to support of the franchise renewal effort.[47]

Although the Rocky Mountain News recommended that voters pass the franchise, one of its reporters, Robert L. Perkin, opposed it. In an article published 5 February 1947 he summed up his contraposition. Perkin believed that the reasons for having a franchise had been reversed. A franchise, in his opinion, should be designed not to guarantee a profit for the company, but to secure benefits for the people at a reasonable cost. Perkin felt that the company was overvalued by at least $22 million, money which Cities Service had bled out of it. He also pointed out that the company intended to pass on only part of the $1,436,437 savings arising from the 1945 repeal of the federal excise profits tax.

Perkin argued that customers should save money by purchasing power from the Big Thompson Project, which had been funded with public tax money. The franchise proposal did not reflect any savings as a result of that project. He also believed that the franchise period should be for a shorter time to allow for adjustments in response to changing economic conditions. In fact, Perkin wrote, perhaps the public interest was best served without any franchise. If the franchise were to be used as a means of regulation, it should be split into separate contracts for gas and electric service. His article also questioned the authority of city council to change rates when the Colorado Constitution stated that that right was reserved for the voters.[48]

While the feelings against the franchise proposal were aired in the newspapers and at public hearings, the Company made its case in a twenty-eight page pamphlet which carefully explained why a franchise was needed as well as describing the various points of the proposal. The franchise was necessary, stated the pamphlet to insure use of the streets and alleys; to allow for the planning of future physical plants and financing; and to guarantee that Denver would have an adequate long-term supply of natural gas. In the words of the brochure, the franchise enabled the company:

> to maintain a trained and competent organization based on continuity of employment, to cover at least the partial life of the physical facilities necessary for expanded and adequate service, and to give the company the reasonable assurance of the right to do business . . .49

Public Service Company reminded people that it was the largest payer of local taxes in Denver, which in 1946 amounted to $2,600,000.[50]

The board of directors of the Denver Chamber of Commerce suggested lowering electric rates by an average of thirteen percent, and supported the provision that would allow the Denver City Council to reduce rates.[51] The Denver Junior Chamber of Commerce supported the franchise because members feared that the supply of natural gas might dry up without it. "While we have no proof that this gas supply is solely dependent upon the granting of the franchise," the Junior Chamber report said, "the attendant risk of not securing an adequate supply of gas by reason of the defeat of the franchise in the coming election supersedes all other considerations."[52]

After months of silence, mayor Benjamin Stapleton, still in office in 1946, finally gave endorsement several weeks before the special election. He said that he was confident that the needs of the city would be met and Denver would remain "one of the best illuminated cities in the country."[53] The voters approved the franchise overwhelmingly 49,746 to 5,960.[54]

Company forecasters were correct in their prediction of continued demand for energy from Colorado's frenetic growth. Promotional efforts of the Denver Chamber of Commerce and other agencies helped attract people to the state during the 1950s. Visitors came in large numbers making tourism the third ranking industry in Colorado. Eighty percent of the people who came spent their time and money on the front range. Industries too came to Colorado in the 1950s. Many of them were high technology businesses that did not have to worry about transporting materials and finished products. They could locate in Colorado and lure employees with the appealing environment. In 1956 Martin Marietta Aerospace Corporation, one of the largest companies to move to the Denver area, settled just south of Denver in Littleton. Martin Marietta established its Colorado operations to build Titan missiles. Other large corporations like IBM, Honeywell, Sunstrand, Ball Brothers Research, and Beech Aircraft came not only for the environmental benefits but also for the benefit of nearby research institutions associated with the University of Colorado and the University of Denver. Industries also valued the large number of college graduates. A highly-educated populace was one of the reasons the metropolitan Denver area became the largest corporate banking center between the West Coast and Kansas City.[55]

Government functions increased rapidly in Colorado during the 1950s. One hundred fifty federal agencies located in the state, employing 20,000 workers in Denver and 10,000 in other parts of

Colorado. Denver gained fame as a summer White House when President Dwight Eisenhower made Colorado his summer vacation site.[56]

The influx of people created a tremendous building boom, particularly in Denver. The previously nondescript capital city began transforming into a more vibrant urban center. Although there was a uranium boom in the Grand Junction and Durango area, most of the growth centered in a corridor between Fort Collins to the north and Pueblo in the south. In fact ninety percent of the increase took place in this front range area which already contained seventy percent of the state's population.[57]

The growth continued well into the fifties forcing the Public Service Company of Colorado to continue its expansion. "As a public utility we cannot wait to plan and construct facilities until applications for service are made," remarked president John E. Loiseau. "We must constantly have ample reserve capacity in our system to meet ever increasing loads of present customers and be ready to service all new customers whether they are small residentials or large industrials."[58] Each year of the decade PSC's board of directors approved large construction budgets, and total expenditures for the ten-year period were more than $260 million.[60]

In 1950 the company completed a new 57-mile, 115,000 volt transmission tie-line from Leadville to Poncha Junction interconnecting the Salida-Alamosa System with the central system. (The company referred to its main power system in the Denver metropolitan area as the "central system.") The interconnection resulted in better utilization of generating capacity, since the Salida-Alamosa system's peak load occurred in the summer months due to irrigation pumping, while the peak load on the central system took place during the winter months for heating. In addition to the Salida-Alamosa/Central System tie, another line was completed in 1950, a fifteen-mile, 69,000 volt transmission line between Palisade and Grand Junction tying the Shoshone Hydro Plant to Grand Junction and providing more capacity to the western end of the Central System.[61] In Denver a high tension loop around the city was completed in 1951 with an eighteen-mile 115,000 volt line from Araphoe Station to the Leetsdale terminal.[62]

In the early fifties, when supplies of materials such as steel and copper were still short, Public Service Company pioneered the use of plastic pipe for gas distribution. When the pipe was first proposed in 1954 the engineers were concerned that it could not safely carry expanding gas. However, after experimenting with 750 installations of plastic pipe leading from streets to homes engineers were satisfied with its performance. The company then made another experiment pulling the plastic pipe through old steel pipes. With its low friction and increased flexibility, it was demonstrated that a pipe only slightly smaller than the metal one could be fished through the latter very easily, thereby saving the time and expense of digging. Although the plastic was not usable in rocky and abrasive soil, it was suitable in most and better than steel in corrosive acid and alkali soils. Begun during the post-war steel shortage, the use of plastic was common thereafter.[63]

Public Service Company of Colorado had of necessity become a pioneer in high-altitude transmission work. Early in the century the Shoshone-Denver transmission line was the first 100,000 volt line to operate at altitudes up to 13,500 feet. In 1956 the company was still researching better ways to transport electricity at high altitudes. A experimental high altitude test line near Leadville, Colorado (10,000 feet in elevation) was set up to carry between 300,000 and 500,000 volts.

The project attracted considerable attention

throughout the nation and in foreign countries. Technical information had been gained from transmission lines at low altitudes, but no one was sure that results would be the same at 10,000 feet. For example, what kind of insulators would work at high altitude, for example, was unknown. Company engineers found that test results at low altitudes did not extrapolate to the high altitudes, and, the experimental line resulted in data that saved the company a good deal of money as well as contributing to engineering knowledge for others to use.[64]

In 1956 Public Service made an agreement with the Southern Colorado Power Company, Pueblo, Colorado, and the city of Colorado Springs to interconnect PSC systems with the other two. This intererconnection, called the Colorado Power Pool, gave the company a second transmission tie to the western portion of its system.[65] The loop linked the three major Colorado utilities in 1958. The three companies subsequently provided power backup for each other during periods of shortage and breakdown.[66]

To meet the requirements of approximately 2,000 new customers per month, Public Service Company expanded many of its generating plants in the 1950s. In the Denver metropolitan area the company put the first phase of its new Arapahoe plant into operation in November, 1950. Construction planning had begun in 1948 for three units, each to provide approximately 40,000 kilowatts. Located west of the Platte River on the southern edge of the city, Arapahoe's 60,000 horsepower steam turbine and boiler for the first unit were housed in a 100 foot high structure. Each of the three units had its own coal pulverizer which consumed more than a ton of coal a minute.[67] The number two unit was put in service April, 1951, followed in December of that year by the number three unit. The entire Arapahoe plant was officially dedicated in 1952 with 132,000 kilowatts of power and only a year later construction crews broke ground for a fourth unit which was placed in service in September, 1955.[68] The 232,000 kilowatt plant was one of the largest generating facilities in the West.

Later in the decade Public Service Company added two new generators. The first was the 100,000 kilowatt turbo-generator at Cherokee Station immediately north of Denver. The other was the $4.5 million, 22,000 kilowatt steam power generating Cameo Station near Grand Junction. In 1952 the company also began work on a new 66,000 kilowatt generating unit addition to the old Lacombe Station, subsequently renamed the Zuni Plant in 1952. Most Public Service Company generating plants were named after Indian tribes, although Cameo's name came from a prominent rock formation near Grand Junction.[69]

In order to raise money for three construction projects PSC, sold issues of preferred and common stock, as well as first mortgage bonds. In 1951 and 1955 the company offered common stock to its employees under the "Employees Subscription Plan," and approximately 700 employees took advantage of each issue.[70] Public Service Company, as it had in the Doherty years, sold stock to employees to raise money as well as giving personnel a stake in the business.

In 1954 Public Service Company bought the Arvada Electric company, which it had previously served with natural gas. The Arvada and Westminster area northwest of Denver had expanded beyond Arvada Electric's capabilities and to provide adequate service Arvada Electric would have had to raise new capital--a task that Public Service Company was better able to handle.[71] On 31 March 1954 Arvada was integrated within the company, bringing 5,967 new customers.

Not only did Public Service Company of Colorado gain numerous customers during the 1950s, but the per capita use of gas and electricity increased. Nevertheless, during the decade the company experienced a year-to-year diminished rate of return on its investment. The costs of construction projects and the impact of inflation more than offset the increase in customer base and usage. Therefore, the Public Service Company launched an aggressive program of business development, or load building.

The promotional department worked with appliance dealers, builders, architects, jobbers, and manufacturers to increase the sale of appliances. The company maintained specialized departments such as Power Sales, Lighting, Gas Industrial Sales and Space Heating to match company services with customers' needs. The company promoted appliances that were not commonly used such as garbage disposals, dishwashers, electric blankets, home freezers, and other less common electrical devices. The industrial department described various ways of saving time and money with greater use of electricity and gas.

Public Service Company also sent salesmen out to the various urban centers to convince city officials that street lighting would make their towns safer and more attractive. As a result, the company installed high-intensity mercury vapor street lights in the business sections of most cities. In Denver mercury vapor lights were also put up in the parks and busier residential streets. The salesmen also worked with commercial customers such as stores, offices, factories and schools to improve lighting of those establishments.[72]

The company looked forward to the advent of television in Colorado, and when it came it did not take long for Denverites to become attached to television. By 1952 surveys indicated that approximately sixty percent of the homes in the Denver area had sets, powered, of course, by electricity.

By 1955 175 employees were full time load builders. They showed rural people ingenious ways to improve home life and farms. They promoted the use of air conditioners in office buidings in the mid-fifties.[73] They worked with the oil industry to meet the substantial new electric load requirements for oil well and pipeline pumping.[74] And, these salesmen worked with the Rocky Mountain Electrical League and the Rocky Mountain Gas Association both of which were active in marketing the increased use of power.

Throughout the country utilities realized that inadequate home wiring was one reason customers did not use more electricity. For that reason PSC began a campaign to encourage customers to rewire. Inserts in monthly bills discussed the advantages of rewiring, as well as the ease with which it could be accomplished.[75]

When Public Service Company was spun off from its parent company in 1943, some said that the community would not be served well without the larger organization managing the operation. The skeptics were proved wrong. When in 1953 John Loiseau looked back at ten years of expansion he could tell his stockholders that the company had dependably and efficiently met the needs a rapidly growing state.[76]
The company and its subsidiaries served sixty-five percent of the electric customers in Colorado through a power network of fifteen generating stations and 820 miles of high voltage transmission lines. Its service area stretched from Antonito on the south to Cheyenne, Wyoming on the north, and from Grand Junction on the west to the Sterling on the east.[77] The company served eighty-five percent of Colorado's gas consumers. With the exception of the city of Grand Junction all its

customers were served through a common transmission pipeline facility.

PSC by 1951 had practically completed electrification of all farms in its service area. PSC's Rural Service Department worked with the outlying residents to demonstrate how to replace manual labor with electricity.[78] By 1953 electricity was available to over ninety percent of Colorado's farms although most were served by Rural Electric Association cooperatives.[79]

Post-World War II inflation skyrocketed the utility's operating costs, leading managers to plan for a rate increase for the first time since PSC's incorporation in 1923-24. For thirty years the company had consistently lowered their rates. Residential electric rates had dropped from 6.05 cents in 1933 to 4.10 cents in 1943 and to 1.678 cents by 1953. Gas rates were also lowered. In 1933 the average residential customer paid 87.2 cents per 1,000 cubic feet of gas. By 1943 that amount had dropped to 76.8 cents and by 1953 it was 47.3 cents.[80]

The increase request was preceded by an interesting piece of history. The Colorado Supreme Court in 1952 ruled that the Public Utilities Commission had sole authority over the regulation of the Mountain States Telephone and Telegraph Company, and that municipalities operating as home rule cities had no power, authority or jurisdiction to attempt such regulation.[81] The court ruling pertained only to the telephone company, but the common interpretation of the law was that it was applicable to any utility operating in a home rule city. The company's rates were regulated by the Colorado Public Utilities Commission in all but the thirteen home rule cities where rates were regulated by the municipalities.

Public Service Company wanted to end this confusion of different regulations.[82] Utility managers realized that their chances of getting rate increases from professionals at the PUC were greater than from the votes of an uniformed electorate. In 1952 the voters had turned down an amendment to the Colorado Constitution to put all utilities under regulation by the Colorado Public Utilities Commission. However, at a special election on 16 June 1953 the voters of the City and County of Denver amended the City Charter placing Denver's utilities under the jurisdiction of the PUC.[83] On 2 November 1954 Colorado voters approved changing the state constitution to allow regulation of all privately-owned utilities, including Public Service

Company of Colorado, by the PUC by a two to one margin.[84]

Although the company announced its intention to raise rates in 1953 the increase took almost two years to accomplish. Even before hearings on the rate case were scheduled, various groups met to take positions. Mayor Quigg Newton and members of the Colorado Municipal League were concerned that the PUC's small staff was not adequately equipped to handle its newly expanded duties. "The league feels it has certain, definite obligations to act as a protective third party." Newton said: "It has one interest--to fairly represent the municipalities involved in the Public Service Company petition."[85] The Municipal League reserved its judgment until it thoroughly scrutinized the proposal.[86]

The Colorado PUC scheduled hearings to begin 4 May 1954 to determine the company's valuation.[87] After listening to the testimony given during the hearings, the PUC ruled that the Public Service Company of Colorado could earn a six percent rate of return on its investment, which amounted to an annual increase of $591,577. The increase was the net of a $1,529,599 increase for electricity, an additional $23,400 increase for steam heating, and a reduction in gas revenues of $961,422.[88]

The company had asked for a 6.75 percent rate increase on a much larger base, and the PUC eventually granted only sixteen percent of the original request. John E. Loiseau questioned whether the company would have the capital to continue its three-year, $69 million construction plan.[89] Nevertheless the company complied with the ruling of January, 1955, by implementing a change in rates and simplified rate schedule effective 1 February 1956.[89] It would not be long, however, before the Public Service Company of Colorado would askd for another raise in rates.

NOTES--CHAPTER 10

[1] William D. Ellis, *On The Oil Lands with Cities Service*, (Tulsa OK: Cities Service Oil and Gas Corporation, 1983), p. 166.

[2] *Securities and Exchange Commission Decisions and Reports* XXVI, May 1947 to 31 October 1947, (Washington: U.S. Government Printing Office,1953), p. 681.

[3] Denver *Post* 28 August 1939, p. 1 and *Securities and Exchange Commission Decisions and Report*, No. 2031 XV (December 16, 1943 to May 15, 1944) (Washington, DC: U. S. Government Printing Office, 1949), p. 543.

[4] Denver *Post*, 28 August 1939, p. 7 and *Securities and Exchange Commission Decisions* (Washington, DC: u. S. Governtment Printing Office, 1941), pp. 837 58.

[5] Denver *Post*, 28 August 1939, p. 7.

[6] Ibid.

[7] Denver *Post*, 18 August 1943, p. 22.

[8] *Securities and Exchange Commission, In the matter of Public Service Company of Colorado, Cities Service Power and Light Company, Report No. 1925, XIV (Washington, DC: U.S. Government Printing Office, 1939), pp. 685-87.*

[9] *Rocky Mountain News*, 20 August 1943, p. 18. In proceedings before the Commission, Cities Service Power and Light Company refused to designate which of its systems it would retain. In default of such a choice the SEC selected the Ohio system.

[10] Ibid.

[11] Public Service Company of Colorado 1943 *Annual Report* [hereafter referred to as PSC *Annual Report* (1944), pp. 1-2 and Denver *Post*, 4 October 1943, p. 1.

12SC 1943 Annual Report (1944), p. 1.

13 *Moody's Manual of Investments* (New York: Moddy's Investment Service, 1943, pp. 625-26.

14 *Lines* (November 1943), 12.

15 PSC 1943 *Annual Report* (1944), pp. 1-2.

16 *Rocky Mountain News*, 20 August 1943, p. 18.

17 Arthur Bosworth, community leader and financier as related in Denver *Post*, 20 January 1943, p. 10.

18 *Rocky Mountain News* 8 October 1943, p. 12.

19 Lyle W. Dorsett, *The Queen City: A History of Denver (Boulder: Pruett Publishing Co., 1976), p. 251.*

20 Denver *Post* 12 August 1941, p. 13.

21 *Denver Post*, 21 December 1940, p. 1 and *Rocky Mountain News* 22 December 1940, p. 1.

22 Denver *Post*, 15 April 1942, p. 24.

23 *Lines*, (August, 1942), 2.

24 Denver *Post*, 10 September 1942, p. 3. and 16 April 1943, p. 30.

25 Denver *Post*, 6 June 1943, p. 16.

26 1943 PSC *Annual Report*, (1944), p. 5.

27 *Lines* (March, 1943), 2.

28 Ibid.

29 PSC 1943 *Annual Report* (1944), pp. 4 & 12.

30 Denver *Post*, 24 January 1945, p. 1 and 5.

31 Denver *Post*, 19 March 1945, p. 21.

32 PSC 1945 *Annual Report* (1946), p. 3.

33 Ibid., p. 4 and 6. On 2 April 1943 the Supreme Court ordered the Colorado Interstate Gas Company to reduce its rates effective the end of 1945.

34
Lines, June, 1946, 3.

35
PSC 1946 *Annual Report* (1947), pp. 3-5.

36PSC 1947 *Annual Report* (1948), p. 3.

37
Gross expenditures for additions and improvements totaled $12,478,338 with retirements of $1,1365,615 leaving a net addition to its property, plant and equipment account of $11,341,723, exclusive of a write off of $14,125,000, according to p. 3 of the PSC 1947 *Annual Report* (1948).

38PSC Annual Report (1948).

39
Denver *Post*, 10 November 1946, p. 8

40
Ibid.

41
Rocky Mountain News, 12 December 1946, p. 8 and "Electric and Gas Franchise Application by Public Service Company submitted to the Qualified Voters of the City and County of Denver at a Special Election on February 11, 1946," (Public Service Company, Denver, Colorado), pp. 34-41.

42
Rocky Mountain News, 13 December 1946, p. 10.

43
Rocky Mountain News, 18 December 1946, p. 6.

44
Electric and Gas Franchise Application, p. 39.

45
Ibid. and Cervis *News Service*, No. 68, Special Supplement, 2 January 1947, p. 1.

46
Rocky Mountain News, 10 January 1947, p. 14.

47
Mary Gibson,"The Long Journey," (unpublished history of the Electrical Workers Union 111), p. 73a.

48
Rocky Mountain News, 5 February 1947, p. 13.

49
The Denver Franchise Proposal. Its Provisions and Benefits (Denver: Bradford Robinson Printing, 1946).

50
Denver *Post*, 2 January 1947, p. 2.

51
Denver: Official Publication of the Denver Chamber of Commerce, Proceedings of the Board of Directors, 16 January 1947 to 30 November 1948 (Western History Room, Denver, Colorado), pp. 1-2.
52
Rocky Mountain News, 17 January 1947, p. 25.
53
Denver *Post*, 25 January 1947, p. 1.
54
Denver Post, 12 February 1947, p. 1 and *Rocky Mountain News* , 12 February 1947, p. 5.
55
Carl Abbott, Stephen J. Leonard, David McComb, *Colorado: A History of the Centennial State*, revised edition (Boulder: Colorado Associated University Press, 1982), pp. 281-83.
56
Carl Ubbelohde, Maxine Benson, Duane A. Smith, *A Colorado History*, Revised Centennial Edition (Boulder: Pruett Publishing Company, 1976), p. 337.
57
Robert G. Athearn, *The Coloradans* (Albuquerque: University of New Mexico Press, 1976), p. 322.
58
Lines, (August, 1956), 2.
59
PSC *Annual Reports* 1950-59.
60
PSC 1950 *Annual Report* (1951), p. 6.
61
Ibid.
62
PSC 1951 *Annual Report* (1952), p. 7.
63
Denver *Post*, 13 February 1953, p. 40 and *Lines* (February, 1953, 3.
64
Robert V. Hugo, Administrative Assistant, Engineering and Planning, Interview, 9 September 1985.
65
PSC 1956 *Annual Report*, (1957), p. 6.
66
Denver *Post*, 26 March 1958, p. 19.
67
Denver *Post*, 25 October 1950, p. 3.
68
Robert V. Hugo, Interview, 9 September 1985.

69 Ibid.

70 PSC *Annual Reports* 1950-59.

71 *Rocky Mountain News*, 28 November 1953, p. 14.

72 PSC 1950 *Annual Report* (1951), pp. 10-11.

73 PSC 1954 *Annual Report* (1955) pp. 8-9.

74 Ibid.

75 PSC 1955 *Annual Report* (1956), p. 5.

76 PSC Annual Report (1954).

77 *Denver Post Empire*, 1 November 1953, p. 6.

78 Denver *Post*, 14 October 1953, p. 39.

79 Denver *Post*, 18 October 1953, p. 1.

80 *Denver Post, Roundup Section*, 26 December 1954, p. 2.

81 *People ex. rel. Public Utilites Commission, et al.* v. *Mountain States Telephone and Telegraph Company et al.* 11 February 1952, Ellsworth Nichols, ed., *Public Utility Reports*, XCIV, Nos. 16709, 16711, (Washington, D.C.: PUR, Inc., 1952) p. 243. Rehearing denied 7 April 1952.

82 *Lines*, October, 1952, p. 2, November, 1952, p. 2, June, 1953, pp. 2-3.

83 Denver. Article III, C.3.4, Denver City Charter, June 16, 1953.

84 All of the Rural Electrific Associations would be regulated by the Colorado Public Utilities Commission in 1961. Before that date some were under the jurisdiction of the PUC and others were not.

85 Colorado Public Utilities Commission hearing date was announced in the Denver *Post*, 25 March 1954, p. 30.

86 Denver *Post*, 26 March 1954, p. 1.

87 Ibid.

88 Denver *Post*, 19 December 1954, p. 1.

89 Ibid.

90 PSC 1955 *Annual Report* (1956), pp. 6-12.

CHAPTER 11

INSIDE PUBLIC SERVICE COMPANY OF COLORADO

A glimpse inside the Public Service Company of Colorado after it separated from Cities Service Company reveals a utility endeavoring to improve its public image. Managers wanted to change the public perception that it was a faceless corporation, more interested in making a profit than the well being of its customers. While attempting to shed the cloak of Henry L. Doherty's improbity, PSC continued many of Doherty's management ideas, particularly his emphasis on training and positive employee relationships.

In an effort to publicize its accomplishments Public Service Company put together an elaborate exhibit of its history to celebrate Colorado's 75th anniversary of statehood in 1951. The display, which traveled throughout the state, won the Freedoms Foundation award[1] for "outstanding achievement in bringing about a better understanding of the American way of life."[2]

The effort to improve public relations included a friendlier treatment of customers. For example, where in the past the credit department had levied a stiff penalty on late payments, it now softened the policy with a second notice. "We appreciate many circumstances can arise to make prompt payment of accounts impossible. If you find it is not possible", the notice said, "to pay the entire amount of this statement, won't you please call our credit department and make some arrangement that will enable us to carry your account?"[3]

Management continued to place significant emphasis on education for its employees. A special company bus traveled from city to city as a mobile classroom to teach employees new methods and techniques for doing their jobs. The company also offered general educational courses on such topics as public utility accounting, memory concentration, public speaking, and the public utility industry. The courses were free of charge to interested personnel.

The Public Service Company has a long tradition of company social activities. The Doherty Men's Fraternity, founded in 1914, brought employees together, with goals of professional improvement, patriotism, and productivity. The fraternity had all the traditional trappings, including lapel pins, secret grips, oaths and inititations. The fraternity organized the company basketball and bowling teams, and the interdepartment and city-league softball teams. It also sponsored an annual summer picnic that attracted as many as 6000 employees and family members. For the Christmas holidays fraternity members supervised filling nearly one thousand boxes with toys and treats for children of employees.

Doherty and his successors knew that the spirit of the company recreational teams and projects carried over to teamwork on the job and an esprit-de-corps with management. It was a blend of paternalism and a desire of the leaders to communicate with all company employees.[4] Although Denver had the first fraternity, there were many other chapters in other Colorado cities and throughout the Doherty empire.

The Doherty Smoker (called the G and E Smoker after 1944), with its mixture of entertainment and camaraderie, was another favorite employee special occasion. The annual event featured nationally-known entertainers and skits by employees. Lines, the employee magazine, reported on the evening and filled the next month's issue with many photographs of convivial company employees attending the gala.

The company sponsored the Henry L. Doherty Educational Foundation which was established in 1939, the year of Doherty's death, to perpetuate the memory of the company's founder. Money for the foundation was raised through voluntary subscription and helped pay the educational expenses of sons and daughters of those who contributed. Subscription amounts began at $0.25 a year and $25 for a life membership. Because Henry L. Doherty was an advocate of education the company considered this an appropriate tribute to him as well as an important way to assist company employees.[5]

Doherty had been a firm believer in allowing employees to share the responsibility of management. He realized that the people who actually worked at jobs had some of the best ideas about how to improve the operation of the company. If employees were allowed to suggest changes they would feel more a part of the company and take more interest in their work. Company executives encouraged all employees to use the suggestion box.[6] Prizes were awarded for the best suggestions of the month and many of the suggestions along, with the management responses, were listed in *Lines*. The large numbers of suggestions, one thousand in 1954, for example, indicated that the employees had faith that managers were willing to listen. The responses to the suggestions showed that the managers took them seriously.

Employee safety was a major concern in the fifties. Each issue of the company magazine contained articles on the subject, along with cartoons illustrating situations that caused accidents. Specific names were used of those whose carelessness precitated accidents, as well as of those who prevented mishaps. Accident prevention was promoted by the unions to protect their members, and by company executives who realized that accidents cost time and, therefore, money.[7] The program worked well, and steadily reduced the accident rate during the decade. In 1960 the National Safety Council gave the Electric Operating Department of Public Service Company special recognition for outstanding achievement in employee safety.[8]

Lines also reported on the award ceremonies for loyal employees who served the company for various periods of time. The number of twenty-five year pins awarded each year was high and, in 1957 the average length of service per employee was eleven years.[9] Public Service Company apparently satisfied the needs of many people with its emphasis on management, educational opportunities, job advancement and collective bargaining through the Electrical Workers Union.

In the 1950s there was a manpower shortage which led the company to recruit employees. The shortage put personnel in a favorable position for bargaining, and the company increased wages almost every year of the decade for both union and non-union workers. In 1951 a funded retirement plan replaced the old disability retirement plan. Employees were eligible for retirement at sixty-five and forced to retire at the age of sixty-eight. Cheyenne Light, Fuel & Power Company and Colorado-Wyoming Gas Company also adopted the retirement plans, although they were deferred until 1953 because of the Korean war. In 1957 the company developed a new life insurance plan and an expanded medical program for all personnel. The life insurance was approximately equal to twice the annual compensation of the individual employee. The costs of the insurance and medical programs were shared by the company and employees.[10]

In a continuing effort to improve the company image Public Service Company managers promoted loyalty to the community and country as well as company spirit. They always encouraged support for war bonds, Mile Hi-United Fund, March of Dimes and other philanthropic efforts. Good corporate citizenship was an important part of public relations.[11]

Public Service Company and its predecessors used a variety of publications to communicate with employees and customers. Denver Gas and Electric Company published the first employee magazine between 1904 and 1909, called "the Booster." In 1907 the Company also produced a bulletin called "Home Topics." with various items of interest for employee consumption. In 1909 Company officials changed the Booster to the Denver Section Bulletin of the National Electric Light Association. This publication continued until 1911. Later, from 1928 to 1930 PSC published "The Lightning Bug" with information principally of interest to operations personnel. In 1930 the Kno-Log, another internal publication, began, and during its six year lifespan gave news of company employees.[12]

In August, 1936 the company established a new publication, *Lines* which listed the various activities of departments and awards being given in still another effort to keep in touch with employees. For example, the first issue announced that PSC's Advertising and Publicity Department was selected for an award from the Advertising Federation of America.[13] In the same issue Guy Faller was recognized for his work in raising money for scholarships in the name of Thomas Alva Edison.[14] Faller always included bits of company policy, and messages such as the one found in November, 1936 which encouraged each employee to speak very positively and often of the company to "increase esteem even more."[15]

Lines gave the managers a vehicle to keep the employees up to date and to have a frequent opportunity to reward them by putting their activities in print. There was also business information concerning sales and district meetings and company statistics. For the most part, *Lines* was intended to communicate with and boost the morale of employees. It was written in the various regions served by the company and contained information of activities throughout the company's territory. It always contained interesting tidbits that provided a personal touch for the company.

Home and Community Service began in 1938. It was a four-page consumer-oriented flyer with recipes and newsy articles not necessarily related to Public Service Company. Two of PSC's subsidiaries, Cheyenne Light, Fuel and Power Company and Pueblo Gas and Fuel also published versions of *Home and Community Service*. *News Briefs* replaced it in 1958 with a similar format but more emphasis on business news.

Guy Faller was the president who established *Lines*. In 1953 the publication noted his death, on 12 February. Faller had joined the Denver utility in 1905.

When Public Service Company became independent in 1943 he gave up the job of president and general manager, and became chairman of the board of the PSC and Cheyenne Light, Fuel & Power Company. Both the company and the Denver community in which he was so actively involved missed his energetic involvement.[16]

In the 1940s Public Service Company signed its first labor contract, even though the union had worked for decades with the company and its predecessors.[17] In the early days of energy development, particularly in the field of electricity, the public was immensely excited about the novel technology. While the inventors received the plaudits the more ordinary workers were responsible for bringing electricity and gas to the populace. Workers willing to string wires were in great demand before the turn of the century. Linemen worked long days of ten to twelve hours, sometimes seven days a week for fifteen cents an hour.[18] It was little wonder that electrical workers wanted to unionize and improve pay, hours, and safety standards.

The National Brotherhood of Electrical workers was established on 28 November 1891 in St. Louis.[19] Thirteen years later, on 19 December 1907, electrical workers in Denver established Local Union 111, at a time when the general mood of the nation was one of hostility toward labor unions. The Denver Gas and Electric Company felt that it could provide benefits for employees without union help. The company established an employee Mutual Aid Association in 1906 to assist personnel in need of financial assistance. The company also sponsored the Medical Service Department to provide the needy with health care. Denver's three utilities, Mountain State Telephone and Telegraph, the Denver Tramway Company and the Denver Gas and Electric Company were opposed to the union.

Labor reform and the coming of World War I diminished antagonism between employees and employers. Management and workers shared a common goal of winning the war while keeping disputes to a minimum. At the end of the conflict the country went through an anti-foreigner mood affecting many ethnic labor groups. When the Ku Klux Klan became powerful in Colorado the antipathy toward unions came out into the open with "hate" lists of various groups including many laborers who fit into the KKK un-American category.[20]

Colorado's newly incorporated Public Service Company was openly hostile to unions in the 1920s. Linemen walked out in 1923 because they were unhappy with wages and working conditions, and the company promptly fired all of the strikers, breaking the strike and consequently the morale of the union. Latent interest in union affiliation remained but twenty years passed before the Electrical Workers formally organized PSC.[21]

The Grand Junction employees of Public Service Company organized early in 1939. They became part of a newly formed Local 925 of the International Brotherhood of Electrical Workers, but the company refused to recognize the group. For three years the union continued to hold meetings and pressured management to accept organization. On 12 February 1942 Public Service Company finally agreed to an election in Grand Junction, and the employees voted to be part of the union. The first IBEW union contract with PSC was restricted to the Grand Junction local. A more cooperative relationship developed; workers and management, through hours of negotiations, agreed to work for their mutual benefit.[22]

Labor's contribution to the war in Europe and Asia in the 1940s brought about an improved public posture towards labor in Colorado and the nation. President Franklin D. Roosevelt insisted that the government award contracts to companies that were fully unionized, and as a result, the union rosters swelled.[23] Despite the President's support, Public Service Company in the early forties was militantly opposed to accepting unionization. Nevertheless, PSC finally yielded to the inevitable, and in 1946 Denver employees and management signed the first union contract.[24]

The Union worked diligently to achieve benefits for its members. It negotiated, and won, periodic pay raises as well as additional paid holidays and vacation allowances. Union and management established a pension plan with the company that was improved in subsequent years. Union leaders instituted an apprenticeship committee and safety program, both of which were extremely active and effective for decades.[25]

Union membership was not required for employment by Public Service Company of Colorado, but all employees, union members or not, benefited from the Electrical Workers negotiation with management. To give the union more clout, officials attempted to organize as many members as possible. Union supporters put subtle and not-so-subtle pressure on employees to sign up. For example, the union maintained a list of non-union linemen and frequently asked those people to join. Sometimes union members did not speak to their non-union colleagues as a kind of social sanction for not joining. Generally one month a year was set aside to actively recruit union members throughout the company.[26]

Union members felt that they contributed to the company beyond their daily work during the 1940's. Their participation during the 1947 franchise renewal most likely helped secure public approval. The company also benefited by the inclusion of a no-strike clause, and management later reciprocated by agreeing to a no lock-out provision[27] The union also believed that when the PSC had to borrow capital from Wall Street financiers, the stability that a union brought to the company was a distinct benefit.[28]

One of labor's few strikes against PSC occurred in 1952 when a smaller union, the Porters struck. Although the Porters had their own organization the Electrical Workers sympathized with the other union. Electrical Worker officials convinced some of their workers to join the picket line in an effort to demonstrate union solidarity to management. Many members disagreed with the decision to picket because they had strong loyalty to Public Service Company. The strike lasted only one day, but the Porters proved that they were willing to walk out in order to demonstrate their power.[29]

In the early 1960s utility unions and management in the western states joined to form a labor-management council called the Labor and Management Public Affairs Committee (LAMPAC). LAMPAC was an effective tool in reducing the numbers of labor-management problems that were sent to arbitration. Robert T. Person, president of PSC at the time, was one of the initiators of LAMPAC. He and others outlined the objectives, making sure that it was an organization to solve industry labor problems not relations within individual companies. The high level of the representative signified the company's positive spirit in working toward avoiding conflicts.[30]

Relationship between management and labor improved considerably over the decades. The Union continued to keep a watchful eye on management to insure that the profit motive did not come at the expense of laborers, while management had to insure that the workers' self-motivated ambitions did not hamstring the company. Each group realized that a strong, well-run company was essential for the benefit of everyone, and could not be achieved without cooperation.

In 1943, during the divestiture of Public Service Company from Cities Service Company, the responsibility of making wise decisions reorganization of Public Service Company lay mainly with the company's new president, John Loiseau. The challenges of creating the necessary financial restructuring for the independent company, of choosing a board of directors, and of making management decisions were great. However, a strong foundation had been laid, and John Loiseau's management skills allowed Public Service Company to establish itself as a strong, publicly-held company.

Loiseau led a private life beyond the scrutiny of the media, and, therefore, it is difficult to create an objective and comprehensive assessment of the man. His successor, Robert T. Person, recalls that Loiseau's broad knowledge of leaders both in the community and in his company helped him put together a strong board of directors. These well-respected men lent their expertise and prestige to the newly independent company for many years.

Although there were many men from Cities Service who wanted to come to Colorado to assume top positions, Loiseau chose carefully, giving opportunities to those at PSC who were talented and who would benefit the organization. He had an uncanny ability to discern a man's abilities, and chose men because they could contribute to the company, not because of his friendship with them, or to advance his own career. He was a fair but exacting leader who expected performance, and astute employees would never consider entering his office unprepared.[31]

In the first year of the company's independence Loiseau made tough financial decisions that would, in the long run make the company stronger, but in the short term were difficult. Since its beginnings PSC had relied on the management and financial planning of Cities Service, it was now essential to make sound policies for the future which Loiseau did. With his financial and accounting background and the strength of his own conviction he was an appropriate leader to make the critical decisions in 1943 and thereafter.[32]

John Elmer Loiseau was born in Colman, South Dakota on 1 January 1891 to Arthur F. and Louise M. Loiseau. His parents moved to Perryville, Missouri where John attended public school. After he graduated from high school he took accounting courses classes at Gem City Business College in Quincy, Illinois. For the most part, however, he was self educated, learning through the experience of his jobs and through books which he enjoyed reading. He is reported to have read all the Harvard Classics.[33]

Loiseau worked at several jobs before joining the Henry L. Doherty interests in 1915 as an accountant of the Citizens Gas and Electric Heating Company of Mount Vernon, Illinois.[34] He held positions in various cities before coming to Denver in 1923.[35] Loiseau's first job in Denver was with the Denver Gas and Electric Light Company. There he was involved in putting together the Public Service Company of Colorado in 1923 and 1924. He held the job of company secretary until 1938 when the board of directors added the job of vice president to his responsibilities.[36]

Loiseau set an example of corporate responsibility for his employees by being active in the community. He was on the aviation committee of the Denver Chamber of Commerce, and helped establish what would become Stapleton Airport and the air mail service at the airport.[37] He also participated in national trade organizations such as the National Electric Light Association and the Edison Electric Institute by which he was elected to the board of directors in 1946.[38]

Loiseau was a private individual who had a great knowledge of the details of his company. He concentrated on business rather than human relations. He believed in training for his employees, and instinctively knew how to assemble a good balance of individuals. For example, he realized that others were better public speakers than he was and relied on his vice president Gaylord Buck, for much of the public speaking. Loiseau's hobbies were golf and bridge, but his life was the company.[39]

The Doherty thread continued to run through the company. Loiseau's emphasis on strong management, education and positive employee relationships was similar to Doherty's, although his personality was not. Loiseau's background was financial which is exactly the expertise needed by the company needed at the time he was elected president. A new emphasis was put on being a good corporate citizen, and letting the public know about PSC community contributions. The company had moved beyond the Doherty era, although his imprint, both good and bad, would remain for many years.

NOTES--CHAPTER 11

1 The Freedoms Foundation was established at Valley Forge, Pennsylvania in 1949. Its purpose is to create and build an understanding of the spirit and philosophy of the constitution and bill of rights, and of the political and economic freedoms inherent in them.

2 *Lines*, (April, 1953), 3.

3 *Rocky Mountain News*, 31 May 1952, p. 15 and Denver *Post*, 31 May 1952, p. 2.

4 William Donahue Ellis, *On the Oil Lands with Cities Service* (Tulsa, OK: cities Service Oil and Gas Corporation, 1983), p. 102.

5 *Lines* (June, 1939), 5.

6 *Lines* (February, 1951), 2.

7 *Lines*, 1950-59.

8 *Lines*, (December, 1960), 20.

9 PSC 1957 *Annual Report* (1958), p. 10.

10 PSC 1950-59 *Annual Reports* and issues of *Lines* 1950-59.

11 Ibid.

12 In 1979 a magazine called "Q" was started with a format like *Lines* but distributed quarterly instead of monthly. In 1980 the public relations department of Public Service Comany gave *Lines* a new format.

13 *Lines*, (October, 1936), 3.

14 Ibid., p. 14.

15 *Lines* (November, 1936), 2.

16 *Lines* (March, 1953), 2.

17 Mary Gibson, "The Long Journey," (unpublished history of the Electrical Workers Union 111), pp. 8-9. This section relies heavily on Mary Gibson's history which she generously allowed the author read and use. She also spent time to be interviewed about union relations.

18"The Long Journey," p. 8. Not only was the work hard, but it was dangerous. A union historian writes that in the 1890s the fatality rate for linemen in some areas was one out of two.

19 Ibid, p. 10.

20 Ibid, pp. 20-25.

21 Ibid, p. 25d.

22 Ibid, pp. 35-37.

23 Ibid., p. 39.

24 Ibid, p. 41.

25 Ibid, pp. 48-61c.

26 Ibid, pp. 76-77.

27 Ibid, pp. 61-71.

28 Ibid., p. 53.

29 Denver *Post*, 23 May 1952, p. 16.

30 Gibson, "The Long Journey,"p. 85.

31 Robert T. Person, interview, 20 September 1984.

32 Ibid.

33 *Lines*, (November, 1943), 3-4.

34 Ibid.

35 "John E. Loiseau," *The National Cyclopaedia of American Biography*. LII (New York: James T. White & Co., 1970), p. 282, and *Rocky Mountain News*, July 17, 1952, p. 37.

36 Ibid, p. 282, and *Journal of Electricity* LIV (1 February 1925), 116.

37 *Lines*, (November, 1943), 4. and *Rocky Mountain News Pictorial Section*, 13 November 1927, p. 2.

38 *Lines*, (June, 1946), 5.

39 Robert T. Person, interview, 20, September 1985.

CHAPTER 12

"CREEPING SOCIALISM"--GOVERNMENT AND THE UTILITIES

The Great Depression ended the spirit of laissez-faire capitalism and faith in an invisible hand to guide the economy. In its place came a managed society in which the government not only passed laws that regulated businesses, but laws that attempted to solve social problems as well. New legislation had a pro-found effect on utilities, breaking up and restructuring most of them. Just as consequential was the government's entry into the power business as more than just a regulator. In reponse Public Service Company of Colorado spent a significant amount of time and effort during and after the depression attempting to contain government expansion into the utility industry.

While electrification had spread rapidly in urban areas during the first third of the century, rural areas had not kept pace in using the new technology. By the 1930s agriculture was the only major industry that was not aided by electricity. Nine out of ten rural homes were not supplied with electric service. The farmer milked his cows by hand by the light of kerosene lamps, and his wife cooked over a wood stove and washed clothing with a washboard. The children drew water with a hand pump at the well, and there was no refrigeration.[1]

President Franklin D. Roosevelt felt a strong desire to help farmers by providing rural areas with electricity. As part of the New Deal, Congress in 1935 passed legislation to establish the Rural Electrification Administration. Under the act the federal government extended electricity to areas which private utilities were unable or unwilling to serve. Roosevelt's interest in providing electricity at a low price to rural areas came from his experience in Warm Springs, Georgia.

> Fourteen years ago a Democratic Yankee came to [Georgia] in search of a pool of warm water wherein he might swim his way back to health. . . . There was only one discordant note in the first stay of mine at Warm Springs. When the first-of-the-month bill came in for electric light for my little cottage, I found that the charge was eighteen cents a kilowatt hour -- about four times what I pay at Hyde Park, New York. That started my long study of public utility charges for electric current and the whole subject of getting electricity into farm homes. . . so it can be said that a little cottage at Warm Springs, Georgia, was the birthplace of the Rural Electrification Administration. 2

Roosevelt felt that government help was needed to halt the desperately poor situation in rural areas. The farmers had been hurt by the recession of 1920-21 when their income had dropped. Added to this was the depression of the thirties which almost bankrupted them. Farmers were so poor that they simply could not afford electricity from the private sector, and yet they could not afford to be without it.

Congress created the Rural Electrification Administration originally for only one year under the Emergency Relief Appropriation Act on 11 May 1935. The following year its life was extended for an additional ten years. In 1939 the REA was put under the Department of Agriculture on a permanent basis.[3]

According to the act the Rural Electrification Administration was authorized to lend money, at two percent interest, for financing the construction and operation of electric generating plants, transmission lines, and for installing electricity in rural homes. Individuals, utility districts, and non-profit cooperatives, as part of a Rural Electric Association, were eligible to receive low-interest loans.[4]

Farmers eagerly received the idea of electrical cooperatives; after all, cooperation was used from the beginning of farm life to help raise barns, supply water, buy seed and fertilizer, and provide markets for their produce. In fact, some rural communities had organized business cooperatives on their own to bring electric service to their areas in the 1920s.[5]

Clyde T. Ellis, general manager of the National Rural Electric Cooperative Association in the 1930s, and an outspoken advocate of public power, believed that private utilities had failed to bring electricity to rural areas simply because there were no profits in doing so. He saw it as a matter of greed. "In those days," he said "the power companies were arrogant, regulation in the public interest was a joke, investors were gullible. . ."[6] Ellis felt that private utilities turned a deaf ear on the pleas of farmers to bring electricity to their areas, because the agricultural people could not afford electrical service. When they did serve rural areas, the private utilities insisted that everyone in a service area be required to connect the power to their homes.[7]

In addition to concern over competition from the REAs, private utilities were worried about plans by the United States Bureau of Reclamation to generate and distribute electricity. The 75th Congress had adopted Senate Document 80 which authorized, in 1937, water diversion projects for flood control and irrigation.[8] The projects would produce enough electricity to support their own operations with some left over to sell. However, the legislation did not limit the amount of generated power which could be sold, and the investor-owned utilities realized that the Bureau's projects might produce enough electricity to provide serious competition.

The effort to prevent government projects from usurping valuable utility business took a great deal of private utility executives' time and energy in the late 1940s, 1950s and 1960s. The presidents of the Public Service Company of Colorado during these decades--John E. Loiseau for most of the forties and fifties and Robert T. Person in the sixties--were advocates of preserving a fair share of the utility business for private firms. Loiseau used much of the editorial space in *Lines* to lobby against what he unabashedly called "creeping socialism."

In 1949 he borrowed from an article written in *Fortune* Magazine by John Davenport on "Socialism by Default."

> . . . we can drift into socialism and collectivism without knowing it. If we do, it will be because we permit the government to become too big and too strong. We are going to have big government in such fields as the military, foreign relief, international relations and so on. But to believe that this must be accompanied by big government in every conceivable activity is to surrender before the battle. The very size of the Federal spending directly endangers economic and political liberty. If we must spent huge sums for arms and kindred purposes, that is all the more reason for

> eliminating every unnecessary domestic expenditure. In this category are the numerous transmission lines proposed to be built by the Federal government which duplicate existing transmission lines of business managed electric power companies as well as proposed government lines which utility companies are willing to build. 9

In the January, 1950 issue of *Lines* John E. Loiseau analyzed the basic building blocks of a private utility as men, materials, and tools. Because of the capital intensive nature of a utility, $40,000 of equipment and facilities (in 1950) was needed for every employee. Of that amount, $20,000 was debt financing coming chiefly from insurance companies, trust funds and thrift institutions. The other $20,000 equity capital coming from venture dollar investments by institutions and individuals. In a free enterprise system the venture dollars, or risk money, made possible new plants, facilities and equipment. Loiseau believed that in order to grow the business was dependent on venture dollars. He pointed out that the venture money was often hard to come by, and when one business was heavily taxed, regulated, or faced governmental competition, those dollars dried up. "For that reason we must strongly oppose those who believe in imposing unfair burdens such as tax-free subsidized government competition or exhorbitant taxation on our industry."[10]

In April 1951 he made an even stronger statement against government competition, reminding his readers that while public power generation projects were built with taxpayers' money, the American taxpayers earned no interest or dividends, nor did they have a voice in the management of the projects. Loiseau believed that the public power projects were uneconomically built and inefficiently operated, a situation over which taxpayers had no control. It was also unfair to the citizens served by privately-owned utilities to support public operations and at the same time pay the twenty percent tax assessed on investor-owned utilities.[11]

In Public Service Company of Colorado's 1951 annual report company executives complained about another discriminatory aspect of public power generation, otherwise known as the "preference clause." In the 1930s Congress had authorized the government to construct reclamation projects with incidental generation of electric power. Such power was to go first to preference customers, such as municipally-owned utilities, rural electric associations, and public agencies, with any excess going to other electric companies. Public Service Company argued that the government's interpretation of incidental power had changed and did not coincide with the legislative intent. Incidental electric power had burgeoned into an excuse for the federal government to produce and transmit large amounts of power in direct competition with private companies. In general, Public Service Company of Colorado believed competition from government projects undermined America's free enterprise system.[12]

The company persisted in fighting "those unsound power policies of the Government which are wasteful of the taxpayers' money and contrary to American concepts."[13] Spokesmen for Public Service Company appeared before hearings of the Interior Department Appropriation subcommittee in 1950 to argue against further allocations to the Bureau of Reclamation for transmission lines that would duplicate PSC service. The result of that testimony was a ten-year agreement by which the Bureau of Reclamation would deliver power to preference customers over the PSC transmission system, and the company would deliver power to its customers in eastern Colorado over Bureau transmission lines. This, the company hoped, would end duplication and terminate further requests for money by the Bureau. The agreement also called for an engineering study to determine the feasibility of pooling other Public Service Company and Bureau of Reclamation systems.[14]

During John F. Kennedy's administration the challenge of restraining the federal government from further intrusion into the utility business intensified. Private utilities were particularly disheartened with the appointment in 1961 of Norman M. Clapp as head of the Rural Electrification Administration. The concern heightened when Mr. Clapp announced his far-reaching policy, i.e.: to increase the capacity of the REA for making loans; to grant more loans for power generation and transmission systems; to make electrical cooperatives and interregional hydroelectric transmission links more permanent; to further advance water, nuclear and tidal power sources; to create an REA Power Supply Division to insure an ample emergency power supply; to establish definite and exclusive territories for cooperatives; and to lobby for favorable state legislation for cooperatives.[15]

The original intent of the REA was to provide electricity to the forgotten rural areas,[16] but by 1960 loans were going to many urban areas. That year Congress held hearings to debate REA appropriations for 1961, and some legislators expressed fear that the competition was beginning to have a negative effect on investor-owned utilities. Responding to the trend toward socialization of the electrical business, Representative Samuel Rayburn, a Democrat from Texas, said, ". . . we are not in that bill, intending to go out and compete with anybody. By this bill we hope to bring electrification to people who do not now have it."[17] Rayburn went on to say that the bill was not written to punish private utilities, parallel their lines, or enter into competition. Local control would be maintained because rates would be controlled by the state, not the federal government. He reiterated that he and his colleagues did not believe in socializing the industry and desired service by private enterprise.[18]

Others were not as confident as Rayburn. In the early years of the Rural Electrification Administration eighty percent of the loans were given to farms, however, by 1960, according to REA statistics fifty percent of its customers were non rural. By 1960 only forty-eight percent of the revenues gained from REA distribution of power came from farm consumers. Twenty-eight percent came from non-farm residences, eleven percent from commercial or small business consumers, eight percent from large power consumers and five percent from a miscellaneous category. Perhaps the most impressive statistic was that three out of four new customers were non-farm people.[19]

In approximately twenty-five years the REA had loaned $4.4 billion to cooperatives to electrify rural areas, resulting in 97 percent of the United States farms being electrified by 1960.[20] Although the rural communities had outgrown their need for huge subsidies, the REA was now looking for new service areas for business expansion. Because cooperatives' return on investment was marginal a private research group, the American Enterprise Institute for Public Policy Research, recommended that both indirect and direct subsidies be reduced until cooperatives were paying a fair price for capital.[21] However, like so many government programs, once the REA had been established it seemed to be in business to stay.

The REA in Colorado followed the national pattern and sought to expand its service area, bringing it in direct conflict with investor-owned utilities. Public Service Company fought the expansion, knowing it was almost impossible to compete with cooperatives which were exempt from state and federal income taxes and had the benefit of two percent loans. To make a bad situation worse, from the Company the cooperatives asked for legislation to restrain any competition in the territories they served.[22]

Colorado Republican Senator Peter H. Dominick joined with Public Service Company in suggesting that the REA expansion violated the free enterprise system. At a Congressional hearing he said:

> . . . I am not unmindful that REA has often been referred to as a "congressional sacred cow". . . . However, I believe a realistic assessment of the program under present day circumstances and policies will show the need for change. I certainly have no quarrel with the accomplishments of REA in bringing low cost electricity to American farms. This was its original objective and a fine one. However, my chief concern is: Where do we go from here? With about 98 percent of all farms presently receiving electricity, a thorough and searching examination of the Rural Electrification Administration is in order. It is now facing increasingly violent attacks which could destroy it unless the most glaring defect, the subsidized interest rate, is eliminated. 23

Senator Dominick's recommendations accomplished as little as did advice from another study. The Hoover report, completed a decade earlier had suggested that the REA be reorganized to be self supporting and seek its financing from private sources.[24]

In addition to the low interest rate charged there were was concerns because of the scarcity of publi scrutiny of such loans. In 1946 the Department of Agriculture ruled that all information regarding an REA loan application could be kept secret, since it was a privileged banker-lender relationship. No public hearings were required, and no data or economic studies were requested by Congress. Expenditures of millions of dollars were approved without facts to determine the effect on other power suppliers or customers, or to analyze the long term cost to the government. For example, in 1961 when the Colorado-Ute Electric Association of Montrose, Colorado submitted a loan application to the REA it would not reveal any details because of the "secrecy policy."[25] However, when private utilities sought to "borrow" money by offering the sale of securities, full disclosure of all factors relating to the utility operation was required.[26]

Robert T. Person, elected Public Service Company president at the beginning of 1959, kept the controversy over public ownership in the forefront of issues challenging the company. He had put his skills as a communicator to good use as vice president of public affairs, and continued to use them effectively as president. In 1965 Person was elected president of the Edison Electric Institute which proved to be an excellent forum in which to express his opinions. The position also carried with it a responsibility to keep the industry abreast of national concerns. One of the main themes of his many speeches was opposition to the expansion of the role of the Rural Electrification

Administration and the United States Bureau of Reclamation.

He also expressed his views in issues of *Lines* and Public Service Company of Colorado's annual reports. Person explained that the investor-owned utilities obtained income from earnings on invested venture capital, while the government acquired its money from taxes, or "captive capital." He thought it ironic that the utility industry paid more taxes than any other industry in the country, and that those same tax dollars went to subsidize the competition.[27]

In a speech before the presidents of Edison Electric Institute member institutions in 1963 he asked, "Are we ready to stand up and be counted?"[28] He reprimanded the utility leaders for sitting back during the Eisenhower administration hoping that a Republican president would be less likely to support government growth, when actually during Eisenhower's administration the REA made more loans than ever before. Person also remarked that, although utilities had worked at lobbying, the end result had been ineffective. "How often have we, as an industry, really teamed up and presented a united, undivided front before the Congress and public?"[29] Asked Person, "Do you think it possible that we could make a more effective presentation of our problems before Congress and the public if we spoke as one?"[30] He entreated the group to stop talking about industry problems and to take action.

One step was the creation of a public relations movie "The Power Within," a film which portrayed the increasingly active role that the government was playing in the utility industry. Edison Electric Institute member companies were prodded to show the film to as many people as possible. The film ended with the question: "Do you agree that unnecessary government competition with private enterprise is bad for America?"[31] The audience often consisted of utility employees who were prompted to send a telegram or write a letter opposing government competition to congressional representatives. Person later noted that by 1963 the film had been shown 194 times to a total of 5,500 people in his area.[32] The movie resurrected overt attempts to shape public opinion, but refrained from the heavy handedness of the 1920s.

In the mid sixties the threat of government competition increased even more. Robert T. Person told PSC stock holders in 1965 that the federal government was encouraging municipalities and cooperatives to distribute their own natural gas, along with the transmission of electrical power. In 1963 the Denver Federal Center, and the Atomic Energy Commission's Rocky Flats plant near Boulder had notified Public Service Company that they were considering buying electricity from the United States Bureau of Reclamation projects. In 1965 Lowry Air Force Base and Fitzsimons General Hospital announced that they, too, were contemplating switching from Public Service Company to power from the Colorado River Storage project, arguing that the cheaper government power would save them money. PSC Executives, however, were determined to stop the Bureau from pirating away customers the company had served for more than a quarter of a century. While the USBR rate was somewhat lower, in the long run the agency would lose because no income taxes would be paid on the USBR project sales. Through long hours of negotiation Public Service Company executives convinced these agencies the service from PSC was more dependable. Furthermore, with power from government projects backup power would have to be arranged and paid for.[33]

There were numerous projects during the 1940s, 1950s and 1960s that made Public Service Company of Colorado feel that it was necessary to defend itself against government encroachment. One of the biggest was the U. S. Bureau of Reclamation's Colorado Big-Thompson project designed to divert Colorado river water from western Colorado through the Continental Divide into eastern Colorado. As an adjunct to this large project, the Bureau planned a hydroelectric plant near Estes Park, anticipating that it would deliver some power by 1950, even though the entire project was not expected to be finished until 1953.[34] According to *Electrical West* original plans called for two pumping plants initially generating 30,000 kilowatts of electricity, and later increasing to a capacity of 142,500 kilowatts. The excess power, over and above the 18,000 kilowatts needed for the pumping plants, would be available for public distribution and sale.[35]

In the mid-1940s the Bureau made plans to expand its transmission system in order to serve northern Colorado towns such as Longmont, Loveland, Greeley, and Fort Collins, the same cities being provided with water by the Big Thompson project. To build the 680 miles of transmission lines to serve these towns the bureau in 1947 requested money from Congress. Public Service Company testified against these appropriations in Congressional committees, and was successful in stopping the funding.[36]

Although at one point the Public Service Company sued the federal government for going beyond its authority in generating and selling Big Thompson power, the Company eventually decided to cooperate and not risk being excluded from the transmission of government power.[37] By cooperating, it believed that it might also persuade Congress not to allot the bureau's 1949 request for $661,000, to pay for almost two million additional dollars for Colorado-Big Thompson transmission lines.[38] Therefore, in 1949, although still disagreeing with governmental competition, Public Service Company, said that it was "ready and willing" to use its existing transmission facilities to carry Colorado-Big Thompson power to certain "preference customers."[39] The company agreed to wheel, or move, public power over its transmission lines to save the taxpayers money and retain a share of the business. By so doing PSC calculated that it would save the taxpayers $2,625,731.[40]

The Colorado Rural Electric Association cooperatives and municipal power plants, protested against this cooperation with a private utility, believing the interjection of a third party would raise their prices and diminish their control. If Public Service Company added a wheeling charge to the existing reclamation rate, distribution expenses for the cooperatives would certainly increase. REA representatives estimated power would cost seventeen to twenty-eight percent more. They contended that "Public Service Company's offer is to [install lines] to 'cream areas,'" and asked, "Would the utility also build high voltage lines to much larger 'skim milk' areas that also must be served?"[41] Despite REA complaints an agreement was reached which allowed Public Service Company to wheel government power over company lines, serving government agencies first.

The federal government brought suit in 1949 against the Public Service Company and other claimants to Colorado river water to consolidate water rights for the Colorado-Big Thompson.[42] Since 1902 PSC's predecessors owned Colorado River water rights at the Shoshone hydro electric plant, and the state courts had adjudicated in the company's favor in 1910 and 1911. Since the statute of limitations for challenging the claim expired four years after the state court ruling, Public Service Company felt confident of its position.

Public Service Company of Colorado decided to use the 1949 Federal Court suit to its advantage by asking the courts to establish the amount of electricity the government was allowed to transmit from Colorado-Big Thompson. In essence, the suit became a judicial test of the constitutionality of the Bureau's right to build transmission lines which would duplicate those of Public Service Company of Colorado.[43] The government argued that its authority was based on Senate Document Number 80, and interpreted the law to mean that the Bureau had a proprietary right to generate, distribute and sell electricity.

Public Service Company challenged this view stating that the U.S. Bureau of Reclamation had gone far beyond the initial intent of the law by planning to construct numerous transmission lines in direct competition with PSC lines. The Bureau, in PSC's view, was stretching the intent of Senate Document Number 80 to a violation of the United States Constitution. PSC lawyers, Lee, Byrnes, Kelly and Stansfield, said that, in building and generating electricity in PSC's service area, the government was "thereby depriving the company of its property, consisting of presently existing transmission and distribution lines adequately and efficiently serving said area."[44] The case was closely watched by both proponents and opponents of public power, who realized that it would set a precedent for electrical generation from other water diversion projects.[45]

In the April, 1949 issue of Lines John E. Loiseau pointed out that the Bureau of Reclamation had increased its original cost estimate for the Colorado-Big Thompson project by 250 percent, from $43,800,000 to $144,581,000. Furthermore, five electric utilities in Colorado had offered to let the government use their existing transmission facilities and lines thereby saving the government $48,000,000. Loiseau wrote: "the government lines would not increase the amount of power available in the area nor would they bring power to a single additional customer not already being served." Concluding he said: "Duplication is always expensive and must be reflected in the ultimate cost of service."[46]

Public Service was encouraged by a small victory in 1953 when the Department of Interior announced a new federal power policy declaring that local people, rather than the federal government had the responsibility of supplying their individual communities with power. The ruling, however, exempted federal reclamation projects and allowed them to continue generating and selling excess power to local utilities. Although a positive step, the new regulation still discriminated against private companies which could not share the government power until all public authorities had been supplied.[47]

Another Company victory came in 1955 after six years of litigation. The suit filed by the United States government to quiet title for water that it wanted diverted from the Western Slope to the Eastern Slope for the Colorado-Big Thompson project. The United States Supreme Court dismissed the portion of the suit related to Public Service Company water rights, and PSC retained the right to use Colorado river water to generate electricity at the Shoshone plant.[48] The suit, however, did not answer the larger question of how much "incidental" power Bureau of Reclamation projects were allowed to generate and sell.

Disputes with the government cooperatives did not end, and when, in 1954 the Union Rural Electric Association of Brighton, Colorado claimed the territory just north of Denver, the PSC objected vigorously. This large expanse of land had long been rural in character, but as Denver grew toward the north, the Public Service Company considered the land part of the greater metropolitan area. In order to insure that the area would be served by PSC the company took direct action. On a Saturday night and Sunday morning in

October, 1954 crews went out to the new north Denver suburb of Western Hills and put up 160 utility poles and began stringing transmission lines. The Union Rural Electric Association was outraged. On Monday morning it accused Public Service Company of "an attempt to grab off a $360,000 a year business plum in its service area . . ."[49]

The Public Service Company work was done more to prove a point and press an issue than to tie up the 6000-house business. Could the REA continue to claim exclusive rights to a rural service area even though a metropolitan area was rapidly expanding into the territory? Or, should cooperatives be guaranteed a market even if the market changes from rural to urban?[50]

The Public Service Company resented the necessity of competing for business with a co-op that functioned like a utility but was not subjected to stringent regulation. The company contended that if the REA wished to serve metropolitan areas, it should come under public utility commission regulation "The REA supplies electric service to its members only, and contends it is not a public utility," remarked Robert T. Person, Public Service Company publicity manager in 1954. "If it holds itself open to serve communities of this type, before it is known who the customers ultimately will be, it therefore must become a public utility and, therefore, subject to the jurisdiction of the Public Utility Commission."[51] The REA was assiduously avoiding coming under PUC jurisdiction because it would face strict regulation. In 1954 the Public Service Company proposed an amendment to the Colorado Constitution requiring REAs to be put under the jurisdiction of the Colorado Public Utilities Commission. Voters approved the amendment at the November election.

At the end of 1954 the Union REA filed suit against Public Service Company because of PSC's bold action in the Western Hills subdivision.[52] In February of 1955 Brighton District Court dismissed the case saying that the dispute was not a matter for district court, and belonged before the Public Utilities Commission.[53] As a result of that decision and the 1954 constitutional amendment, Union filed an application with the Public Utilities Commission of the State of Colorado to become a public utility. Union REA wanted to apply for a certificate of public convenience and necessity to serve territories north of Denver including Western Hills.

On 7 January 1957 the Commission declared Union to be a public utility, and defined the service territories of Union and Public Service Company. In some cases the two utilities were given non-exclusive rights to sell electricity in overlapping areas, which prompted both to file petitions with district court to review the PUC order.[54] The court refused to rule, and the case was appealed to the Colorado Supreme Court in 1960, which also refused to rule leaving the matter under the jurisdiction of the public utilities commission. Union Electric took the case to the United States Supreme Court, but it too declined to review the decision.[55]

Eventually Union Rural Electric Association and Public Service Company of Colorado settled their differences outside of the court system. After a series of meetings from 1960 to 1964 they agreed on mutually exclusive boundaries and on 8 May 1964 petitioned the PUC to issue certificates of public convenience and necessity for the agreed upon north Denver boundaries. The Commission approved the agreement on 20 July 1964, ending the long battle.[56]

Public Service Company experienced other challenges from Bureau of Reclamation projects. Two such projects, the Colorado River Storage Project and the Fryingpan-Arkansas Project, were of major concern. In 1949 Colorado, Wyoming, Utah, and New Mexico agreed to make full use of their half of the Colorado river system decreed to them in the 1922 Colorado River Compact. These states, the so-called Upper Basin group, proposed to Congress the Colorado River Storage Project (CRSP), consisting of twenty-one dams for irrigation power generation. Funds requested for the Colorado River Storage Project would also be used to build an all-federal power grid of transmission facilities from existing hydro-electric plants in Utah, Arizona, New Mexico and Colorado.

Public Service Company of Colorado supported the basic concept of water storage and the irrigation aspects of the project but was adamantly opposed to power grid transmission. A long battle ensued with the Public Service Company actively advocating private development of transmission lines to carry electricity from the hydroeclectric generators. The company offered in 1960 to cooperate with the USBR to combine private utility and Federal construction and avoid wasteful duplication of facilities. "Our proposal would provide for full integration and interconnection of all the Federal generating facilities in the area at a direct savings in construction cost to the government of some ninety million dollars."[58] Person continued by saying that: "Federal money saved in Colorado alone by the adoption of the Company plan would amount to nearly ten million." He concluded by promising that: "The proposed plan is fully capable of marketing all the power from the Colorado River Storage project and assures delivery of the project power to preference users."[58]

At the June, 1961 Senate hearings private utilities vehemently argued that lines could be built and operated by private firms without financial damage to the Colorado River Storage Project.[59] Proponents of public power argued, however, that there were several concerns about private transmission lines. First, the investor-owned private utilities might control the billion dollar Colorado River Storage project by investing only ten percent of the total cost. Secondly, Colorado Ute Electric Association did not want private utilities wheeling power to them because of previous poor experience with private firms. The Colorado River Basin Consumers Power, Incorporated and the Inter-mountain Consumers Power Association stated that the cooperative and municipally-owned electric systems had been established because of lack of service or poor performance by private utilities.[60] Private utilities had lost their chance.

Public Service Company was determined to fight

"those who cloak and disguise their efforts to federalize America's power industry behind the worthy objective of resource development . . ."[61] The company made five main points in its detailed proposal to share in transmitting electricity from the Bureau project. First, the company projected a savings of $137 million in government construction costs for transmission lines. Second, the company was prepared to abide by requirements of reclamation projects by providing power to preference customers, rural customers and cooperatives. Third, the PSC would provide an integrated network of generation and transmission systems. Fourth, private water users were prepared to repay some of the construction costs, thereby enabling an early completion of the project. Fifth, the company would contribute millions of dollars in taxes at the local, state and national level.[62]

Despite PSC efforts the House Appropriations committee in 1961 approved initial appropriations to build a bureau transmission line from Glen Canyon Dam to Phoenix, Arizona, one from Vernal to Provo, Utah to connect with the Flaming Gorge Dam, one from Sinclair, Wyoming to connect with the Missouri Basin transmission lines, one from Four Corners to Albuquerque to connect with the Rio Grande River system and one from Curecanti

Dam on the Gunnison River in Colorado to Midway, Colorado.[63]

Nevertheless, the following year, on 9 May 1962 the Bureau of Reclamation and Public Service Company signed a reciprocal power transmission agreement. The company agreed to wheel government power over its transmission lines for a very reasonable cost and without charge in some cases. The Bureau's concession was to use company's transmission system to the fullest extent to reduce construction of federal lines. This compromise agreement superseded all other reclamation agreements between PSC and the government, with the exception of pumped storage projects. It became the basic contract with the federal government which, with only minor modifications continues to this day.[64]

The other bureau project of concern to the Public Service Company of Colorado was the Fryingpan-Arkansas project, another large water-diversion and power generation facility. The bureau of reclamation planned to take water from the Fryingpan Creek, a Colorado river tributary, and divert it under the Sawatch Mountains of the Rocky Mountains into the Arkansas River to supply water for the rapidly growing municipal areas of Pueblo, Colorado Springs, and southeastern Colorado. The project included five major dams, and reservoirs, seventeen smaller diversion dams a 200-megawatt pumped-storage power plant, and a major conduit to supply municipal water systems.[65] Bureau officials claimed that water users could not support the project by themselves, and that the hydroelectric plant was necessary to enable the project to support itself.[66]

Fryingpan-Arkansas was proposed for the first time in 1953, but for nine years failed to be approved by Congress. Ironically, PSC appeared before Senate hearing in support of the government project with two primary motives. It sought to promote development of the Rocky Mountain region, it also wanted to be in a better bargaining position to wheel government electricity over company transmission lines. With PSC help the Fryingpan-Arkansas project was authorized and signed into law 16 August 1962, and finally became operational in the 1970s.[67]

The Rural Electrification Administration continued to be a thorn in the side of PSC and one project in particular had a significant impact on the company. The Colorado Ute Electric Association, an REA cooperative, filed a formal application with the Public Utilities Commission in 1962 to build a $31 million steam turbine electric generating plant in the northwestern Colorado town of Hayden. It planned a series of interconnecting transmission lines to connect the plant with the Colorado River Storage Project.[68] It was the first time that REA loans would be used to integrate cooperative plants with U.S. Bureau of Reclamation transmission lines.[69] Ute proposed to borrow $22,876,000 from the government at two percent interest, with the balance of $8,610,000 coming from the Salt River Project Agricultural Improvement and Power District in Arizona, a direct beneficiary of the project. If approved, the loan would be the largest ever granted by the Rural Electrification Administration for a single project.

The Senate Agriculture Committee reviewed the loan application and concluded that it would make for unfair Rural Electric Association competition with investor-owned utilities by using public tax money for financing. The committee strongly advised that public funds not be used for this project. Their recommendation however, went unheeded,[70] and the Congress approved the request in 1962.

In opposing the project at the 1963 Colorado Public Utilities Commission hearings, the PSC argued that since the Salt River Power District was not eligible for REA loans, it was not proper to supply the area with electricity from an REA-financed plant. The Salt River District was inelegible because of its urbanization and adequate service from private utilities. Transmitting power 700 miles to Phoenix from the Hayden plant was in PSC's view a blatant infringement of the REA charter.[71]

As noted, the Colorado Ute Electric Association had already obtained approval for REA financing of the venture and only needed the Colorado Public Utility Commission's approval to begin. Public Service Company and Western Colorado Power Company both protested the application because the potential duplication of plant, lines and systems. Western Colorado Power Company had also applied to the public utilities commission to build a transmission line to Arizona. The two companies argued that they had in the past provided adequate service in the area and were willing and able to continue.[72]

The hearings lasted twenty days and testimony filled 2,536 pages of transcription. To help in making a decision, Colorado PUC Commissioners asked questions such as: Will granting permission be in the public interest? Is the Hayden plant necessary for future public convenience and necessity? and, if so, is it immediately necessary? Is it in the public interest to build up and integrate the United States Bureau of Reclamation power project with REA power projects?[73] On 21 February, the commissioners approved most of the Colorado Ute Electric Association request, denying only the line from Shiprock, New Mexico to Bayfield, Colorado.[74]

It was not an easy decision for the three commissioners to make. Each wrote a separate opinion. Commissioner Ralph Horton concluded that although the Ute case was "supported by a preponderance of . . . diametrically conflicting evidence,"[75] the benefits to the economy of the western part of the state warranted the strengthening of the Colorado River Storage Project. There would, he said, be significant savings (because of the two percent loans) which would benefit the people of the Western Slope, and for that matter the entire state. Horton remarked that it was not the duty of the PUC to rule on whether the REA had the authority, under the federal act, to make a loan for to the project.[76] It was federal business that was not within commission jurisdiction.

In a concurring opinion Commissioner Howard S. Bjelland stated that he had arrived at the same view but for different reasons. Bjelland believed that the project, rather than benefiting the whole state, would profit 40,000 Colorado farm families that purchased electricity from cooperatives. It was also clear to him that the construction of the Hayden Plant with REA money would contribute to the entire Colorado River Storage Project by allowing the United States Bureau of Reclamation to reduce its construction costs per unit of electricity produced.[77] Construction, would also bring additional employment and tax base to the town of Hayden.[78]

Bjelland conceded that this Colorado River Storage Project would have a definite advantage over private utilities because of the low-interest rate tax advantages,[79] however, the application must be judged on its own merits, and the applicant had proved an established need and proved that the project would meet that need.[80] The adverse affects to private utilities from the growth of the rural electric cooperatives could not be considered by the PUC in Bjelland's opinion.[81] "The Public Utilities Commission of the State of Colorado is not a proper forum before which to debate the merits of private power or public power."[82]

Chairman Henry E. Zarlengo wrote a twenty-three page dissenting opinion, objecting primarily to the fact that Colorado-Ute would have no equity in the project because all the contruction money would come from loans.[83] He also pointed out that both Public Service Company and Western Colorado Power were serving Colorado with electricity long before Colorado Ute incorporated; Public Service, through its predecessors for almost a century and Western Colorado Power Company as early as 1907.[84] Zarlengo said that some of the "new" members of Colorado Ute such as Holy Cross, Grand Valley, San Luis Valley and Sangre de Cristo, (all REAs) had been served previously by Public Service Company, and it was only after completion of the Big Thompson project that they began purchasing cheaper electricity from the Bureau of Reclamation.[85]

Unlike the other two commissioners, Zarlengo was willing to tackle the issue of appropriateness of the loan. The stated purpose of the Rural Electric Associations he said, was "for the furnishing of electric energy to persons in rural areas who are not receiving central station service. . ."[85] He firmly believed that Colorado-Ute was not a "person" in a rural area unable to receive central station service. Commissioner Zarlengo chastised the applicant for its hypothetical figures implying significant savings for its customers which contrasted with more believable figures from Public Service Company. He concluded that there was no substantial proof of either need or savings.[86]

The Colorado-Ute Electric Association, Inc. proceeded to construct a steam electric generating plant at Hayden while Public Service Company and Western Colorado Power Company appealed the Colorado Public Utilities Commission decision. The Colorado Supreme Court ruled on the case 14 February 1966, overturning an earlier decision of the state District Court which upheld the Colorado Public Utilities Commission decision. The judges concluded that there was, in fact, adequate service available in the state without the Colorado-Ute project.[87] They summed up their decision by saying that to affirm the commission decisions by the court would be "inconsistent with the doctrine of regulated monopoly and would ... render regulation wholly ineffective and meaningless."[88]

Colorado-Ute Electric Association appealed this decision to the Federal Power Commission, objecting to the closing of the Hayden plant ordered by the Colorado Supreme Court. In 1966 the United States Supreme Court refused to review the Colorado Supreme Court decision for lack of jurisdiction. In 1967 the Federal Power Commission also declined to make any decision about the case.[89]

Colorado-Ute now had a serious problem deciding what to do with its illegal 150-megwatt generating plant. After a period of negotiation Colorado-Ute and PSC arrived at an agreement with regard to operation of the plant which was mutually beneficial. The twenty-five year contract signed on 9 October 1967 provided for the following: Colorado-Ute to retain ownership and operation of the Hayden plant and associated transmission system; Colorado-Ute to buy from nine and one half to fifty megawatts per year from PSC to service the growing needs of its member systems; the Hayden plant to become part of the PSC grid for emergency and backup purposes; Public Service Company to provide transmission for Colorado-Ute to serve the San Luis Valley and Holy Cross Rural Electric Cooperatives; and the PSC to buy 75 million kilowatt hours of surplus energy from the Hayden plant each year from 1968 through 1974, unless there was of a below-average runoff year in the Colorado River Basin. A final provision of the agreement gave the Bureau of Reclamation the first right to purchase any surplus energy available from the Hayden plant from 1975 through 1985.[90]

Thus, while the Public Service Company was

certainly not entirely successful in eliminating the "creeping socialism," it had won some victories and put the government competition on notice that the PSC would not give in easily.

NOTES--CHAPTER 12

1
Jack Doyle, *Lines Across the Land: Rural Electrification Cooperatives, The Changing Politics of Energy in Rural America* (Washington, DC: The Rural Land and Energy Project Environmental Policy Institute, 1979), p. 1.

2
John D. Garwood and W. D. Tuthill, *The Rural Electrification Administration: An Evaluation* (Washington, D.C.: the American Enterprise Institute for Public Policy Research, 1963), p. 2.

3
Colorado State Planning Division, *Colorado Year Book 1939-1940* (Denver: Colorado State Planning Division, 1941), p. 338.

4
Guide to National Archives of the United States (Washington, DC: General Service Administration, 1974), p. 440. An act of October 28, 1949 authorized the REA to make loans for extension and improvement of rural telephone service.

5
Doyle, *Lines Across the Land*, pp. 2-3.

6
Clyde T. Ellis, *A Giant Step*, (New York: Vintage Books, 1966) p. 28.

7
Ibid.

8
"Colorado Big Thompson Project," Sen. Doc. 80, 75th Cong. 1st Sess (Washington, DC: U. S. Government Printing Office, 1937), pp. 1-33.

9
John Loiseau, *Lines*, (March, 1949), 2.

10
Lines, (January, 1950), 2.

11
Lines, (April, 1951), 2.

12
PSC 1951 *Annual Report*, (1952), pp. 13-15.

13
Ibid., p.15.

14
U.S. Senate, 81st. Cong. 1st Sess, Statement of John E. Loiseau, president of Public Service Company of Colorado before Hearings before the Subcommittee on

Appropriations on H.R. 3838, "A Bill Making Appropriations for the Department of Interior ending 30 June 1950, part 1 (Washington, DC: U S. Government Printing Office, 1961), pp. 475-476.

15

Garwood and Tuthill, *The Rural Electrification Association*, p. 17.

16

The American Enterprise Institute for Public Policy Research, a non-partisan research and educational organization which studies national policy problems, ilustrated this departure. John D. Garwood and W. C. Tuthill writing for the institute, pointed out what the REA was and what it had become, often through the words of those who established the program. Garwood and Tuthill's references are invaluable in understanding the change.

17

U.S., Congress, House, *Congressional Record*, 74th Cong. 2d sess. Vol. LXXX, part 5 (Washington, DC: U.S. Government Printing Office, 1936) pp. 5281 and 5283.

18

Ibid.

19

Rural Electrification Administration Annual Statistical Report, August, 1960, p. xv.

Not only were loans going to non-rural customers but the REA was being redesigned to remedy the negative effects of electrification. According to the Denver *Post* 13 August 1961, p. 3, section 1AA, in the 1960s, as electricity provided relief from manual labor on farms, farm workers were being put out of work. In response to this situation President John F. Kennedy expanded the REA's role to one of creating jobs for the 1.4 million underemployed rural Americans. With new responsibility the REA tried to help local groups improve their rural communities in order to attract new industry. It was hoped that with improved water, sewerage, police and fire protection as well as eductional, cultural and recreational facilities, businesses would be more inclined to choose a rural community in which to locate rather than an urban area. The new REA also aimed its efforts at stopping the exodus of youths to the city.

20

Ibid.

21 Garwood and Tuthill, *The Rural Electrification Association*, p. 69.

22 *Lines*, January, 1961, p. 2.

23 *Congressional Record*, 10 July 1963, p. 11675.

24 84th Congress 1st Session, House Reports, Vol II, "Report of the Committee on Interior and Insular Affairs (Washington: U S. Government Printing Office, 1962), p. 11963.

25 Garwood and Tuthill, *The Rural Electrification Association*, p. 54.

26 Ibid.

27 Robert T. Person, "Seagulls and Salesmen" a speech delivered to the Annual Sales Institute of the Edison Electric Institute, 3 April 1963, pp. 2-7 of the transcript.

28 Robert T. Person, remarks delivered at the Edison Electric Institute's Presidents' meeting, Chicago, 11-12 December 1963, p. 5 of the transcript.

29 Ibid.

30 Ibid.

31Ibid.

32 Ibid.

33 Public Service Company of Colorado 1965 Stockholders meeting, p. 3 of the transcript.

34 M. S. Bitner, "The Colorado-Big Thompson Project," *Reclamation Era* XXX (September, 1940), 267-269.

35 *Electrical West*, LXXXI, (July, 1938), 44.

36 PSC 1948 *Annual Report* (1949), pp. 9-10.

37 *Rocky Mountain News*, 26 June 1949, p. 8.

38 *Denver Post*, 4 May 1949, p.1. and 19 May 1949, p. 2.

39
Denver *Post*, 4 May 1949, p. 1.
40
Ibid.
41
Denver *Post*, 19 May 1949, p. 2.
42
Denver *Post*, 26 June 1949, p. 1.
43
Editorial, Denver *Post*, 30 June 1949, p. 10.
44
Denver *Post*, 26 June 1949, p. 1.
45
Rocky Mountain News, 26 June 1949, p. 8.
46
Lines, (April, 1949), 2.
47
PSC 1953 *Annual Report*, (1954) pp. 9-10.
48
PSC 1955 *Annual Report*, (1956) pp.7-8.
49
Denver *Post*, 18 November 1954, p. 3.
50
Denver *Post*, 24 January 1961, p. 14.
51
Denver *Post*, 20 November 1954, p 6.
52
Union became a public utility in 1955, but it was not until 1961 that the Colorado Public Utilities Commission had jurisdiction over all REA cooperatives in Colorado. *Session Laws* passed at the first regular session of the 43d General Assembly of the State of Colorado, (Denver: Bradford Robinson Printing Co., 1961), p. 627.
53
Denver *Post*, 2 December 1954, p. 30 and 15 February 1955, p. 16.
54
Ellsworth Nichols, ed. *Public Utilities Report* XXX (Washington, DC: P.U.R., Inc., 1960), pp. 222-242 and Colorado Public Utilities Commission decision No. 63771, 25 September 1964, and *Electrical West* CXXVI (February 1961)1-2.

55*Electrical West* CXXVI (May, 1961), p. 3.
56
Lines, August, 1964, p. 2.
57
Ibid.

58 Ibid.

59 Hearings before the Subcommittee of the Committee on Appropriations, House of Representatives, 87th Cong., 1st Sess, Part 2, Department of Agricultural Appropriations for 1962 (Washington, DC: 1961), pp. 475-476.

60 Ibid.

61 *Lines*, April, 1961, p. 2.

62 Ibid.

63 Denver *Post*, 7 September 1961, p. 1.

64 Robert V. Hugo, Administrative Assistant, Engineering and Planning, Interview, 9 September 1985 and Contract for Interconnections and Transmission Service with Public Service Company of Colorado and the United States Department of the Interior Bureau of Reclamation, p. 1.

65 Denver *Post*, 31 May 1962, p. 3.

66 *Denver Post Perspective*, 23 November 1969, p. 1H.

67 Terence Brace, compiler, The History of the Fryingpan-Arkansas Project." (no publisher, no date, Western History Department of the Denver Public Library), p. 28.

68 It proposed to interconnect another USBR generating plant, also located near Hayden with the Yampa Valley Electric Cooperative; interconnect circuits from Oak Creek to Craig; to interconnect transmission lines from Hayden to Hamilton to Meeker to Rifle and interconnect with Moon Lake Electric Association from Meeker to Rangely; to construct a substation in The Carbon-Basalt area and circuits to Eagle and Aspen; a circuit from Rifle to Collbran and interconnection with the Reclamation Bureau's Molina plant; to interconnect facillities with the Reclamation Bureau Morrow Point plant at Montrose; to construct a substation west of Gunnison to interconnect the USBR substation to existing Gunnison County rural electric lines; to serve the San Luis Valley Rural Electric Cooperative near Monte Vista over the Reclamation

circuit from Montrose to Poncha Junction, Colo (and wheeling arrangments with PSC); to serve Arkansas G & T at Pueblo over Reclamation circuit from Montrose to Poncha Junction and then to Pueblo; to provide a circuit from the Reclamation Bureau's Shiprock, New Mexico substation to Bayfield, Colorado and terminal facilities to interconnect with an existing REA circuit from Nucla to Bayfield. Denver *Post*, 18 May 1962, p. 3.

69 Denver *Post*, 18 July 1962, p. 22.

70 Hearings before the Subcommittee of the Committee on Appropriations, House of Representatives 87th Cong. 1st Sess., Aprigcultural Appropriations for 1962 (Washington, DC: U. S. Government Printing Office, 1961), pp. 475-476.

71 Public Utilities Commission of the State of Colorado, Decision No. 60156, 21 February 1963, p.4. San Miguel Power Association, Inc., Empire Electric Association, Inc., La Plata Electric Association, Inc., Delta-Montrose Rural Power Lines Association, San Luis Valley Rural Electric Cooperative, Inc., The Grand Valley Rural Power Lines, Inc., Holy Cross Electric Association, Inc., White River Electric Association, Yampa Valley Electric Association, Gunnison County Electric Association, Inc., another generating and transmission cooperative Arkansas Valley Generation and Transmission, all of Colorado Bridger Valley Electric Association, Inc. of Wyoming, Salt River Project Agricultural Improvement and Power District of Arizona.

72 Ibid., p. 4.

73 Ibid., p. 7.

74 Ibid., p. 18.

75 Ibid., p. 21.

76 Ibid., p. 22.

77 Ibid., p. 29.

78 Ibid., p. 31.

79 Ibid.

80 Ibid., pp. 34-35.

[81] Ibid., p. 33.

[82] Ibid., p. 31.

[83] Ibid., p. 40.

[84] Ibid., p. 50.

[85] Ibid, p. 59.

[86] *Rocky Mountain News*, 17 July 1966, p. 44.

[87] Denver *Post*, 12 August 1967, p. 3.

[88] *The Western Colorado Power Company and Public Service Company of Colorado* v. *The Public Utilities Commission of the State of Colorado, Ute Electric Association*, Supreme Court of Colorado, December, 1957, pp. 16-17.

[89] PSC 1967 Annual Report (1967), p. 21.

[90] *Electrical West* CXXXIV (October 1967), 29.

CHAPTER 13

NATURAL GAS 1945-1969

Like its electrical power counterpart, the natural gas industry was challenged by tremendous demand for its product in the post-war years. In order to transport a sufficient amount of natural gas to the growing Colorado population, Colorado Interstate Gas, Public Service Company's main supplier, began a major construction program immediately after the Second World War. The rapidly increasing demand also put great pressure on supplies, and caused CIG to request four price increases in the 1950s, which in turn forced Public Service Company of Colorado to raise its own rates. The twenty-five year post-war period for PSC is a story of these two efforts, to meet the demand for gas and to receive a reasonable price for the product.

In the mid-1940s Colorado Interstate Gas began a fifteen million dollar construction project to double its pipeline capacity, and the Public Service Company followed suit by approving plans to expand its distribution system.[1] As part of the expansion project Public Service Company and Colorado Interstate Gas Company signed a twenty-year contract in 1946 whereby

PSC would buy gas from a 240-mile pipeline to be constructed to the Hugoton gas fields in west-central Kansas. CIG felt some urgency in beginning the project because its 340-mile pipeline to the Amarillo field in the Texas Panhandle carried only 83 million cubic feet a day. During one day in 1946 Denver used 69 million cubic feet of natural gas.[2]

Before construction could begin, however, Colorado Interstate Gas Company required a certificate of public convenience and necessity from the Federal Power Commission, which opened hearings at the City and County Building in Denver on 21 April 1947. In addition to the proposed 240 mile pipeline to Kansas the commission considered Colorado-Wyoming Gas Company's application to build an eight-inch pipeline from Denver to Cheyenne, Wyoming, as well as CIG's twenty-inch pipeline circling the city of Denver and connecting the main pipeline from Kansas with Colorado Springs. During the formal hearings gas distribution companies testified to the critical need for more gas in both Colorado and Wyoming.[3] Since there was no protest to the applications the Federal Power Commission granted the certificates for all three projects on 23 May 1947.[4]

Construction crews had been waiting for the hearings to end, and a day after the applications were granted workers began digging a trench for the Kansas gas line. The line was completed in 1947, increasing CIG's capacity by 100 million cubic feet of natural gas per day.[5] The Colorado-Wyoming Gas Company completed its eight-inch pipeline from Denver to Cheyenne in May, 1948 and the loop around Denver was finished in 1949.

In 1951 Colorado Interstate Gas completed another twenty-inch transmission pipe line a distance of 215 miles from the Amarillo gas field in Texas to Kit Carson in eastern Colorado, half way between the Hugoton field in Kansas and Denver. In order to qualify for the financing required for this project it was necessary for Colorado Interstate Gas, the transporter, to merge with Colorado River Gas Company, the producer. The merger gave CIG sufficient property values to enable it to borrow funds to finance the expansion project.[6] The Federal Power Commission authorized the merger on 16 March 1951.[7] The two companies consolidated because Colorado Interstate Gas was experiencing limits on its borrowing capacity.

On the Western Slope, repeated attempts to bring natural gas to Grand Junction had been unsuccessful in the 1920s, 1930s and 1940s. However, when Public Service Company applied to renew its franchise to supply electricity and manufactured gas to the area in the late 1940s residents indicated that the city would turn the company down unless Public Service Company agreed to bring natural gas to the city. As a result, the company created a new subsidiary, the Grand Valley Pipe Company, with most of its directors coming from the executives ranks of Public Service Company.

Before construction of a natural gas pipe line could begin, however, material became scare because of the Korean war. As a result, Grand Valley Pipe Company was dissolved in 1951. In the meantime the residents of Grand Junction had voted to renew Public Service Company's franchise with a provision that the company would make natural gas available within two years from the date of renewal. In order to meet this commitment Public Service Company on 15 March 1952 created another subsidiary called the Western Slope Gas Company. In the fall of 1952 that company began laying a ten-inch pipe line to the nearby Asbury gas field. The line was completed in the winter of 1953, and it was not long after that the residents began receiving a supply of natural gas for home cooking and heating.[8]

In 1953, after ten years of independence from Cities Service Company, Public Service Company had realized increases of 118 percent the in the number of gas customers and 179 percent in gas revenues. The cost of the natural gas to Public Service Company, however, was rising rapidly due to several Colorado Interstate Gas price increases between 1948 and 1952.[9] In 1953 CIG requested a twelve percent increase, and the Federal Power Commission gave preliminary approval in December. Public Service Company estimated the rate hike would cost the company an additional two million dollars per year, and responded with an immediate rate increase request to the Public Utilities Commission. The company argued that it simply could not afford to absorb any more cost increases.[10]

Opponents, including Denver city officials, calculated the proposed increase would add ten percent to customer bills and vigorously lobbied against it. Mayor Quigg Newton objected to the price increase, saying there had been too little time to study the proposal. He also claimed that Public Service company had been earning from 7.3 to 7.8 percent interest on its gas investments in recent years, a return which he considered excessive.[11] Despite these arguments the PUC granted the Company temporary $1,800,000 gas rate hike in January, 1954.[12] Further hearings began in August of that year, and continued well into 1955, at which time the higher rates were made permanent.[13]

On 31 October 1954 Colorado Interstate Gas requested another increase from the Federal Power Commission, this time a thirty percent hike. This increase was tentatively approved by the Federal Power Commission on 1 February 1955, and led to another PSC rate increase request to the PUC in 1955. Coupled with the prior twelve percent increase the new request raised gas prices to many Coloradans by forty-two percent.[14]

In 1954 the United States Supreme Court ruled in the Phillips Petroleum Company Case (concerning the nation's largest natural gas producer) that the wellhead prices charged by gas producers, such as Phillips and Colorado Interstate Gas, for intrastate gas transactions fell under the jurisdiction of the Federal Power Commission. (Before that ruling, gas producers had been regulated by the 1938 Natural Gas Act which only gave FPC commissioners jurisdiction over interstate sales of natural gas.)[15] This judicial decision had a major long-range impact on the natural gas industry and companies such as CIG protested being regulated by the Federal Power Commission. The inclination of the Federal Power Commission was to use outdated figures to determine the costs of finding and processing gas. These figures were then used to set prices to be paid by interstate pipeline companies to the independent producers. These artificially low prices tended to stimulate the demand for natural gas without providing an incentive to producers to search for new gas. From the mid-1950s on, drilling activity declined, and by 1970 a shortage of natural gas appeared.

Although Colorado Interstate Gas Company was forced to be regulated by the Federal Power Commission, it won a battle to avoid coming under the jurisdiction of the Colorado Public Utilities Commission. In 1954 the PUC began hearings to determine whether CIG should be considered a public utility and in January, 1959 ruled that CIG, when it sold gas directly to customers within Colorado, was, indeed, a public utility. The gas company would, therefore, require a certificate of public convenience and necessity from the Colorado PUC for the extension, construction, or operation of pipelines. Colorado Interstate Gas appealed the PUC decision and in 1960 the Colorado Supreme Court ruled that CIG was not subject to regulation by the Public Utilities Commission.[17] The Court essentially determined that regulation by the Federal Power

Commission was sufficient to protect the public interest. It was a six year battle that the gas company was grateful to win.

Colorado Interstate Gas Company planned to buy part of its natural gas supply from producers in the Rock Springs, Wyoming area. The Wyoming gas cost about eighteen cents per thousand cubic feet compared with approximately 16.9 cents for gas from Texas, Kansas, or Colorado.[18] Another rate increase was, therefore, in the offing. CIG applied to the Federal Power Commission to build a line from Denver to Rock Springs to connect with a new pipe line from the San Juan Basin in the four corners area of Colorado, through Rock Springs to the Pacific Northwest. This interconnection would make an additional one hundred million cubic feet of natural gas available to CIG per day, and although the gas was more expensive, the new line (completed in 1957) insured an ample supply of natural gas for Denver and other Colorado consumers.[19]

Colorado Interstate Gas also established a subsidiary company in 1954, Natural Gas Producers, Inc. to construct a pipe line from Denver to the northeast Colorado oil and gas fields near Fort Morgan and Brush. When completed, the pipe line added significantly to

CIG's natural gas supply, making an additional 50,000,000 cubic feet of gas available a day.[20]

While Colorado Interstate Gas was occupied with new construction, the United States Supreme Court reviewed a challenge to the pre-1952 CIG rate base. In March, 1955 the Court upheld the Federal Power Commission's decision of 8 August 1952 that the company used too high of a rate base to establish its rate. According to the FPC decision the company incorrectly calculated the amount of depreciation to subtract from the operating costs, thereby arriving at a higher rate base. FPC guidelines allowed a 5 3/4 percent return on the rate base, but with the new base, the actual rates charged by CIG yielded a 6 1/2 percent return, or $3,111,187 too much during 1952 alone. As a result the company was ordered to refund the overcharge to its customers during a four-year period[21] and the Public Service Company received a refund of $4.4 million.

It is interesting to note that the ruling was one of the last rate reductions ordered by the Federal Power Commission. After Republican President Eisenhower was elected in 1952, the Federal Power Commission developed a new system of calculating rates which had the effect of raising gas prices.[22] Even though the policy changed, the Federal Power Commission would rule against Colorado Interstate Gas Company in the future.

The March, 1955 Supreme Court ruling negating the 1952 rate hike did include CIG's two price increases that had gone into effect on 1 January 1954 and the 1 February 1955. A year later in 1956 Colorado Interstate Gas went back to the Federal Power Commission asking for third rate increase which would take effect 1 July 1957. Public Service Company of Colorado had anticipated the increase but not as soon as mid 1957. To avoid an estimated net two million dollars extra expense to obtain gas PSC immediately asked the Public Utilities Commission for its own rate increase, or "pass-on,"[23] and the request was granted.

Although consumers did not like these gas rate increases most knew that prices of gas transported from Texas, Kansas and Wyoming had caused higher prices. Some customers, nevertheless objected to all increases whatever the reason. One justification for higher rates was particularly bothersome to Colorado customers. Soon after Colorado Interstate Gas was established to bring natural gas to Colorado, a deal was made in 1927 for Cities Service, Standard Oil of New Jersey and the Southwestern Development Company to furnish the city of

Amarillo natural gas for the life of the Panhandle gas field. Amarillo was to pay only the cost of producing the gas without any additional investment return or surcharges.

In return, the three companies were allowed to develop the gas field and pipe the gas to areas outside of Texas, including Colorado. Any profit that expected to make had to come from its own customers, for example, those in Denver. As a result, the cost of gas to PSC consumers doubled, while the cost for Amarillo residents remained low. By 1958 Denverites paid $9.03 for 15,000 cubic feet of gas while townspeople in Amarillo paid $4.25.[24]

In early 1957 Colorado Interstate Gas received unwelcomed news that the presiding examiner of the Federal Power Commission had issued an order that Colorado Interstate Gas's 1954 and 1955 preliminary rate increases should be scaled down. CIG's appeal of the order was denied, and in the spring of 1959 the company was forced to refund to Public Service Company and seven other utilities approximately $40 million in overcharges.[25] The Public Service Company in turn distributed $16 million in refunds to its gas customers.[26]

The refund orders continued. The Federal Power Commission at a meeting in July 1960 determined that Colorado Interstate Gas had earned $2,699,121 too much for the year 1959, and it ordered that amount returned to the customers. Colorado Interstate Gas, now somewhat accustomed to refunding money, developed a plan for consideration by the FPC. It was approved on 31 December 1959[27] and the money was distributed soon thereafter.

During the winter of 1958-1959 Public Service Company of Colorado became concerned about the ability of CIG to provide adequate amounts of gas for PSC customers. Colorado Interstate Gas's building program after the end of World War II was barely keeping up with demand. Because of the problems with rates they charged between 1954 and 1959 CIG did not want to expend large amounts of money on construction and had added very little to its system after the mid-1950s. Fortunately, the winter of 1958-1959 was not particularly harsh, and Colorado Interstate Gas was able to deliver enough gas to meet consumer requirements. Public Service Company decided that the only way to insure sufficient natural gas reserves was to develop storage capacity. In response to the problem, the engineers and executives came up with one of Public Service Company of Colorado's most innovative ideas. They were the first in the country, and perhaps in the world, to demonstrate that gas could be stored very conveniently in an abandoned mine. Colorado was full of old mines and the idea had great promise as a low cost method of storage.

Public Service Company hired a geology firm to search the Denver area for a suitable mine. Geologists identified sixteen mines that might be appropriate for gas storage, and after further study they selected the Leyden Mine, fourteen miles northwest of Denver. The Leyden Mine was a coal mine which had been operated from 1903 until 1950. It was close to the metropolitan area, was relatively easy to test and develop, and had an enormous storage capacity.[28]

Gas would be stored during the summer months when demand was low and extracted during periods of heavy use in cold weather. Several tests were made to determine if the mine would hold gas without leakage. Geological surveys indicated that a shale strata above the working levels was gas tight, and the tests confirmed the favorable conditions. By the end of 1959, much of the water had been pumped out of the mine and 165,000,000 cubic feet of gas was injected into the old mine for storage. During the following year more gas was injected bringing the total stored to 750,000,000 cubic feet. Later a compressor station was added to distribute gas.[29] By 1964 2.3 billion cubic feet of gas was stored.[30]

In addition to having its own emergency reserve, PSC had another reason to store gas in the Leyden mine. Colorado Interstate Gas charged Public Service Company a two part rate for gas, a commodity charge and a demand charge. The commodity charge was a flat rate based on the total amount of gas used over a long period. The demand charge was based on the volume of gas used on the highest demand day of the year, and was added to the commodity charge. Colorado Interstate Gas always had to be prepared to provide the highest demand level of gas, and it was, therefore, necessary and reasonable to charge for that reserve capability. The demand charge was added even in the summer, when there was no call on the reserve. By providing its own reserve from the Leyden Mine, Public Service Company was able to reduce the amount paid to Colorado Interstate Gas for peak demand and, therefore, keep the demand charge lower. The demand charge had accounted for almost one-third of the company's total gas costs, and the new storage concept saved a considerable amount of money.[31]

The Leyden Mine Project brought much national and local praise to the company. It was commended for the ingenuity with which it stretched the gas supply for Colorado.[32] President Robert T. Person said that the project illustrated the need for pure scientific research and development in the utility industry, "not only to provide universal service but also to cope with inflation, reduce the effects of rising costs and increase our markets in competition with other industries."[33]

As a member of the American Gas Association, the Midwest Gas Association and as a contributor to the Institute of Gas Technology, the Public Service Company actively participated in research and development in areas other than gas storage. The research included the manufacture of high quality synthetic gas from raw materials, such as coal and oil shale. Development of new gas equipment and improvements in utilization of gas for refrigeration, air conditioning and incineration was also part of the research. These efforts were aimed primarily at human labor reduction, as well as the extension of natural gas service into remote and semi-remote areas of the state.[34]

In 1962 Public Service Company's subsidiary, Western Slope Gas Company, built a 240-mile pipeline with high-pressure gas pipe to serve the central mountain valley towns of Saguache, Salida, Buena Vista, Leadville and Climax, Colorado.[35] The first leg, completed in 1961, an eight-inch gas transmission line from the Ignacio field near Durango to Del Norte, brought service to the San Luis Valley of southwestern Colorado. The second leg was a 150-mile line that was said to be the nation's, and perhaps the world's, highest high-pressure gas pipe line. From Del Norte to Climax, Colorado, the line crossed the Continental Divide three times.[36]

In 1964, two Public Service Company subsidiaries merged, Colorado-Wyoming Gas Company which had become a subsidiary in 1931 and Western Slope Gas Company which had been established in 1952. The Wyoming portion of the business had been sold, so that it functioned only in Colorado. The combination of the the two companies created the largest intrastate gas transmission enterprise in the United States.[37]

The Leyden Mine was so successful that in 1965 the company, through its Western Slope Gas Company subsidiary, developed underground storage in the Grand Junction Area. The depleted Asbury Creek gas field where natural gas had been extracted over a decade before, was selected as the storage site. It had a potential of holding 3.2 billion cubic feet, although only 1.6 billion cubic feet of natural gas was injected the first several years. Once in operation the company withdrew nearly four million cubic feet of gas per day to meet peak requirements during the winter months.[38]

Two years later the company purchased the depleted Fruita gas reservoir and used it as a gas storage facility as well. The Fruita reservoir, which was close to the Asbury Creek site, had an maximum storage capacity of one billion cubic feet of natural gas. Asbury Creek and the Fruita Field together had an ultimate storage capacity of 4.2 billion cubic feet, and saved the company millions of dollars.[39]

Underground storage capacity was particularly important in the 1960s as gas supplies dwindled. Suppliers such as Colorado Interstate Gas and Public Service Company feared the inability to meet future consumer demands. During the difficult years of the sixties gas producers and distributors reorganized their operations to cut expenses. Because of budget consciousness and storage programs customers in Colorado obtained all the natural gas they required.

NOTES--CHAPTER 13

1
Denver *Post*, 28 April 1945, p. 1.

2
Rocky Mountain News, 5 December 1946, p. 17.

3
Denver *Post*, 23 March 1947, p. 1A, 22 April 1947, p. 26, and 25 April 1947, p. 3 and Wallace Thackery, "Early Colorado-Wyoming Pipeline History," (Denver: c. January 1953), p. 4.

4
Denver *Post*, 24 May 1947, p. 1.

5
Rocky Mountain News, 27 May 1947, p. 8.

6
Federal Power Commission, Decisions and Reports X, "In the matter of Interstate Gas Company and Canadian River Gas Company," decided 16 March 1951 (Washington, DC: U.S. Government Printing Office, 1953), 105-135. *Rocky Mountain News*, 3 January 1952, p. 23 and PSC 1951 *Annual Report* (1952), p. 8.

7
Denver *Post*, 27 March 1951, p. 36.

8
"A Short History of Western Slope Gas Company (Denver: Pulic Service Company of Colorado, no date), pp. 1-2 and *Public Service Company: Providing Energy for More than a Century* (Denver: Public Service Company, 1976), 18. The Colorado-Wyoming Gas Company was formed 1 December 1925 to transport gas coming from the Wellington field. Two pipelines were built by the Colorado-Wyoming Gas Company. One extended south to Fort Collins and was completed 9 December 1925; the other carried gas north to Cheyenne and was completed 7 July 1926. The Colorado-Wyoming Gas Company became the property of Public Service Company 22 September 1931 when its 50,000 shares of common stock were turned over to PSC in settlement of debt owed by Cities Service Company. p. 14. In 1984 Western Slope Gas Company changed its name to Western Gas Supply Company.

9
Denver *Post*, 23 December 1953, p. 1.

10
Ellsworth Nichols, ed., Colorado Public Utility Commission decision re: Public Service Company of Colorado 7 January 1954, *Public Utility Reports*

(third series) II (Washington, DC: Public Utility Reports, Inc., 1954), pp. 65-74.

11 *Rocky Mountain News*, 31 December 1953, p. 5.

12 Denver *Post*, 21 July 1954, p. 13.

13 Denver *Post*, 30 March 1955, p. 14.

14 *Rocky Mountain News*, 31 October 1954, p. 14 and Denver *Post*, 31 October 1954, pp. 1 and 20.

15 Charles L. Phillips, Jr., *The Economics of Regulation, Theory and Practice in the Transportation and Public Utility Industries*, revised edition, (Homewood, IL: Richard D. Irwin, Inc., 1969), p. 195

16 Ernest J. Oppenheimer, *Natural Gas: the New Energy Leader* (New York: Pen and Podium Productions, 1980), pp. 91-92.

17 Ellsworth Nichols, ed., Colorado Supreme Court Decision, *Colorado Public Utilities Commission, et al v. Colorado Interstate Gas Company, Public Utility Reports* (third series) XXXIII (Washington, DC: Public Utility Reports, Inc., 1960), p. 254.

18 Denver *Post*, 30 March 1955, p. 14.

19 PSC 1954 *Annual Report* (1955,), p. 4.

20 Ibid.

21 Federal Power Commission "In the Matter of Colorado Interstate Gas," XI (1 January 1952 - 31 December 1952) (Washington, DC: U. S. Government Printing Office, 1957), pp. 324-363.

22 Denver *Post*, 30 March 1955, p. 14.

23 Denver *Post*, 7 June 1957, p. 1.

24 Denver *Post*, 29 June 1958, p. 2AA.

25 Denver *Post*, 2 April 1959, p. 1. and *Rocky Mountain News*, 3 April 1959, p. 5.

26 PSC 1960 *Annual Report* (1961), p. 3.

27
Federal Power Commission Reports, Opinions, Decisions, Orders. XXXIV, 1 July 1960 to 31 December 1961. (Washington, D.C.: United States Printing Office, 1964), 300-01.

28
Lines, April 1961, p. 8, and Robert T. Person, Sr. speech delivered to the St. Louis Society of Security Analysts, 18 September 1964, p. 19.

29
Ibid.

30
Robert T. Person, a speech to the St. Louis Society of Security Analysts, 18 September 1964, p. 19 of the transcript.

31
Robert T. Person, a speech to Gyro Club of Denver, 24 September 1965, p. 1 of the transcript.

32
PSC 1966 *Annual Report* (1967), p. 13.

33
Robert T. Person, speech, 18 September 1964, p. 13.

34
PSC 1966 *Annual Report* (1967), p. 10.

35
Rocky Mountain News, 7 September 1962, p. 91.

36
Denver *Post*, 8 September 1962, p. 26.

37
Dan McNellis, "Heat, Light, and History, in the Colorado Cattleman's Centennial Commission, *The Cooperative Century, (Denver: privately printed, 1967), p. 63.*

38
PSC 1966 *Annual Report* (1967), p. 10. In 1961 Colorado Interstate Gas set up the Natural Gas Producers, Inc., as a completely owned subsidiary. Located in northeastern Colorado, it was set up to develop the Fort Morgan Field as a storage reservoir and to serve northeast Colorado towns as an intrastate pipeline. The field was ready for storage in 1966.

39
PSC 1968 *Annual Report* (1968), p. 10.

CHAPTER 14

THE 1960S - REWARDS AND CHALLENGES

The decade of the sixties was one of mixed blessings for the utility industry. Prosperity brought high revenues, but inflation created high costs and profits were reduced. "Inflation is eating us out of house and home," remarked a spokesman for Public Service Company at the beginning of the 1960s.[1] However, inflation then was only an inkling of what it would be in the 1970s. Utilities were adding rapidly to their facilities but construction required large amounts of capital. It was also a period in which people raised questions about the social costs of producing enormous amounts of energy.

In the 1960s Colorado was the ninth fastest growing state and had the ninth highest level of personal income in the nation.[2] Public Service Company of Colorado experienced a sustained period of growth, building a new headquarters and, the year before the decade began, appointing a president who would head the company longer than any of his predecessors. In 1962 Fortune Magazine, for the first time, included Public

Service Company on its list of the fifty largest utilities in the nation.[3]

The cost of keeping up with growth had risen dramatically since the company's last rate increase in 1955. Between 1955 and 1959 the public utility construction cost index for the region increased 26 percent for electric and 31 percent for gas construction. Fuel costs rose fifteen percent and wages increased a like amount. The ratio of capital investment to revenue also increased.[4] Because of rising costs, PSC made an application in September 1959 to the public utilities commission for a rate increase. In making the request, executives pointed out that a utility must preserve financial integrity in order to compete with other, mostly unregulated enterprises, in the capital markets. The company maintained that a return of 6.75 percent was justified in order to avoid rate increase requests each time economic conditions changed.[5] Many federal agencies, however, considered 5.43 percent a fair minimum rate of return and exerted pressure to limit Public Service Company to that amount.[6]

After receiving Public Service Company's application for an increase the Public Utilities Commission of the State of Colorado scheduled hearings and notified the appropriate elected officials of all the larger communities being served by PSC. The PUC also sent notices to all of the company's wholesale electric purchasers; to the Colorado Municipal League; to a competitor, Union Rural Electric Association, Inc., and to various newspapers.[7] The hearing before the Colorado Public Utilities Commission started 18 November, 1960 and lasted twelve days.

Before determining the rate of return the commissioners had to determine the value of the company, i.e., the rate base. There were three basic theories of valuation that the Commission considered: "original cost," "reproduction cost," and "reasonable value." The "original cost" value was determined by reviewing the company books and determining the original cost of all facilities. The second value, the "reproduction cost," was established by calculating the cost to reproduce all the plants at current prices. In both methods, an amount was subtracted for depreciation. "Reasonable value," was determined through a fair market value analysis, i.e. the price a willing buyer and a willing seller would establish for the facilities.[8] The commissioners decided to adopt the original cost value approach because it was straight forward and based on the actual amount of money invested in facilities.[9] With an adjustment for attrition of old plants, the commissioners using original cost arrived at a rate base of $260,754,667. On this amount the rate of return was established.

After weighing the various opinions on how much profit should be permitted the commissioners decided to increase it from 6.15 to 6.35 percent. (They excluded the portion of the steam department that was used for back up.) The electric department was allowed to file rates that would yield gross revenues of $54,671,366, an increase of $3,200,264. The gas department was permitted to produce a gross revenue of $41,288,101 or an adjusted increase of $1,188,875.[10]

While on the one hand the PUC complimented the company for delaying a rate increase as long as possible, on the other hand it approved an increase which was only forty percent of the requested ten million dollars. A former Denver city attorney even disputed that amount, and filed an official protest against the Public Utilities Commission decision. He believed that the allowance for inflation included in the rate of return was too high. The commissioners defended their decision saying that the current rate of inflation would continue to erode profits, and that it was their duty to establish a rate which would prevent the financial deterioration of the company.[11] District Court Judge Don D. Bowman rejected the protest and upheld the Commission's order in February, 1961.[12]

Public Service Company expanded its service area in the early 1960s by merging with the Colorado Central Power Company. "For many years our company and Central have been serving many of the same customers," said president Robert T. Person, "CCP with electricity and our company with gas. By combining these services, greater efficiencies will result which will benefit our customers."[13] Stockholders of both companies voted almost unanimously to approve the combination. The merger was, in turn, approved by the Public Utilities Commission and was accomplished 29 December 1961. Central's 189 employees became part of the PSC staff.[14] Colorado Central Power Company's 42,151 electric customers located in south suburban cities of Littleton and Englewood were added to Public Service Company's 351,634 electric customers and 330,236 natural gas customers.

The time was right to acquire Colorado Central because the president of the company was approaching retirement and management had to be reorganized when he did. Colorado Central benefited from Public Service management and stock position. But, the most significant aspect of the merger was that it gave PSC a territory of high growth to the south and west--Littleton, Englewood, Golden and Evergreen. Had it not merged Colorado Central would have circumscribed PSC's operation.[15]

With extensive growth, Public Service Company executives decided that the corporation needed a larger corporate headquarters, In 1957, the company commissioned the architectural firm of Berne, Muchow, Baume and Polvnik to design a building. Construction began on 1 September 1959 and was completed late in 1961. The facade was made of natural red granite arranged in offset columns to create a vertical pattern. Inside, in addition to five elevators and a sophisticated heating and cooling system, every imaginable type of light fixture was included inside. All of this contributed to the 5600 kilowatts of electricity used by the building.[16] In 1962, fifty-one years after Mayor Speer pushed the button to turn on the lights at the old Denver Gas and Electric Building, another mayor, Richard Batterton, conducted a similar ceremony for a new twelve-story building at Fifteenth and Welton streets. The company received top honors from Downtown Denver, Inc. for making a "lasting contribution to the community with its new building."[17]

The economic boom kept Public Service Company engineers busy planning numerous construction projects. In 1961 the PSC Board of Directors approved plans for an additional 150,000 kilowatt generating unit at the Valmont Steam Electric Station near Boulder. The expansion was completed in three years.[18] Two large lakes used for cooling at the Valmont plant were always warm and attracted thousands of game birds, providing a particularly startling contrast between nature and technology. They became a popular wildlife refuge for both birds and animals.[19]

Two new steam generating units were also added to the Cherokee plant in North Denver, which with the existing two units, raised the total capacity to 710,000 kilowatts. Cherokee was the most efficient of PSC plants, producing more energy per ton of coal than any other. Nevertheless, it still consumed 150 tons of coal per hour and was one of the reasons the Public Service Company was the largest coal consumer in Colorado.[20]

The company added to its facilities on the Western Slope with the construction of a second 44,000 kilowatt unit at its Cameo plant in Grand Junction. Another addition was a 76-mile high-voltage transmission line from Cameo to Glenwood Springs as the first link in a new 230,000 volt line over the Continental Divide. Completed in 1967, with assistance from information gathered in the 1956 high altitude research at Leadville, the new line operated in conjunction with the Shoshone-Denver 115,000 volt line.[21]

One of Public Service Company's most innovative projects was the Cabin Creek hydroelectric system. Located four miles south of Georgetown, it included two dams and reservoirs with a pumping system between them. During hours of low power consumption, generally from 1:00 to 7:00 a.m., power from steam plants in Denver was used to operate the reversible pump-turbines to transfer as much as 326 million gallons of water from the lower reservoir to the upper reservoir through a 3600 foot tunnel. During high power demand the water of the upper reservoir was released through three hydroelectric generators to produce 324,000 kilowatts of electricity more efficiently than could the steam plants. Cabin Creek was designed to provide peaking power to supplement the output of the company's steam generating stations.[22]

At the November, 1967 dedication, L. M.

Robertson, engineering vice president, explained that the great advantage of Cabin Creek storage facility was the speed with which it could be put into action, less than fifteen minutes in an emergency. To bring a steam-electric plant up to full power from a cold start requires as much as two days. Illustrating the point, Robertson pushed a button and water immediately began flowing into the turbine. Within minutes the generator was at normal operating speed of 360 revolutions per minute.[23]

Cabin Creek's total generating capacity was 325,000 kilowatts making it the largest hydroelectric plant in the state and second only to the Cherokee coal-fired plant in output. The power was transmitted over a 35-mile double-circuit 230 kilovolt transmission line to Denver. It also interconnected with the Leadville line for backup service to the western part of the state.

The elevations of Cabin Creek's two reservoirs were 10,000 feet and 11,200 feet above sea level making it the highest pumped storage project in the United States.[24] Edison Electric Institute gave its highest award to Public Service Company of Colorado for Cabin Creek project, stating that it was "an outstanding and successful undertaking, involving courageous and ingenious concept engineering and construction under severe conditions of altitude, climate, and terrain . . ."[25] Pumped storage was a fairly new concept and many investor-owned utilities subsequently studied the project's operations for their own possible use.[26]

In mid-1965 the company completed a new computerized control center. The $394,000 "brain center" regulated the transmission of power from four generating plants and twenty-three substations. The computer kept track of all the power in the Colorado Power Pool, including the Colorado Springs Municipal Power Company, the Southern Colorado Power Company and two of the United States Bureau of Reclamation projects. All of these were interconnected and served as a mutual backup system. Having all the controls under one roof saved PSC an estimated $100,000 a year.[27]

Public Service continued to take pride in its street lighting program, and in 1968 a five-year project of converting all of Denver's street lighting to mercury vapor from incandescent was completed. The project required 4700 separate fixture replacements. Since this was the first major city to be completely lighted in this way the Denver Post proudly reported that Colorado's capital had become the brightest city in America.[28]

Almost a postscript to the 1960s was Public Service Company's operation of the Boulder bus system. Public Service Company had taken over the transit line as part of the 1927 franchise agreement. PSC tried to sell the system but there were no buyers. The company also offered to give it to the city of Boulder, but was turned down. Public Service Company operated the buses at a small loss, making up the difference in gas and electric rates. In 1958 when Boulderites complained about poor service to new suburbs the company added additional buses and raised fares.[29] In 1968 PSC added two more buses making a total of six to handle regular routes, rush hour and some charter service.

PSC was determined to get rid of the bus system when the Boulder franchise was renewed in 1968. The city of Boulder was very reluctant to assume the deficit of the bus operation. Only by more than a year of negotiations, delay of the franchise renewal, and the insistence of PSC did the city take some of the responsibility. Boulder agreed to absorb half the losses of the operation. However, it would not be until the 1970s when the Regional Transportation

District (RTD) came into being that the company completely disposed of the Boulder bus system.[30]

Robert T. Person took over the helm of Public Service Company when John Loiseau retired at the age of 68 in 1959. Person had started his career in the utility business in 1935 at the Albuquerque Gas and Electric Company, working on a part-time basis before graduating from the University of New Mexico in 1936. His father, Howard A. Person, had spent the bulk of his life in the utility business. It was the close relationship with his father that inspired Robert T. Person to work for a utility. (He too passed on the tradition to one of his sons, Robert T. Person, Jr. who works for Public Service Company of Colorado.) Because of his father's influence Robert Person was exposed to various public utility leaders and concepts of utility management which were to his advantage.[31]

In 1940 Person moved to the Pueblo Gas and Fuel Company as its commercial manager. The Pueblo company was struggling at the time. It was three years behind on its revenue bonds and was unable to issue dividends. Person was asked to serve on the company board of directors at the age of twenty-five, an outstanding learning opportunity for a young man. The board reorganized Pueblo Gas and Fuel Company and the company began to progress.

Person left the company during World War II to serve in the Navy, spending seventeen months in the Pacific as a navigation officer.[32] At the war's end he returned to Pueblo, and in 1947 was named vice president and general manager of Pueblo Gas and Fuel Company which had, in 1943, become a subsidiary of Public Service Company of Colorado.[33] In 1953 Loiseau asked Person to come to Public Service in Denver as manager of advertising and publicity. Four years later he was elected to the board of directors, and was named executive vice president in 1958. A year later he became president.

Robert Person considered himself a generalist, stressing the importance of a balanced company. His background provided a good foundation for such a perspective, since he had been involved in almost every facet of the utility business, working as a laborer between terms of college, and then holding several jobs before being selected for a policy-making position at the age of twenty-five. Early on he realized that managers who specialized in one or another aspects of the business had difficulty making good overall decisions. For example, a manager who thought only in terms of finances and ignored sales might eventually not have any finances with which to work. Person strove not only for balance but also for excellence in operations, engineering, financial, marketing sales, and every other function.[34]

An important role of an executive, Robert Person believed, was to make every employee feel essential to the organization. To do that, he was convinced that a manager must have a clear understanding of goals and objectives, to communicate them well, and to keep reminding the organization of them. He was cognizant of the fact that there was a tendency for objectives to become fragmented while a company endeavored to develop new methods and techniques, and to improve production, efficiency and service. Person reminded his managers that an effective leader kept everyone working together despite the challenges.[34]

Striving for excellence through training was an important goal of the new president and one established long ago by his predecessors. Before becoming president he believed strongly the importance of developing competent managers for the future. Person was somewhat concerned that the low birth rate during the Depression might result in a shortage of 40 to 55 year olds in the 1980s and, therefore, a lack of managers. Since three people might be asked to do what four did before the choice of people for management positions and training of them was crucial.[35] He listed six items to help insure future managers:

> Aggressive recruiting in all categories to assure men of sufficient caliber to meet our needs.
>
> Constant evaluation of our organizations so that an accurate personnel inventory will factually and objectively reveal the specific training needs of our organization.
>
> Provide the leadership and management training vehicles to meet these needs. First through internal training programs and, secondly, through the generalized academic areas available either by correspondence or residence instruction.
>
> Keep your supervisory forces well informed at all times, assign them ever-increasing responsibility and allow them to participate in and carry out policy decisions.
>
> Encourage them to participate in community affairs and recognize their achievement in this field. By so doing they will not only broaden and improve their own abilities in the human relations field, but they will also make a material contribution to your corporate public relations.
>
> Last but not least, do not overlook training opportunities in the nebulous areas of the humanities--such as human relations, public speaking, philosophy and the fine arts. While we might disagree on the degree of importance the liberal arts play in decision making and administration, I'm sure we'd all agree they are a factor in broadening the viewpoint of the so-called well-rounded executive personality. 36

As manager of Education and Employee Communications, and Advertising and Publicity, before becoming executive vice president, Person stressed methods of communication as well as the ideas to be communicated. He was an effective public speaker with an ability to express his thoughts clearly. When asked a question, he was quite skilled at turning the answer into a positive statement about his company or the utility industry. It was a valuable quality in a business that must live with considerable adverse publicity. He once remarked,

> [we may have] the most efficient electric power system in the world, but it will do us precious little good if the public attitude is such that we have to build and operate that system at someone else's behest or dictate.37

In a speech given to celebrate the sixteenth anniversary of the founding of the Public Information Program (PIP) for electric companies Person repeated his strong commitment to enlightening the public. He believed that the public relations departments of utilities was such an important function that it should be an integral part of a company's decision-making structure. A public relations person, as a spokesman for the company, must acquaint himself with the engineering, financial, legal, accounting and other aspects of the business. If he expected to be taken seriously as a policy counselor he must perform as a company executive, and be familiar with and knowledgeable about all phases of the company.

The information manager, to be effective, must understand management's goals and act as a filter for proposed policies and programs, and be able to explain to management how the public is likely to react to a given idea or course of action. The public relations manager had to be familiar with public opinion in order to tailor information about the enterprise to the changing moods of the people. Management was primarily concerned with formulating policy and being guided by it, while the public relations man was the link between the executive and the public.[38]

In many of his speeches Person used the word "power" as a framework to illustrate his points. "P" represented people and a preference for the free enterprise system. "O" stood for opportunity and optimism. "W" meant hard work in cooperation with others. "E" was for excellence. And, "R" signified research, reminding managers that they had to plan for the future and not be caught up in day-to-day details.[39] He was also fond of ending his speeches with a quote from Englishman Edmund Burke: "The public interest requires doing today the things that men of intelligence and good will would wish, five or ten years hence, had been done."[40]

Person was also committed to social responsibilities in the community, such as metropolitan planning, resource conservation and environmental protection.[41] The economic prosperity of the community went hand in hand with the well-being of the company.[42] The range of Robert T. Person's community and professional activities was broad. He served as director of several organizations: the American Gas Association, the Advanced Reactor Development Association, Atomic Industrial Forum, Breeder Reactor Corporation, and the Colorado Association of Commerce and Industry. Person was president of the Edison Electric Institute (the major national trade association for utilities), and also chairman of the National Association of Electric Companies (the legislative branch of the industry which eventually merged with EEI). He was on the board of the Federal Reserve Bank, Denver Branch and served on the Federal Reserve Bank of Kansas City, the last two years as chairman. He served on the board of directors of the Denver Chamber of Commerce from 1958 to 1961 and was its president in 1961-1962. Other community organizations such as the Central City Opera House

Association, the Colorado State Fair Commission, the Denver Symphony Orchestra, and the Denver Museum of Natural History have also benefited from his knowledge and leadership skills. Robert T. Person was named "Outstanding Jaycee Boss of 1957," the American Legion (L-C-W Post No. 1) "Man of the Year" in 1964, and the recipient of Regis' "First Citizen" award for distinguished citizenship.[43]

In 1966, Public Service Company started to plan for renewing its twenty-year franchise with Denver. The company began discussing a new proposal with city officials. In response to questions from the press about changes the city wished to make, Mayor Thomas Currigan replied that Denver would consider the possibility of purchasing the Denver facilities in order to better serve its residents. The Denver Post conjectured that Currigan's statement was a negotiating ploy to strengthen the city's bargaining position[44] and nothing much was heard of the idea thereafter.

Mayor Currigan appointed a four-man committee to review the franchise and negotiate the best contract for the city. He also hired a Washington, D.C. utilities consultant to assist the committee with technical matters. Denver was short of revenue and one objective in negotiating a new franchise was to increase the franchise fee. To do this, the consultant wanted to determine how much more city property PSC used in 1967 than in 1947, and to estimate how much the company's revenue would grow in the upcoming twenty-year franchise period.[45] The Washington consultant knew that he had to achieve a balance of protecting the city without "unduly burdening the utility or impairing its ability to grow and competitively attract utility-using industries to Denver."[46]

Each franchise renewal, first in 1906, then 1927, 1947 and 1967 illustrated the evolution of the company into a more responsible corporate citizen. It was, perhaps, the past misdeeds of utilities, including PSC and its predecessors, that created social pressure forcing a beneficial franchise. No longer would citizens tolerate the wheeling and dealing that had gone on in previous franchise renewals. Business in general had changed from the robber baron era to one in which companies practiced social responsibility if they expected to survive in the community.

The committee and the consultant were successful in negotiating some important changes in the franchise and when the Denver City Council considered the new proposal in November, 1966, it was well accepted and easily approved.[47] In the absence of any organized opposition the Denver voters followed suit and overwhelmingly approved the franchise on 7 February 1967.

Bargaining by the city brought about several changes in the new proposal. First, company under the old franchise paid three percent franchise tax on only the first $2,500 collected annually from a customer for each kind of services (city lighting was not included). In the new contract the amount was raised to $10,000, plus two percent thereafter. The company, therefore, contributed a larger amount of money to the cost of operating the city and provided a considerable difference to the city coffers.[48]

Second, the company agreed to buy 4000 ornamental street lighting poles which had been installed in downtown Denver. It also agreed to keep the price of city lighting at its present rate even though costs of producing electricity had risen.[49] The company wanted to help preserve the capital city's reputation as a well-lighted city,[50] which added a positive element to the company's image.

Third, the new proposal required the company to install and operate hydroelectric generators on the Denver water system when requested by the Water Board to do so. Furthermore, if the company installed a generator on Water Board property the Water Board had the right to buy the generator, at a depreciated cost, any time it wanted to.[51]

Fourth, the franchise acknowledged that the Colorado Public Utilities Commission regulated rates and refunds rather than the taxpayers. This was a change from the 1947 franchise resulting from amending the city charter in 1953 and the state constitution in 1954. All public utilities, even those in home rule cities, were put under the jurisdiction of the PUC.[52]

Fifth, the 1967 franchise provided for a policy of city beautification. The company was required to put newly constructed electric distribution lines under ground in residential areas if it was required by subdivision rules. This was a minor concession to environmentalists who were beginning to put pressure on the company at that time.[53]

The 1965 interruption of electric power from the blackout in the northeast United States, along with nuclear power discussions brought to a head issues such as electric reliability and social consequences of producing vast amounts of power. Although the less populated Rocky Mountain West was not in immediate danger from a blackout, utilities in every area began to question traditional dependence on energy. The general populace, and environmentalists in particular, wondered about the price society paid for its insatiable energy appetite.

Scientists projected that during the fourth quarter of the century energy demands in the United States would double its present usage, and world wide this figure might even be three times the amount at the end of the century as it was in the late 1960s. These predictions prompted utilities to discover ways to find resources to produce more energy, as well as transport them safely, and dispose of wastes. In addition, power producers had to find land for electric generating stations and transmission lines which was increasingly less available and more expensive. However, the greatest challenge was not to discover resources and land, and to dispose of the refuse, but to do it with the least damage to humanity.[54]

As the utilities built more and more power plants in the 1960s, environmentalists became vocal in publicizing the effects of pollution on the quality of life. Anti-establishment and anti-business sentiments arose during a decade in which people began to push big businesses to reform in a number of ways including their seeming lack of respect for the well being of the environment. Utility officials responded to these environmental critics with an effort to take care of the environment as long as they did not have to change too much too fast at the expense of profit.[55]

Although the automobile was the chief contributor to air pollution, industry was second, and power plants were responsible for about fourteen percent of air pollutant emissions in the 1960s.[56] Because fossil-fueled steam plants produced 76 percent of electric generation in the 1960s, the sulfur oxides, nitrogen oxides, and particulate matter that they discharged played a significant part in fouling the air.[57]

Even though western power plants burned low sulfur coal, air pollution was still a problem in Colorado because of its high altitude and temperature inversions. The burning of fossil fuels also generated tremendous residues of ash which had to be disposed of The Public Service company found a practical way to get rid of the mounds of ash. Fly ash was separated from coarse ash and sold to masoners to mix with concrete which reduced the amount of cement and made the concrete stronger, lighter, and cheaper.[58] Mining of the coal also presented environmental problems, particularly surface mining which damaged the landscape, filled streams with acid run-off and produced enormous hills of low grade rock. Underground mining created acid runoff and rock dumps.[59]

Hydroelectric plants, although probably the least environmentally damaging way of producing electricity, still had adverse affects. These plants changed the velocity and seasonal flow cycles of streams and increased the surface evaporation from reservoirs which was a serious problem in arid areas. In addition, silting behind dams decreased the amount of water that could be stored. All hydroelectric projects affected the aquatic environment in one way or another.[60]

Transmission lines were eyesores, particularly in areas of natural beauty, and the utilities were criticized for their seeming lack of sensitivity to the visual problems.[61] High-tension transmission lines caused a particular problem in the West where predatory birds, such as eagles and hawks, with their tremendous wingspans were electrocuted by landing on a post and touching two lines with their wings. As a preventive measure the Public Service Company installed special high perches on poles to provide the birds a safe resting spot and won an award for protecting them. At the White House Conference on National Beauty in May, 1965 conferees discussed putting power transmission lines underground, but the twenty to one cost ratio of underground to above-ground wires and an estimated cost of $220 billion nationwide was prohibitive. The term "beautility" was coined about this time as a common objective to beautify the surroundings of transmission lines and utility plants through the use of underground lines and extensive landscaping.[62]

Despite its one-time reputation for healthy air, Denver developed a serious pollution problem with its concentration of population and industry in the Platte Valley. Public Service Company has attempted to help by retrofitting anti-pollution devices on its plants, and was successful in removing 75 to 85 percent of the particulants.[63] In 1963 the company announced a $2.5 million program to install electrostatic precipitators on the Zuni, Cherokee, Arapahoe and Valmont plants. These preciptators were designed to collect extremely fine particles. The flue gas passed through an electric field in a series of plates, taking on a negative charge causing them to move to the electrified plate. The ash built up on the plates and was periodically shaken off into bins.[64] Although the electrostatic precipitators helped they were not 98%

effective as predicted,[65] and in 1968 the company hired the Denver Research Institute at the University of Denver to improve the performance.[66]

In 1963 Public Service was using sixty percent coal and forty percent natural gas, and each year the percentage of coal increased, making it more important for the company to reduce the plant pollution. The company spent millions of dollars to lessen the pollution problem.[67] Denver awarded PSC its "Clean Air Award" in 1963 for the low pollution performance of one of the Arapahoe Plant generating units.[68] By 1968 it had invested five million dollars over a six-year period on antipollution equipment. PSC was also careful to point out that its dispersal plumes from cooling towers were composed almost entirely of water vapor not harmful to the environment.[69]

The decision of utilities to spend millions on protecting the environment was an effect of the pressure from environmentalists in the 1960s which would intensify in the following decade. The fact that utilities polluted the environment in generating energy was only one of the industry's problems. A more philosophical perplexity was that utilities provided energy which was the foundation on which economic expansion was based. Affluent societies were disrupting the balance of nature, but people seemed unwilling to institute a policy of no growth to diminish damage to the environment. Most people believed that their jobs and material well being were dependent on an expanding economy which relied on cheap, plentiful energy.

Both business and society grappled with questions such as, when do the adverse effects of energy demand outweigh social benefits? The use of energy had played an important part in shaping society, now it seemed to be mishaping it. In the more developed Western nations people used air conditioners, clothes dryers, hair dryers and other luxuries with little consideration for the adverse effects of energy production on society. In power-poor countries developing energy sources were essential for the advancement of third world cultures. Society had to face up to choices about the benefits and detriments of energy usage and also determine who should make those decisions.

Was it the responsibility of a utility, which was in the business of making money from the sale of gas and electricity, to decide how much energy is good or bad, or is it the people served who should collectively regulate businesses to balance power production with profit? If society decided that energy consumption should be limited, should the amount of energy used be determined by the federal government, state or local entities or people themselves. At any level it was realistic to assume that politics will play a part in skewing the fairness of any policy.

Environmental concerns caused delays in construction and although protecting ecosystems the delays and modifications lead to more expensive energy costs. Overuse of energy caused new plants and lines to be built or--as peak usage time to put in operation older, less efficient systems that are used for back up but pollute and waste more. A balance had to be achieved in what is protected and the value of what is saved. In many cases environmentalists made valuable contributions; in some cases they added to costs and delays for very little worthy results and almost immobilized energy production.

The United States Congress influenced by the rising voices of those concerned with a proper balance in nature enacted legislation in the 1960s some of which affected the utility industry. The National Wilderness Preservation Act set standards for preserving wilderness areas, making it much more difficult, if not impossible, to develop resources or cross such land. The Motor Vehicle Air Pollution Control Act of 1965 was the first law to control automobile emissions, and fostered an argument between mobile and stationary pollution sources as to which was worse. The Water Quality Act of 1965 and the Clean Water restoration Act of 1966 sought to clean up, and preserve waterways in the United States, including those used by hydroelectric and steam generating plants. In 1968 Congress passed the Radiation Control for Health and Safety Act in response to the expanding use of nuclear reactors for power generation.

In 1969 Congress enacted the National Environmental Policy Act, a significant law because it required action by various federal agencies to develop positive plans to improve the environment.[70] Finally, the Environmental Protection Agency, created by Congress in 1970, was an agency which would have considerable authority over the construction of power facilities. The Colorado Legislature followed suit in 1963 and 1964 with pollution control measures, and an even stronger law in 1966.[71]

The proposition of cutting back on energy use had its difficult aspects. Less energy would change Americans' lifestyle. For example, many argued that air conditioning, although a luxury, made workers more efficient, productive, and safer. Just as electrically powered vacuums and washing machines lessened the time women had to spend on housework early in the century, more sophisticated technology such as microwave ovens, clothes dryers, and computers now helped them balance the dual role of homemaker and paid employee or head of a household. Were women willing to leave the market place? Could they?

If the government were to decide to demand that people reduce their energy consumption laws could be passed to ration energy to require appliances and machinery to be built to minimize energy use, to build homes, offices, and plants that are energy efficient. The government could also impose a tax on energy to discourage use. Each method to save energy would have its drawbacks and different economic groups would suffer from each of the policies. Laws might make it a privilege of the rich to use energy saving devices when the poor might need them more. Reducing energy too quickly would hurt the utility industry which in capital assets was sixty percent larger than any other industry in the United States in 1960. Although changes can be demanded slowly, forced rapid changes not only effect the industry but the entire American economy as well.[72]

Thorny issues like these compelled utilities to search for alternative methods of producing energy. One in which people could use as much electricity as they wished, and as much as the industry could convince them to use, but one that would let man and nature exist harmoniously. What ever the alternative, the costs and benefits must be considered. That would prove true with one of their alternatives, the new technology of nuclear energy.

Thus, the decade of the 1960s was an era of a growing social consciousness on the part of the Public Service Company of Colorado, and an increasing environmental consciousness on the part of those concerned with what seemed to be an imbalance in nature. PSC was viewed as doing a creditable job developing more social responsibility, but had only just begun to respond to the environmental challenges as the decade ended.

NOTES--CHAPTER 14

1 Lines, (February, 1960), 11.

2 Robert G. Athearn, The Coloradans (Albuquerque: University of New Mexico Press, 1976), p. 321.

3 Lines, (October, 1962), 2.

4 Lines, (July, 1960), 2.

5 Colorado Public Utilities Commission Decision No. 54367, Statement and Findings, 27 May 1960, p. 8.

6 Ibid., p. 8.

7 Ibid, p. 2.

8 Ibid., pp. 10-11.

9 Ibid., p. 13.

10 Ibid., pp. 47-49.

11 Denver Post, 29 May 1960, p. 1.

12 Denver Post, 5 February 1961, p. 3A.

13 Denver Post, 22 November 1961, p. 22.

14 Ibid., and Lines, (December, 1961) and the Rocky Mountain News, 26 November 1961, p. 18.

15 Interview with Robert T. Person, 22 December 1985, Denver Post, 8 August 1961, p. 1, 17 September 1961, p. 5D, 29 December 1961, p. 11, and 11 July 1963, p. 2.

16 PSC 1957 Annual Report (1958), 7-13 and Denver Post 1 March 1962, p. 74.

17 Denver Post, 24 May 1963, p. 3. American National Bank was a dual recipient that year.

18 Lines, (January, 1961), 5.

19 Lines, (March, 1960), 1.

20 Denver Post, 14 February 1965, p. 3.

21 PSC 1960 Annual Report (1961), p. 6 and Robert T. Person, speech delivered to the Leadville Chamber of Commerce, 9 January 1965.

22 Electrical West, CXXXII (April, 1965), 46.

23 Denver Post, 26 November 1967, p. 47.

24 Rocky Mountain News, 7 March 1963, p. 5 and Electrical West CXXXI (August, 1964), 29.

25 Denver Post, 6 June 1968, p. 27.

26 Lines, (April, 1963), 7.

27 Denver Post, 6 December 1965, p. 50.

28 Denver Post, 23 August 1968, p. 4J.

29 Denver Post, 2 April 1958, p. 21, 16 April 1958, p. 19, and 4 April 1968, p. 42.

30 Robert T. Person, interview 22 December 1985

31 Robert T. Person, interview, 20 September 1984.

32 Lines, (December, 1958), 5 and (January, 1959), 4.

33 Robert T. Person, interview, 20 September 1984 and Lines, (January, 1959), 4.

34 Robert T. Person, interview, 20 September 1984.

35 Robert T. Person, "People Engineering," speech delivered to the 18th Annual Round Table Conference, Industrial Relations Committee, Edison Electric Institute, 27 September 1965, Chicago, Illinois, p. 1.

36 Robert T. Person, "Tomorrow's Management," Rocky Mountain Electrical Convention, Colorado Springs, Colorado, 14 October 1957, p. 18.

37 Robert T. Person, speech delivered to the Electric Companies Public Information Program 1965 Workshop Conference, p. 5

38 Ibid., p. 6.

39 Speech by Robert T. Person, for the Eighteenth Management Conference, Des Moines, IA., 4 October 1965.

40 Speech by Robert T. Person, Electric Companies Public Information Program, 1963 Workshop Conference, p. 16.

41 Speech by Robert T. Person, for Public Information Program, p. 6.

42 Robert T. Person, address before the New York Financial Members, no date, p. 2.

43 Robert T. Person, 1984 resume.

44 Editorial, Denver Post, 30 March 1966, p. 20.

45 Kosh-Glasman Associates, Inc., "Report to the City and County of Denver, Regarding Renewal of the Franchise of Public Service Company of Colorado (Washington, DC: Public Utilities Consultants, 1 January 1967), p. 6.

46 Ibid. p. 58.

47 Denver Post, 29 November 1966, p. 15.

48 Kosh-Glasman Association, Inc. "Report to the City and County of Denver,", p. 6 and Denver Post, 11 December 1966, p. 1G:

Public Service Company's Franchise Tax

1947	$ 232.876	1967	$1,814,900
1948	467,236	1968	1,880,000
1949	546,608	1969	1,947,800
1950	577,992	1970	2,018,500
1951	635,290	1971	2,092,400
1952	690,717	1972	2,169,500

1953	727,476	1973	2.249,800
1954	756,646	1974	2,333,800
1955	831,491	1975	2,421,400
1956	960,645	1976	2,513,000
1957	1,014,410	1977	2,608,500
1958	1,083,572	1978	2,708,500
1959	1,134,481	1979	2,812,600
1960	1,171,943	1980	2,921,500
1961	1,204,237	1981	3,035,600
1962	1,269,941	1982	3,153,700
1963	1,251,106	1983	3,277,700
1964	1,325,589	1984	3,407,300
1965	1,341,626	1985	3,542,600
1966	1,383,200	1986	3,683,800
Total	$18,607,082	Total	$52,592,300

[49] "Street Lighting Agreement" in Kosh-Glassman, Associates, Report to the City and County of Denver, pp. 94-105.

[50] Denver Post, December 11, 1966, p. 1G.

[51] Section IX of the 1967 Electric, Gas and Steam Franchise of the Public Service Company of Colorado, (Public Service Company, Denver, Colorado).

[52] Ibid. and Kosh and Glasman, p. 58

[53] Denver Post, 11 December 1966, p. 1G.

[54] Chauncey Starr, "Energy and Power, the Role of Energy in Human Life: Past, Present, and Future," Energy and Power, (San Francisco, CA: W. H. Freemen Co., 1971), p. 3.

[55] John Davenport, "Industry Starts the Big Cleanup." Fortune Magazine LXXXI, February, 1970, 118.

[56] Wilfrid Bach, Atmospheric Pollution (New York: McGraw Hill Book Co., 1972), p. 3 and Amos Turk, Jonathan Turk, and Janet T. Wittes, Ecology, Pollution, Environment (Philadelphia, London,, Toronto: W. B. Saunders Company, 1972), p. 79.

[57] Ibid., p. 5.

[58] Denver Post, 17 June 1965, p. 56.

[59] The Association of the Bar of the City of New

York Special Committee on Electric Power and the Environment, Electricity and the Environment: The Reform of Legal Institutions, (St. Paul, MN: West Publishing Co., 1972), pp. 28-29.

60 New York Bar, Electricity and the Environment, p. 32.

61 Ibid., p. 43.

62 Leonard S. Hyman, America's Electric Utilities: Past, Present and Future (Arlington, VA: Public Utilities Reports, Inc.), p. 30.

63 Denver Post, 27 January 1962, p. 1.

64 Rocky Mountain News, 2 November 1964, p. 30 and Air Pollution in the Denver Area, p. 20.

65 Public Service Company of Colorado: Providing Energy for More than a Century, (Denver: Public Service Company of Colorado, no date), p. 24.

66 PSC 1968 Annual Report (1969), p. 8.

67 Denver Post, 27 January 1963, p. 1 and Air Pollution in the Denver Area, p. 18.

68 PSC 1968 Annual Report (1969), p. 8.

69 Air Pollution in the Denver Area, (Denver, Public Service Company of Colorado, no date), p. 18.

70 W. Elliot Brownlee, Dynamics of Ascent: A History of the American Economy (New York: Alfred A Knopf, 1974), p. 364.

71 Air Pollution in the Denver Area, p. 24.

72 New York Bar Association, Electricity and the Environment, p. 28.

CHAPTER 15

NUCLEAR POWER AND PUBLIC SERVICE COMPANY

"GOOD NEWS TODAY" read the front page headline of the Denver Post on 14 March 1965. Public Service had announced its intention to build the world's most advanced nuclear power plant in Colorado.[1] The company had begun to participate in nuclear research in 1954 when Congress passed the Atomic Energy Act to allow civilian access to information about nuclear energy. John E. Loiseau, president of the company at the time, expressed great interest in and hope for the peaceful use of atomic energy.[2] He said:

> Our long established policy is to keep abreast of all technological developments so that our customers may have the advantage of the most economic source of electric energy which we can obtain.[3]

Radiation technology dates back to the mid-1890s when the X-ray and radioactivity were discovered. The study of nuclear physics began in 1905 when Albert Einstein, one of the greatest intellects in history, advanced the theory that mass and energy were equivalent. Einstein, born in Munich, Germany on 14 March 1879, was an indifferent student as a youth student and showed little promise of becoming a famous theoretical physicist. Encouraged by his uncles, however, he entered the prestigious Polytechnic Academy in Zurich, and four years later was awarded a Ph.D.[4]

Einstein was a confirmed pacifist and vocal zionist. When Hitler rose to power in Germany in the 1930s life became very dangerous for Einstein, and so he emigrated to America to accept a position at the new Institute for Advanced Studies in Princeton, New Jersey in 1933. There he continued his research on various projects, one of which was nuclear fission. When physicist Lisa Meitner, using earlier discoveries of other scientists, first demonstrated the splitting of a uranium atom in 1939 scientists realized that a controlled chain reaction of splitting atoms could cause an enormous explosion. Knowing that war was close at hand Einstein was aware that Hitler's scientists might also discover the explosive powers of nuclear fission, and feared that it could lead an weapon which could threaten the free world.

Einstein wrote to President Franklin D. Roosevelt encouraging him to start United States scientists in research on an atomic bomb.[5] Roosevelt agreed, and shortly thereafter, in 1942, the United States War Department established the Manhattan Engineering Project to create superexplosives. Under the project, physicist Enrico Fermi set up a controlled chain reaction in the first nuclear reactor at the University of Chicago. Although Einstein's name has been linked with the atom bomb, he did not work on the first project, nor did he know of its success until the bomb was dropped on Japan.[6]

After the end of World War II the United State government continued to develop atomic energy. Military leaders were interested in improving nuclear technology to produce more sophisticated weapons, while many scientists saw uses of uranium for peaceful purposes. Government leaders soon realized that engaging in a nuclear program for non-military purposes provided an acceptable rationale for spending millions of dollars for research.[7] For that reason the government in 1946 established a national policy of nuclear development for the maximum welfare of the country.[8]

When the House of Representatives passed the Atomic Energy Act of 1946 (McMahon Bill) creating the Atomic Energy Commission, it gave the United States government the exclusive right to develop nuclear energy. The Atomic Energy Commission was established to oversee and control all nuclear activity, with the responsibility to protect the public's health and safety from any dangers inherent in nuclear materials.[9]

Private energy development did not take place until a new Atomic Energy Act was adopted in 1954. This permitted government subsidies for the private construction and ownership of nuclear reactors. Until that time, utility companies were reluctant to invest money in an unproven technology that carried a potential for serious accidents. The government's willingness to assume some of the financial and safety risks made it more feasible for private business to participate in the development of nuclear power.[10]

Public Service Company of Colorado was one of nine companies to form the nonprofit Rocky Mountain Nuclear Power Study Group in 1954 for investigating the potential of nuclear energy for generating electric power.[11] Each of the nine companies (Arizona Public Service Company; Ebasco Services, Inc. of New York; Fluor Corporation, Ltd., of Los Angeles; Idaho Power Company; Minnesota Mining and Manufacturing (3M) Company; Phillips Petroleum Company; Riley Stoker Company of Massachusetts; Utah Power and Light; and PSC) contributed $5000 to pay for the initial costs of research. The newness of the technology made research essential to determine which reactor designs merited further research and development.

The Edison Electric Institute, a trade organization of electric companies, also set up a task force comprised of leaders in both the utility business and the atomic energy field to study energy in 1956. During their investigation into the various types of nuclear power plants throughout the world the study group disseminated information about reactor types and designs to help companies which were considering entering the nuclear field.[12]

President John E. Loiseau commented about Public Service Company's involvement in the research, saying it was not as interested in fuel saving benefits because it was located in a coal-rich area, as it was in making a worthwhile contribution to the technology. The investigation into the use of nuclear energy for power plants was consistent with the company's long established efforts to develop new technology through research and development.[13]

The United States government had done most of its research with water-cooled reactors, but a gas-cooled system attracted the attention of the Rocky Mountain Nuclear Power Study Group. In 1958 Public Service Company, with seven other western utilities, formed the Rocky Mountain-Pacific Nuclear Power Research Group which entered into a contract with the General Atomic Division of General Dynamics Corporation to sponsor a high-temperature gas-cooled, graphite-moderated reactor (HTGR) design.[14]

The principal difference between fossil and nuclear power plants is the way in which the steam is produced. In a conventional steam plant coal or oil is burned to produce steam. In a nuclear plant the furnace is replaced by a nuclear reactor, and heat is produced by fission. In most nuclear reactors water is used as a coolant to remove the heat energy from the reactor core so that it can be used for producing electricity.

In a high temperature gas-cooled reactor helium is used as the coolant. The gas is blown through the reactor emerging at 1,400 degrees Fahrenheit. It is then pumped through the steam generator circulating around the water pipes to produce steam at 1,000 degrees Fahrenheit and 2,400 pounds per square inch of pressure. The superheated, high-pressure steam is then condensed and pumped back to the steam generator to begin another cycle.[15] The cooling water is in a closed cycle to be reused after being sent through a cooling tower.

An HTGR was appealing for several reasons. Helium transfers heat better than water, and, therefore allows nuclear reaction to occur at a higher temperature than a water-cooled reactor. The higher the temperature of the reaction the more efficient it is to produce power. It was estimated that a high-temperature, gas-cooled reactor could convert forty percent of the potential heat of the fuel into electrical energy, which is approximately the same rate as fossil fuel plants and more efficient than conventional light water reactors. Another advantage of a high-temperature reactor is the use of graphite, which increases its strength at high temperatures. The uranium is encased in graphite cladding to act as a neutron moderator and as a sufficiently strong container for the fissionable material. Helium, the gas used in the reactor, has an additional advantage over water in its ability to remove heat from the core without slowing down the neutrons. Helium has other advantages over water in that is inert and will not react chemically with any structural material or with steam, water or air, nor can it become radioactive.[16]

Later in 1958 The Rocky Mountain-Pacific group joined with other companies throughout the country to establish another non-profit organization, High

Temperature Reactor Development Associates (HTRDA), to develop a helium-cooled fast-breeder nuclear reactor prototype. The HTRDA submitted a proposal to the Atomic Energy Commission in response to legislation passed by Congress calling for the development of a high temperature gas-cooled, graphite-moderated power reactor.[17] Fifty-three utilities planned to share in the costs of construction of the prototype plant which was to be built in Pennsylvania. The Philadelphia Electric Company, on behalf of the whole group submitted a proposal to build a small, 40,000 kilowatt, high temperature, gas-cooled nuclear power plant at Peach Bottom, Pennsylvania. This new group entered into an agreement with the General Atomic Division of General Dynamics Corporation to carry on its research and development at Peach Bottom cooperatively.[18]

As Peach Bottom was being built, simultaneous testing on the plant by General Dynamics was extremely positive, proving the theoretical predictions that scientists had made. Those predictions were that the reactor would provide an efficient heat source with an adequate shutdown margin during the core life, and that it would produce a steady power output with strong built-in safety devices.[19] Public Service Company was the lead company in the Advanced Reactor Development

Associates (ARDA) which launched studies to determine the feasibility of building a commercial HTGR nuclear plant eight times larger than the one at Peach Bottom. The experience gained from membership in these two nuclear groups led to the PSC's decision to build a nuclear plant in Colorado.

The Colorado plant was to be built under the Atomic Energy Commission's cooperative power reactor demonstration program.[20] An agreement signed by the AEC, Public Service Company, and General Dynamics, the contractor and plant operator, stated that any of the three organizations could back out if Peach Bottom failed to operate properly for a period of one thousand hours over nine months.[21] Glen Seaborg, chairman of the AEC, said that building a nuclear power plant to demonstrate the importance of peaceful atomic power was part of the Atomic Energy Commission's long-range plan. He considered it a necessary research and development project "for providing demonstration of technical performance and reliability and economics of large high temperature, gas cooled reactors."[22] Public Service Company contributed $45.8 million of its own money and received $47.3 in a government research and development grant, an additional $6 million from the government was to be used to purchase fuel to run the reactor.[24]

After the Atomic Energy Commission approved the funds, Public Service Company began a search for a site for the proposed 330,000 kilowatt nuclear plant. The company found a 1600-acre piece of land in Platteville, 33 miles north of Denver near the confluence of the St. Vrain Creek and South Platte River, ideally located to serve the Denver customers, who were the bulk of the population served by the company. There was convenient transportation nearby and the land had an adequate supply of water.[24] The site was close to the old Fort St. Vrain which was built in 1837 during the fur trapping era, and named after two brothers, Marcellin and Ceran St. Vrain, who operated a fur trading post. When fur trapping disappeared the fort became a general store, and then later during Colorado Territory days a county seat and post office.[25]

Public Service Company's plant, named Fort St. Vrain, was a larger version of the Peach Bottom prototype. Heat was produced by fission in the reactor utilizing a uranium-thorium fuel cycle. Graphite was used for the moderator, fuel cladding, core structure, and reflector, and helium was the primary coolant. Fort St. Vrain was designed with a conventional turbine generator utilizing superheated steam at 2400 pounds of pressure per square inch, and 1000 degrees Fahrenheit.[26] The plant, scheduled to open in 1970 or 1971, would be the first commercial-sized nuclear installation to take advantage of high steam temperature and pressure, generating more power per pound of fuel than any commercial nuclear plant operating in the United States.[27]

Robert T. Person spoke with pride when he enumerated the benefits of the nuclear plant to Colorado. Construction of the ninety-five million dollar reactor[28] began early in 1968, employing three to four hundred people and using as many suppliers from the state as possible. The state and local governments received taxes on the construction material and equipment. This innovative effort in the nuclear field attracted world-wide attention to the state and promoted efforts to bring scientific companies to Colorado. Person felt that the plant's most important contribution would be to provide continued dependable and economical supplies of power to present and future residential, commercial and industrial customers.[29] United States Senator Gordon Allott, a Republican from Colorado, praised "the vision and planning of this progressive Colorado utility and its management team."[30]

Reports in newspapers indicated the early positive response Colorado had for a nuclear plant. "The world's most modern electricity generating plant . . . will be built 33 miles north of Denver near Platteville in Weld County,"[31] exclaimed the Rocky Mountain News. "The spotlight of nuclear science has swung sharply into focus on Colorado"[32] limned a Post editorial. The Atomic Energy Commission announced that it would close its own power-plant experiment with a medium gas-cooled reactor at Oak Ridge National Laboratory in Tennessee, because private technology had surpassed the Oak Ridge experiment and represented the trend of the future.[33]

"To Colorado now, the United States electric industry looks for the next step after Peach Bottom," said a Denver Post editorial, "a step which ultimately should lead to million kilowatt high temperature gas cooled reactor plants in large centers of the population."[34] Public Service Company's zealous public relations department did their part to insure an enthusiastic reception. Within a year of announcing the project the speakers bureau had explained the nuclear story to six thousand people at 118 meetings of civic, technical and academic groups.[35]

President Robert T. Person had appeared before the Joint Committee of Congress on Atomic Energy in 1965 to explain the Public Service nuclear plant proposal to the committee in support of the forty million dollar appropriation request. A year later he returned to bring the committee up to date, describing the research into, and acquisition of the site at Platteville. Person also apprised the committee of developments at Peach Bottom which Public Service Company was carefully monitoring.

At the time of his statement Peach Bottom was behind schedule and was not expected to generate electricity by its target date of 15 September 1965. Person reminded the committee of the provision in the agreement that allowed any of the three participants in Fort St. Vrain to withdraw if Peach Bottom did not perform on time. He stated that the delay would not cause PSC to withdraw, as long as no serious technical problems were encountered.[36] Although late, the prototype plant went into commercial operation on 1 June 1967, becoming the first HTGR commercial nuclear plant in the United States to produce electric power with high heat and pressure.[37]

Before commencing construction on the new plant, the Public Service Company had to obtain a state license from the public utilities commission. The PUC held hearings in Denver in February, 1967 and on-site at Platteville in March. On 14 September 1967 the PSC filed an application for a certificate of public convenience and necessity with the PUC for construction and maintenance of the electric generating plant, as well as a 230-kilovolt transmission line from Fort St. Vrain to the Valmont Steam Plant and a 230-kilovolt transmission line to Fort Lupton.

Several groups came to the hearings to argue against issuing a certificate. Originally the PUC had not allowed these opponents to participate, but district court Judge Saul Pincheck ruled that they had to be heard.[38] The United Mine Workers came to protest the concept of nuclear energy, because it would hurt the coal industry. Union Rural Electric Association and Tri-State Generation and Transmission Association opposed the plant, because they were afraid that electricity from the new plant would encroach on their territory. The Colorado Electric Consumers Association, Inc., was concerned that electricity generated by nuclear power would result in higher rates. Finally, Elbridge G. Burnham, speaking as an individual stated nuclear technology was not well enough developed to be considered safe. An environmental group, the Colorado

Open Space Coordinating Council, made a statement about environmental issues, but did not speak against licensing the plant.[39]

While Union REA and Tri-State Generation were eventually satisfied with the application, the United Mine Workers tried to block the plant. This was the same union which, in the 1920s, protested bringing natural gas to Colorado for fear that it would eliminate the need for coal. In the 1960s the miners objected to the government's spending millions of dollars on an unproven source of power that might replace coal-fired generating plants. Not only, they claimed, were the coal-fired generating plants good for the community, there were none of the dangers with coal that arose from nuclear energy.[40] With the new technology there would be a potential danger to the eight hundred UMW members who lived near the plant site, as well as an economic loss to the coal miners who would forfeit jobs when atomic energy replaced coal.[41] Actually, an organized campaign against all nuclear plants had been stirred up by the leadership of the United Mine Workers of America under the banner of safety and job security.[42]

In April, 1968 the Colorado PUC approved construction plans and issued a license after

Commissioners' questions about safety had been answered. They were satisfied that the most modern devices would be installed in Fort St. Vrain, and that there were enough safety checks to prevent a dangerous accident. The commissioners, however, voiced their concern about cost, because producing power with nuclear energy was more expensive than other methods. Their hope was that with experience and technological improvements the costs of nuclear energy would drop. The public utilities commission ordered the utility not to pass on to its customers any unforeseen expense of building and operating the plant. A Denver Post editorial warned that there was a limit to what the consumers could pay because of costly mistakes, and therefore "any mistakes will come home to roost with everyone--the Public Service Company, Public Utilities Commission and the public."[43]

Before construction began the Atomic Energy Commission had to perform safety inspections at the site and grant final approval. In the fall of 1968 the AEC granted Public Service Company a permit for the nuclear reactor.[44] The AEC's atomic safety and licensing board and advisory committee on reactor safeguard ruled that the Fort St. Vrain designers had provided for all reasonably foreseeable risks.[45] In response, Robert T. Person said that the company was particularly pleased that the Atomic Energy commission examined each objection raised by the United Mine Workers and found that their questions about safety and operating procedures were without merit.[46] The UMW had appealed the decision of the PUC to the district court. When Denver District Judge Sherman G. Finesilver dismissed appeal in November, 1968 as without merit, it allowed construction to finally begin.[47]

There was great hope during the 1950s and 1960s for nuclear energy as an advanced technology to meet rapidly growing energy demands. According to a 1967 article in Business Week electrical consumption had been rising consistently at seven percent each year. In 1966 the demand for electricity from homes, offices and factories was rising at an even faster rate of nine percent.[48] The League of Women Voters noted that between 1950 and 1970 the United States population grew by 34 percent, but per capita energy consumption grew by 56 percent.[49] Because of this accelerating demand for energy, Robert T. Person, predicted that the electrical industry would build the same amount of power production in the 1970s capacity that it had constructed in all its eighty-five year history.[50]

Each year more and more of our resources were being used to generate electricity. The Federal Power Commission pointed out that generation of electricity accounted for one-fourth of the total energy consumed in the United States in 1970, and was projected to increase to one-third in 1980 and one half in 1990.[51] The need for power was doubling every ten years while the resources of fossil fuels--coal, oil, and gas--were diminishing.[52]

The power shortages in the East and Midwest during the mid-1960s hastened the building of power plants and gave further impetus to finding new technology for power generation. Of the new plants being constructed in 1967, only one percent was nuclear. Business Week estimated that fifty percent of new utility installations by 1980 would be using nuclear fuel.[53] Although the investment required for a nuclear plant was more than the cost of a fossil fuel plant of similar size, substantial savings in fuel costs were anticipated to more than offset the original investment.[54]

Nuclear power was well suited for supplying energy in large quantities. "Nuclear plants increased in efficiency and widened their advantage over fossil-fuel plants when they were operated nearly continuously. . . ."[55] This meant big utilities could let large nuclear plants handle the "base load" part of its operations around the clock and use other plants as needed for peak load.

> The growing trend toward very large installations definitely favored nuclear plants, with high capital costs and low fuel costs. Size was to be a significant factor in giving nuclear power a competitive edge over fossil fuel, even in the middle of coal-producing regions of the United States. . . . Fuel transportation is not a significant part of the cost of nuclear power. . .[56]

In fact, nuclear power was not practical for anything but a large population center, because the technology does not reach full economy except in large units.[57]

Engineers from the utility industry had developed nuclear energy in the 1960s with great expectations, hoping that this new technology would produce an abundance of energy without harming the environment. The nuclear fuel gave utilities the flexibility of having an alternative resource to take the place of fossil fuels and hydroelectric power. Environmentally, nuclear power was a two-edged sword. Nuclear energy was cleaner to generate, i.e., there is no sulphur dioxide or fly ash released. However, the small amounts of radioactivity which escaped in the air or water could be more damaging than larger amounts of fossil fuel pollutants.

The Sierra Club initially endorsed nuclear energy as better for the environment than fossil fuels, but as more information became known about the potential hazards, it withdrew their support. In the years to come, objections by environmentalists would cause many delays in building nuclear plants across the nation and greatly add to the expense of the projects. Utilities had to begin to carefully weigh environmental impact and cost against energy needs.[58]

The grave consequences of a possible nuclear accident made many people very cautious. A nuclear accident could cause thousands of deaths, billions of dollars of property damage and contamination of land for many miles. Although a reactor required design safety checks before receiving a state license or operating license from the Atomic Energy Commission, many people felt there were no safety standards strict enough to meet the potential dangers. Furthermore, environmentalists criticized the AEC, and some courts agreed, that the commission subscribed more to industry's demands than to protecting the public.[59]

Even if there were enough safeguards to avoid a serious disaster, nuclear opponents pointed out that not enough was known about the consequences of the small amounts of radiation emitted into the air or water over a long period of time to risk nuclear power generation. Even the health risks attendant with uranium mining may not be worth the energy produced.[60] Core meltdown, in which inadequate cooling would allow the uranium core to melt, causing a catastrophic release of radioactive material was the most serious danger,[61] but this was not possible with the high-temperature gas-cooled reactor.

Waste disposal was another serious concern. The Fort St. Vrain plant, when completed, would produce approximately one-fourth of a ton of radioactive waste each year. Richard F. Walker, Public Service Company's expert on nuclear energy said that the bulk of waste from an HTGR was contained in the spent fuel elements. These elements would either be recycled at a distant chemical processing plant or buried and kept under surveillance for a century. Opponents, however, believed that neither recycling nor burial was completely safe.[62]

Public Service Company incorporated numerous safety controls into their nuclear plant, including a system to monitor twenty-seven different areas within the plant for radioactivity. In addition, engineers closely monitored any amounts of radioactive material which would escape into the air or water. The amounts released from Fort St. Vrain have been well below the limits established by the Atomic Energy Commission.[63] The plant has special storage components for the spent fuel, which will be cooled and shipped to a permanent fuel storage facility. The HTGR is designed with an enormous steel and concrete casing, called a Prestressed Concrete Reactor Vessel (PCRV) which enclosed the reactor steam generators and helium circulators. All operations will take place within this 106 foot high, sixty foot wide vessel. An accident could not raise the pressure of the helium to a level that would crack the concrete.[64] The vessel was designed and constructed with reinforced concrete to withstand all conceivable accidents caused by system malfunctions.

Fort St. Vrain has several cooling systems, operating independently of each other, to prevent the loss of coolant that could result in damage to the reactor fuel. Considering the worst possible scenario of heat build up, it would take an HTGR more than an hour to reach a temperature level that would seriously damage the core, thereby allowing time to respond to the danger.[65]

The graphite core is another protection from a radioactive accident. Graphite containers cannot melt and even if the helium escaped from the core, heat from the uranium-thorium fuel would first be absorbed by the graphite (which can absorb much more heat than a conventional light water reactor). Even if the core was then able to transfer heat to the entire 17,000 ton concrete casing, the uranium-thorium mixture would produce less and less fission as the temperature rose in the core.[66] A final fail-safe is an automatic shutdown of the reactor at a certain core temperature.[67]

Other safeguards were built into the plant to prevent an accidental buildup of heat within the reactor. The reactor could be "scrammed" or shut down in two and a half minutes by either automatic control systems or two manual control systems. Even if all these controls failed, the water-cooled PCRV walls would prevent damage to the reactor containment vessel. The ceramic encased fuel particles are virtually rupture proof.[68]

At the time Public Service Company was designing and constructing Fort St. Vrain, nuclear reactors had a far better safety record than other chemical and fuel processes. There had been nuclear accidents, but all involved plants with different designs than Fort St. Vrain, and people associated with the HTGR felt that it was designed for utmost safety. But as the hazards of nuclear fission began to reveal themselves, perplexing social, ethical, and political questions about energy were raised.

Is it better to use fossil fuels, with all the accompanying problems, or use nuclear technology with possible consequences such as higher cancer rates and genetic defects? Is it ethical to use a technology whose health hazards are unknown? Are people entitled to receive the cheapest, safest form of electricity, and are nuclear reactors that source? Will nuclear fission enable the United States to become less dependent on other countries for our fuel supply? Should the government be allowed to limit an individual's right to energy in order to avoid sabotage, theft or radioactive leakage? If there is a reasonable level of safety is it ethical to disallow energy growth in other countries, particularly third world countries for which nuclear energy is the most practical option?[69]

By the time of the company's centennial celebration in 1969, most of the questions had not yet been answered. However, the Public Service Company had, in developing the particular kind of nuclear power that it did, taken steps to address some of the problems. PSC had entered the nuclear energy field in an attempt to use a new technology to produce more efficiently reliable and economical energy.[70] This bold action continued the company's tradition of developing and using experimental generation and transmission methods. It was also an opportunity to generate more electricity and, therefore, more profit. Despite the problems and criticisms of nuclear power, Public Service Company of Colorado remains convinced that it is the technology of the future.[71]

NOTES-CHAPTER 15

1 Denver Post, 14 March 1965, p. 1.

2 Lines, (January, 1954), 16.

3 Denver Post, 29 October 1954, p. 1.

4 K. S. Shrader Frechette, Nuclear Power and Public Policy: The Social and Ethical Problems of Fission Technology (Dordrecht, Holland: D. Reidel Publishing Company, 1980), p. 7.

5 Ibid.

6 Ibid.

7 Ibid., p. 8.

8 Public Law 79-585 (60 Stat755) 1946.

9 Frank G.Dawson, Nuclear Power: Development and Management of a Technology, (Seattle and London: University of Washington Press, 1976), pp. 19-20. In 1964 the Act was amended to gradually allow private ownership of nuclear fuel for power plants.

10 Shrader-Frechette, Nuclear Power, pp. 10-11.

11 PSC 1955 Annual Report, (1955), 11.

12 PSC 1956 Annual Report, (1957), 9-10.

13 PSC 1957 Annual Report, (1958), 10.

14 PSC 1958 Annual Report, (1959), 11.

15 Milton McBride, Nuclear Fuel and Analysis Manager, Public Service Company of Colorado, interview 13 September 1985.

16 Edwin Vennard, The Electric Power Business, second edition (New York: McGraw Hill book Co., 1970), pp. 290-91.

17 Statement of Robert T. Person before the Subcommittee on Legislation of the Joint Committee on

Atomic Energy, Congress of the United States, 89th Cong. 1st Sess. on Reactor Development Program, March 1965, pp. 1-2.

18 From Arrows to Atoms, (Fort St. Vrain Nuclear Information Center, no date, no pagination and the Rocky Mountain News, 25 July 1965, p. 54.

19 Statement of Robert T. Person before the Subcommittee on Legislation of the Joint Committee on Atomic Energy, Congress of the United States, 89th Cong 1st Sess. on Reactor Development Program, March, 1965, pp. 1-2.

20 U.S. Congress, 89th Cong., 1st Sess on Reactor Development Program, Statement of Mr. R. T. Person, president of PSC of Colorado, Hearings before the Joint Committee on Atomic Energy, March 1966, part 3 (Washington, DC: U. S. Government Printing Office, 1965), pp. 1707-1714 Also From Arrows to Atoms and Denver Post, 12 May 1965, p. 1.

21 Rocky Mountain News, 14 April 1965, p. 5.

22 Quoted in Ibid.

23 Rocky Mountain News, 12 May 1965, p. 5 and Denver Post 25 May 1965, p. 1.

24 Rocky Mountain News, 24 November 1965, p. 10.

25 From Arrows to Atoms.

26 Introductory statement by the Public Utilities Commission of the State of Colorado, Decision No. 71104, p. 3.

27 PSC 1965 Annual Report, (1966), 10.

28 Actual cost was $762 million, of which PSC paid $131.2 million. Denver Post, 28 November 1982, pp. 1A and 15A.

29 Denver Post, 2 November 1965, p. 29.

30 Senator Allott quoted in Denver Post, 1 November 1965, p. 1.

31 Rocky Mountain News, 24 November 1965, p. 10.

32
Denver Post, editorial, 21 January 1966, p. 24.

33
Ibid.

34
Ibid.

35
Statement of Robert T. Person before the Subcommittee on Legislation of the Joint Committee on Atomic Energy, Congress of the United States, March 1966, p. 4.

36
Ibid., p. 3.

37
Fort St. Vrain (San Diego: General Atomic Co., 1974) 13.

38
Denver Post Perspective, 4 February 1968, p. 2.

39
Public Utilities Commission of the State of Colorado Decision 71104, in the matter of the application of Public Service Company of Colorado for a certification of Public Convenience and Necessity for the construction, operation and maintenance of a 330 MW electric generating plant to be known as the Fort St. Vrain Nuclear Generating Station, 2 April 1968, p. 2.

40
Denver Post, 4 August 1965, p. 22 and letter to the editor from Fred Hefferly, President, District 15 United Mine Workers of America in the Denver Post, 13 September 1966, p. 31.

41
Rocky Mountain News, 18 September 1968, p. 5.

42
Denver Post, 4 February 1968, p. 2.

43
Denver Post, editorial April 4, 1968, p. 20.

44
Rocky Mountain News, 18 September 1968, p. 5.

45
Ibid.

46
Denver Post, 18 September 1968, p. 3.

47
Denver Post, 29 November 1968, p. 3.

48 "Nuclear Plants Turn Up the Juice," Business Week, 11 March 1967. p. 65.

49 Energy Dilemmas: An Overview of U.S. Energy Problems and Issues, League of Women Voters Education Fund, 1977, p. 5.

50 Remarks by Robert T. Person, Sr. before the Edison Electric Institute Accounting Conference 5 April 1965, p. 2.

51 Dawson, Nuclear Power, p. 140.

52 Barnard Kelly, "Atomic Power for Colorado," Denver Post Empire Magazine, 7 May 1967, p. 30.

53 Week, 11 Mary 1967, p. 64. The estimates were wrong, by 1973 oil and natural gas provided 77 percent of our energy (46 percent from oil and 31 percent from natural gas). Coal provided 18 percent and hydropower and nuclear made up the other 5 percent. Energy Dilemmas, p. 5.

54 PSC 1965 Annual Report, (1966), 12.

55 Business Week, 11 March 1967, p. 65.

56 Dawson, Nuclear Power, p. 138.

57 Business Week, 11 March 1967 p. 65.

58 Dawson, Nuclear Power, p. 204.

59 Shrader-Frechette, p. 12.

60 Turk, Turk, and Wittes, Ecology, Pollution and Environment, pp. 67-75.

61 Denver Post, 24 May 1970, p. 27 and Kelly, Denver Post Empire Magazine, 7 May 1967, p. 30.

62 Cal Queal, "Super Safe Fort St. Vrain Plant a Question." Denver Post, 24 May 1970, p. 27 and Kelly, Denver Post Empire Magazine 7 May 1967, p. 35.

63 From Arrows to Atoms.

64 Peter G Miller, "HTGR, a Safer Way to Nuclear Power," Popular Science, (February, 1975), pp. 68 and 128.

[65] Ibid., pp. 128-29.

[66] Ibid., p. 129.

[67] Denver Post Perspective, 4 February 1968, p. 3.

[68] Queal, Denver Post, 24 May 1970, p. 27.

[69] Shrader-Frechette, pp. 19-20.

[70] Miller, "HTGR," p. 68.

[71] Interview with Richard F. Walker, President of Public Service Company, 3 January 1985.

PART IV

A POSTSCRIPT ON THE FIRST CENTURY

1970-2000

EPILOGUE

For more than a century the Public Service Company of Colorado has been the state's major supplier of power. Since 1869, when its first predecessor was established to provide manufactured gas to a fledgling town, the company has evolved and matured in response to changes in technology, regulation and economics. Throughout its history the Public Service Company has played an important role in the development of Colorado by supplying the power that has allowed the state to grow and prosper. By 1969 the company was supplying natural gas and electricity to eighty percent of the people in the state that had become the growth leader of the Rocky Mountain region.

Public Service Company has had a long tradition of strong executives whose decisions about the use of men, money and materials have determined the direction of the enterprise. Three men in particular have shaped the company during its first one hundred years. Outstanding was Henry L. Doherty, an entrepreneur extraodinaire. He was an aggressive promoter, brilliant scientist, creative financier, and innovative manager. Doherty's penchant for trying new technology, developing strong managers, and training employees often provided examples for other utilities to follow.

When the utility industry was young it was advantageous to have a leader who was powerful and unrestrained. Doherty's personality and manner of doing business fit the climate of the time. Acting through holding company, Cities Service, he was instrumental in creating several successful utilities. Doherty played a large part in developing the industry, but at the same time it was his wheeling and dealing and financial manipulation that lead in part to stringent utility regulation and a reshaping of the industry in the thirties and forties.

After the Great Depression a new type of leader was needed. John E. Loiseau, who took the helm in 1943 during divestiture from Cities Service, was the right person to deal with a changing political climate. He, like many of his peers throughout the country, was a professional manager with a keen sense of both the social and economic environment. Because of close scrutiny by the public and by regulatory agencies, the company's methods in setting goals and making policies under Loiseau were much more above board than during previous years. Furthermore, financial liability rested on a broader base of stockholders who also had a part in the decision-making process. Loiseau's expertise made him particularly qualified to become president during the establishment of a financially independent utility.

Sixteen years later, in 1959, when John E. Loiseau retired, the company had different requirements Robert T. Person was elected president primarily because of his broad knowledge of the utility business and his unique ability to communicate. He led the company through a demanding period of inflation and a exploding demand for energy. It was under Person's leadership that innovative projects such as Cabin Creek, Leyden mine, and the Fort St. Vrain nuclear plant were developed. He was also successful in limiting the encroachment of the federal government into the investor-owned utility business, not only in Colorado but also across the country.

The fact that each of three leaders had a long tenure of office made their mark on the company more profound. Each had different fields of expertise and styles of management, but they all had the necessary skills to deal with people and adapt to a changing environment.

Public Service Company has had a significant impact on the community it serves because people have become dependent on energy to maintain modern lifestyles. Public Service Company, like most utilities, was a monopoly and consumers could no easily turn to another supplier for electricity or natural gas, or generate power themselves. Without the services that PSC provides, Colorado would come to a standstill. Actually, utilities have in many ways shaped society developing and promoting new energy uses.

In addition to providing essential services, Public Service played important financial and social role in its service area. As a capital intensive business it provided opportunities for investment (twenty percent of all capital in the United States is invested in utilities), and as Colorado's largest taxpayer it financed education and other community services. The company also benefited society through corporate donations to many philanthropic organizations and by encouraging its employees to volunteer time to civic activities.

Just as a utility affected the community, a community played important roles in the success of a utility. Public Service Company has reaped the benefits of being located in an economically healthy area. For most of the years between 1869 and 1969

Colorado's prosperity was equal to or greater than the rest of the nation. The continually expanding population and business created a strong demand for gas and electricity. The company also benefited from the state's rich resources of coal and natural gas which are the necessary raw materials of its production process.

A utility, more than other businesses, is dependent on its community, because it cannot pick up its wires and pipes and move to another location. Once a utility is granted a franchise and makes the large capital investment necessary to operate, it is wholly dependent on its area for success. For that reason, it is especially important to promote customer good will and to seek the respect of the entire community. The Public Service Company of Colorado has followed this strategy and has always been very conscious of its public image.

For most of its history the company has tried to influence public opinion. Denver Gas and Electric Company was one of the first utilities in the country to use advertising on an extensive basis to sell its products and to promote good will with its consumers. Public Service Company continues to promote a positive corporate image through media campaigns and active participation in civic associations. It is also very careful about the information it releases to the public. It has a relatively large public relations department which issues press releases and responds to media questions, among its many responsibilities.

Unless a utility such as PSC can convince the public that it conducts business in an efficient, cost-effective manner, the public will not vote to renew its franchise. Unhappy customers can put pressure on regulatory agencies to reject rate increases and to turn down applications to construct new facilities. Ultimately, if public opinion were allowed to become extremely negative, municipal or state ownership of a utility might ensue. When PSC elected a president from its public affairs department in the late fifties, it was quite conscious of the importance of public opinion to the company. The company is, therefore, guided by a positive public image.

Because utilities are monopolies, regulation is more encompassing for them than for other enterprises. Since government regulation seems primarily to protect the consumer rather than to benefit the utility, PSC is usually defensive in its dealings with the regulators. The company persuades voters to grant a franchise in order to sell gas and electricity. At the state level it must prove that there is a demand for its products and meet strict financial requirements to receive a certificate of necessity and convenience from the Public Utilities Commission. It is also dependent on approval of the PUC for rate increases. At the federal level Public Service is regulated by the Federal Energy Regulatory Commission (formerly the Federal Power Commission), the Securities and Exchange Commission, the Nuclear Regulatory Agency (formerly the Atomic Energy Commission), and the Environmental Protection Agency.

In other words, increasingly stringent regulation at all levels influences the way PSC does business. It shapes the company's financial structure and its future planning. Sometimes the pressures of regulation stifle the ability of the company to make a profit or plan for the future, and force it to concentrate on immediate problems and short-term goals. Regulation also tends to keep the price of energy lower than in an unregulated industry. Utilities are much more likely to build larger generating plants which produce power at a lower cost per unit, than smaller plants. With deregulation this might not be the case because the price of power is kept fairly low, it is more difficult for competitive technologies to enter the field. Thus, in some ways regulation perpetuates the monopoly. In the evolution of utility development Public Service Company of Colorado has reached the cooperative stage. There is never a clear beginning or ending to any stage of development, but since the battles between public and private power in the 1950s and 1960s have subsided, there has been more cooperation. The sharing is probably justified on economic more than ideological grounds, but it has been accomplished. The Public Service Company is a member of the Rocky Mountain Power pool which exchanges power among its members which are both privately and publicly owned. PSC is also a part of the Western United States Power Network which exchanges power in a much larger region. Finally natural gas producers and distributors cooperate in financing, storage and marketing efforts.

The end of Public Service Company's first one hundred years in 1969 also was the conclusion of an unprecedented twenty-year period of growth in which the utilities kept pace with the demand and provided a quality of service that few industries could equal. On the national level, the 1970s, however, was a different situation, when with rapid inflation and growing environmental concerns, costs rose and productivity fell. The industry overspeculated on the rate of growth and use of energy, and as a result, overbuilt. The cautious public attitude towards nuclear energy also hurt the industry. When regulatory agencies set low rates of return, utilities could only meet their profit goals through reduced costs.[1]

The 1970s ended a thirty-year period during which utility bonds and stocks were considered premium investments. However, when bond interest rates increased from three percent to thirteen percent, utilities, being large borrowers of funds, were significantly hurt.[2] The resulting higher price of building power generating plants reduced the opportunities for economies of scale and made the production of energy less efficient. Because of the Natural Gas Policy Act of 1978 the gas industry changed dramatically. That Act created price incentives for the discovery and sale of new gas, and the shortages that the industry had been experiencing were quickly alleviated.

Congress, in 1978, enacted the Public Utility Regulatory Policies Act (PURPA). This law ordered utilities to buy alternative power from suppliers such as windmill, solar, small hydroelectric operators, joint ventures of other utilities or cogeneration from industry. PURPA's goal was to reduce the country's dependency on oil, but it forced the utilities to buy power they often did not need. The percent of electricity produced from alternate sources will continue to rise.[3]

In a management audit requested by the Colorado Public Utilities Commission in 1982 PSC was given high marks on the manner in which it survived the seventies. The report by the Washington, D.C. firm of Cresap, McCormick and Paget[4] revealed that Public Service Company provided reliable service at below-average rates with an unusually small work force. When the consultants observed that PSC was behind in its long-range planning, it did not place the blame as much with the company as it did with regulatory agencies and other external factors. The company had suffered from inflation, high energy costs, environmental controls, and public resistance to rate hikes. As a result it was preoccupied with short-term problems and profits.

According to the study, salaries for some managers did not keep up with inflation and some talented employees went elsewhere. The company, said the study, then had to hire consultants, which turned out to be more expensive than paying large salaries. The utility also decided not to invest as much capital as perhaps was needed in new facilities and, therefore, ended up buying expensive electric power from other utilities.

The consultants felt that the Colorado Public Utilities Commission was overly protective of consumers during the 1970s, leading to many battles between PSC and the Commission. Cresap, McCormick and Paget also criticized the state law which allowed only formal public meetings between the Commission and the utility. The auditors proposed that if the staffs of each organization could meet informally, fairer policies would be devised and implemented. Clearly the regulatory system hampered the company from making reasonable profit as well as making long-range plans.

A number of recommendations were made by Cresap, et al, to improve Public Service Company's management and finances, all of which would require customer rate increases. The consultants believed the changes were necessary for PSC to break away from the national trend toward lower profits and lesser service. ". . . few utilities have achieved allowable rate of return in recent years, but Public Service Company's experience has been unusually adverse."[5] Richard F. Walker, who became president of Public Service Company in 1976, agreed with the consultants' conclusions.

> [Utilities] no longer talk about the character of business in terms of predictability, low cost fuel

> supplies, economies of scale and stable customer bills. The delicate balance between financial and service obligation has been tipped out of proper proportion by rampant inflation, high interest rates, above industry average growth in our service territory and impractical government regulation. 6

Walker joined Public Service Company as an assistant engineer in 1949, the same year he was graduated from the University of Colorado with a degree in electrical engineering. From 1957 to 1959 he was involved in nuclear research for the company. As he gained experience, Walker was given more management responsibilities. In 1966 he was named Assistant Vice President of the Electric Department. In 1968 he became vice president of Engineering and Planning and was named president in 1976. Like his predecessors he has been very active in the community.[7]

Public Service Company named a new chief executive officer October 1988, Delwin D. Hock, who was then elected chairman of the board 28 February 1989. Hock has worked for the company since 1962, serving in accounting operations, information management, customer service and senior executive positions for twenty-six years. He was elected to the board of directors in 1985, and was named president in June 1986.[8]

The 1980s have returned some prosperity to the utility industry. President Ronald Reagan's economic policies reduced inflation and interest rates. Environmental and consumer groups were less vocal. Public Service Company's earnings rebounded after several rate increases were approved. Previously PSC had begun to diversify to achieve financial stability by seeking earnings opportunities outside the regulated utility business. The company established an oil and gas subsidiary, Fuel Resources Development Company (Fuelco), for exploration of natural gas, and the Bannock Center Corporation was formed to engage in a variety of non-utility real estate activities in Denver. The benefits from diversification are limited because it was almost impossible for a large utility to develop sufficient outside business to significantly affect its finances. The directors anticipated that diversification would at least help offset inflation, give strength when searching for new capital, and make the company more competitive in the market place.[9]

Nuclear energy, innovation of the 1960s has been a debacle in the 1980s. In December 1988 Public Service Company of Colorado adopted a plan to discontinue nuclear operations. The company will terminate Fort St. Vrain in mid 1990, after all fuel segments currently in the reactor are utilized. The

Company may then convert the plant to a fossil fuel operation.[10]

A number of reasons account for the closing. Fort St. Vrain, which achieved criticality in 1974, did not generate the amount of energy it was expected to. For the first five years of the 1980s, for example, it produced forty-five percent of capacity. Output decreased after that.[11] Some authorities say that the large size of the 330 megawatt plant has caused most of its problems.[12] In addition, the company has had to meet regulations that were not law when it began constructing Fort St. Vrain, and has found it difficult to make modifications to comply with changing rules. Two well-publicized accidents in other plants have increased public apprehension about nuclear power facilities. The accident at Three Mile Island took place in 1979 and a disaster at Russia's Chernobyl nuclear reactor occured in 1986. The Chernobyl nuclear reactor had a graphite core as does Fort St. Vrain.

The Nuclear Regulatory Commission, in its 1986 audit, gave Public Service Company a rating of 2.3, or below average. The NRC also pointed out management weaknesses which they blamed for poor nuclear performance. Expense added to the problems. During 1986 the Company lost $101.4 million resulting from writing down a substantial portion of the total investment in Fort St. Vrain in expectation of decommissioning the reactor.[13]

While dramatic changes in the utility industry in past years make it difficult to forecast the next ten years, some things seem probable. Environmental issues will remain important with acid rain at the top of the list, especially in the Midwest and East. Coal-fired generating plants using high sulfur coal can cause damage to lakes and plants. The burden does not fall solely on utilities. In order to solve the problems of acid rain consumers must also be willing to pay more for energy.

Since the utility industry believes that nuclear energy is a reasonable means of producing electricity, it will have to continue to sway public opinion to its way of thinking. Building nuclear plants has virtually stopped because of cost and safety concerns, but as the economy suffers because of the high cost of imported petroleum, and the warming of the planet due to the greenhouse effect, in part caused by fossil fuel pollution, America may change its mind about the hazards of nuclear plants, and construction could begin again. If it does, nuclear technology will be more advanced, and parts will be standardized, making facilities more efficient to build and operate.[14]

The government might also consider some degree of deregulation which, despite the capital intensive nature of utilities, could bring more competition. Even now the electric and gas industries compete against each other, and some large industrial users have been able to produce their own power. Deregulation could encourage more innovation because different enterprises and technologies would be competing for the same market. With deregulation companies would be free to set their own rates and there would be less lag between need and rate increases. Some have concluded that competition can be introduced into the electric industry by separating the generation and transmission functions. Distribution would remain regulated because multiple lines and pipes are not needed. It is unlikely that generation will be broken down into small units. There is still an economy of size in producing power. Deregulation might simplify the process by letting competition "regulate" the industry, but that may not be the case. It will be hard to judge when there is enough competition to sufficiently protect the public's interest.

Electricity has become the principal source of power in this country, and may consume as much as forty percent of the primary fuel by the year 2000.[15] Nevertheless, growth in electrical usage will be moderate for the next decade and will not require the enormous outlay of capital for construction that PSC expended in the 1950s and 1960s. The increasing price of power will keep researchers seeking new sources of energy such as nuclear fusion, solar energy, the fuel cell, wind generators geothermal energy, as well as advanced techniques for storing energy, but a breakthrough is not on the horizon.

Strategic planning will be essential for the future. Successful leaders will be those who understand all the variables--financial, political technological, social, and resource--and are able to readily adapt to changing situations. They will be forced to deal with the contradiction of an insatiable appetite for energy and a desire to live in a healthy environment. It is a dilemma utilities cannot resolve by themselves. The solutions, however, will have a major impact on the industry.[11] A major problem for management will continue to be that of raising the tremendous amounts of capital necessary to meet the demand for service.

Cooperation among the various types of ownership in the utilities will continue. Investor-owned utility competition with federal or municipal power projects will continue, but it will not be as combative as in the past. It should also be in the industry's best interest to cooperate in developing new energy technologies to discourage domestic and foreign competition so that utilities are not shut out of a competitive process.

By the year 2000 people will be even more dependent on utilities to support the American lifestyle. There may be a greater understanding that the consumer and producer of power are dependent on each other, creating a less adversarial relationship. With such cooperation perhaps the conflict between the great benefits of energy and the negative consequences of power production can be solved.

1 Andrew S. Carron and Paul W. MacAvoy, The Decline of Service in the Regulated Industries (Washington, DC: the American Enterprise Institute for Public Policy Research, 1981), pp 1-2.

2 Cresap, McCormick and Paget, Inc., "A Management Audit of the Public Service Company of Colorado, April, 1982. (Public Utilities Commission of the State of Colorado, Denver, Colorado).

3 Business Week, 20 June 1988, pp. 133-134L.

4 Cresap, et al., "A Management Audit," p. 2.

5 Peter G. Chronis, "Electric Utilities Urged to Become More Competitive," Denver Post, 26 July 1984, p. 1C.

6 Richard F. Walker, 1979 Public Service Company Annual Report (1980), p. 4.

7 Richard F. Walker, 1985 resume.

8 Public Service Company of Colorado Annual Report, 1988, p. 4.

9 Public Service Company of Colorado has several subsidiaries that fall outside the jurisdiction of the public utilities commission. Green and Clear Lakes Company was incorporated 13 November 1886 and accumulates, stores, and sells water around Leadville; 1480 Welton Corporation founded on 11 April 1958 acquired real estate property including PSC's headquarters which it leases to the company; and the Bannock Center Corporation established 8 September 1981.

Subsidiaires which fall under the purvue of the Colorado PUC are Home Light and Power Company in Greeley, incorporated 2 January 1909; Cheyenne Light, Fuel, and Power Company, incorporation 21 May 1900; Pueblo Gas and Fuel Company, incorporation 1 August 1902; and Westgas (formerly Western Slope Gas Company).

[10] Public Service Company of Colorado Annual Report, 1988, p. 36.

[11] Rocky Mountain News, 25 July 1986, p. 6.

[12] U.S. News and World Report, 21 July 1986, p. 60.

[13] Public Service Company of Colorado Annual Report, 1988, p. 4.

[14] Time Magazine, (13 February 1984), pp. 34-45.

[14] P. M. Boffery, "Energy Crises: Environmental Issues Exacerbates Power Supply Problems," CLXVII Science (26 June 1970), 1554.

SELECT BIBLIOGRAPHY

ARCHIVAL AND MANUSCRIPT REPOSITORIES

PUBLIC SERVICE COMPANY OF COLORADO

MINUTES

Arvada Electric Company, 1908-1937.

Brighton Ice, Light and Power Company, 1911-1926.

Central Power Company, 1906-1910.

Central Colorado Power Company, 1907-1914.

Cheyenne Light, Fuel and Power Company, 1900-1950.

Colorado Power Company, 1913-1924.

Colorado-Wyoming Gas Company, 1925-1962.

Denver Consolidated Gas Company, 1891-1911.

Denver Consolidated Electric Company, 1889-1911.

Denver Gas Company, 1869-1909.

Denver Gas and Electric Company, 1899-1909.

Denver Gas and Electric Light Company, 1907-1923.

Denver Highlands Electric Company, 1891-1911.

Denver Light, Heat and Power Company, 1887-1889.

Doherty Operating Company, 1908.

Eastern Colorado Power Company, 1907-1925.

Edison Electric Light Company, 1887-1911.

Fort Collins Electric Company, 1888-1902.

Lacombe Electric Company, 1900-1911.

Leadville Illuminating Gas Company, 1879-1900.

Public Service Company, 1923-1937.

Pueblo Gas and Fuel Company, 1902-1952.

Western Electrical Construction Company, 1889-1911.

Western Light and Power Company, 1919-1923.

SPEECHES

Robert T. Person, 1957-1965.

OTHER MATERIAL

"Brief History of Public Service Company. 1 December 1931.

Denver Gas and Electric Company "Memo to Stockholders", 8 April 1905.

"History of the Company Steam System," (mimeographed copy, no date.)

COLORADO STATE ARCHIVES

ARTICLES OF INCORPORATION

Colorado Electric Company 25 February 1881.

Denver Gas and Electric Light Company. 29 November 1905.

Public Service Company of Colorado.

Colorado Land and Mineral Association.

Denver Gas Company.

Denver Gas Water Company.

Denver City Council Minutes.

OTHER MATERIAL

Contract between the Denver Gas Company and the City of Denver.

Jefferson Territory. Provisional Laws and Joint Resolutions passed at the First and Called Sessions of the General Assembly of Jefferson Territory, 1859-1860.

DENVER PUBLIC LIBRARY

"The City Beautiful." a book of caricatures reproduced from Public Service Company newspaper advertisements.

Denver Chamber of Commerce Proceedings, 1924-1928.

Denver Franchise Proposal. Its Provisions and Benefits. Denver: Bradford Robinson Printing, 1946.

Kosh-Glasman Associates, Inc. "Report to the City and County of Denver, Regarding Renewal of the Franchise of Public Service Company of Colorado." Washington, DC: Public utilities Consultants, 1 January 1967.

Report of the Commission. Charters for Electric Service in Denver and Other Cities. (no date)

"Report on the Public Service company of Colorado in Connection with the Proposed Franchise for the Supplying of Electricity and Gas to the City and County of Denver: 3 November 1926." Denver Chamber of Commerce Proceedings.

COLORADO STATE HISTORICAL SOCIETY

Mosley, Earl. History of the Denver Board of Water Commissioners, 1859-1919." Denver: mimeographed, 1960.

Writers Program, Colorado "Public Utilities in Denver," part III, "Denver's Gas and Electricity."

CITY AND COUNTY OF DENVER ARCHIVES

City Council Proceedings

"Report of the City Attorney on Proposed Franchise to Denver City Council." 17 March 1925 Denver City Council Proceedings.

PUBLIC UTILITIES COMMISSION OF THE STATE OF COLORADO

Decisions, 1959-1967.

INTERVIEWS

Denious, William P. III, May, 1985.

Hugo, Robert J. (Administrative Assistant, Engineering and Planning), Public Service Company of Colorado, 10 September 1985.

Fitzmaurice, William , Public Service Company of Colorado, 1979-1985.

Galligan, Harry. (Executive Secretary, Colorado Public Utilities Commission), 28 May 1985 12 September 1984, and 9 May 1985.

Gibson, Mary, (historian for the Electrical Workers Union III), 14 September 1984.

McBride, Milton, 20 September 1985. Public Service of Colorado.

McMahan, Peg. Interview with author, 13 September 1985, Fort St. Vrain Nuclear Energy Plant, Platteville, Colorado.

Olson, Lee (Denver Post) interview with author

September 1985.

Person, Robert T. Chairman of the Board, Public Service Company of Colorado, 0 September 1984, 15 November 1985, 22 November 1985.

Taylor, Shirley, 5 October 1985.

Walker, Richard F. Interview with author, 4 January 1985.

UNPUBLISHED MATERIAL

Gibson, Mary. he Long Journey. unpublished manuscript of the history of the Electrical Workers Union III.

Morris, Arval A. "An Analysis of Some Recent Developments of Public Utility Regulation Principles. A Master's Thesis. University of Colorado,

1957.

Vetter, A. R. "Some Doubtful Financial Practices in Public Utilities." A thesis for a Master's Degree in Business Administration at the University of Colorado, 1932.

GOVERNMENT DOCUMENTS

Colorado. House Journal, 1909-1910.

Colorado. Session Laws, 1876-1969

Colorado State Planning Commission. "Development of Electric Power Industry in Colorado 1916-1936. Conducted under the auspices of the Works Progress Administration. Denver: Colorado State Planning commission, 1938.

Denver. Charters and Ordinances of the City of Denver.

Federal Power Commission. Reports, Opinion, Decisions, Order, VIII, in the Matter of Colorado Interstate Gas Company, decided 2 November 1949. (Washington, DC: U.S. Government Printing Office, 1952).

Federal Power Commission. Reports, Opinions, Decisions, Orders. XXXIV, 1 July 190 to 31 December 1960 (Washington, DC: U. S. Government Printing Office, 1964).

Federal Power Commission. National Power Survey I Washington, DC: U. S. Government Printing Office, 1964.

Federal Power Commission. World Power Data. Washington, DC: U.S. Government Printing Office, 1968.

Security and Exchange Commission. Decisions and Reports, V, Appendix 3, 1 June 1939 to 30 September 1939 (Washington, DC: U.S. Government Printing Office, 1941.

Security and Exchange Commission. Decisions and Reports, XXVI, 16 May 1947 to 31 October 1947

(Washington, DC: U.S. Government Printing Office, 1953).

State Railroad Commission of Colorado. First Annual Report, 1907-1908. Denver, 1908.

U.S. Congress. Department of Agriculture. Department of Agriculture Appropriations for 1962. Hearings before the Subcommittee of the Committee on Appropriations, 87th Cong., 1st Sess, part two, Washington, DC. U.S. Government Printing Office, 1961.

U.S. Department of the Interior. Bureau of Reclamation. Contract for Interconnections and Transmission Service with Public Service company of Colorado. 9 May 1962.

U.S. Department of Interior, Bureau of Reclamation,. "Fryingpan-Arkansas Project," CPO: 1983.

U.S. Congress. House. Committee on Interstate and Foreign Commerce, Public Utility Holding Companies, part III before a subcommittee on the Committee on Interstate and Foreign Commerce, House of Representatives, on H.R. 5423, 74th Cong., 1st. sess., 1935. Washington, DC: U. S. Government Printing Office, 1936.

U.S. Congress. House. Congressional Record. 74th Cong, 2d Sess., LXXX, part 5. Washington, DC: U. S. Government Printing Office, 1936.

U.S. Congress. House. Report of the Committee on Interior and Insular Affairs, to accompany H.R. 3383. 84th Cong., 2d sess., 1960. Vol. II.

U.S. Congress. Joint Committee on Atomic Energy. Reactor Development Program, Civilian Power Program, 11, 18 March 1924 and 13 April 1965, part 3, 89th Cong., 1st Sess. Washington, DC U.S. Government Printing Office, 1965.

U.S. Congress. Joint Committee on Atomic Energy. Environmental Effects of Producing Electric Power, Part 1 and Part II, vols, I and II. Hearings Before the Joint Committee on Atomic Energy, 91st Cong. 1st sess. 28-31 October and

4-7 November 1969 and 2d sess. 27-19 January and 24-26 February 1970.

U.S. Congress. Senate. Report of the Federal Trade Commission. S. Doc. 92, 70th Cong., 1st sess., 1934.

U.S. Congress. Senate. Department of Interior. Hearings before the Subcommittee of the Committee on Appropriations. A Bill Making Appropriations for the Department of Interior for the Fiscal Year Ending 30 June 1950, part 1. 81 Cong, 1st Sess.

U.S. Congress. Senate. Congressional Record 10 July 1963.

COLORADO SUPREME COURT

Castle Rock Railroad v. Denver Tramway Company, 1919.

East Denver Business and Public Association v. Denver Tramway Company, 1917

UNITED STATES SUPREME COURT

Munn v. Illinois, 1877

Wabash, St. Louis and Pacific Railway Company v. Illinois, 1886

Smyth v. Ames, 1898

Denver v. Mountain States Telephone and Telegraph Company, 1920

Colorado Interstate Gas v. Federal Power Commission, 1945

Federal Power Commission v. Hope Natural Gas Company, 1945

Phillips Petroleum Company v. Wisconsin, et al, 1954

BOOKS

Abbott, Carl; Leonard, Stephen J.; and McComb, David. Colorado: History of the Centennial State. revised edition Boulder: Colorado Associated University Press, 1982.

Anderson, Douglas D. Regulatory Politics and Electric Utilities: A Case Study in Political Economy. Boston: Auburn House Publishing Company, 1981.

The Association of the Bar of the City of New York Special Committee on Electric Power and the Environment. Elecricity and the Environment: The Reform of Legal Institutions. St. Paul, MN: West Publishing Co., 1972.

Athearn, Robert G. The Coloradans. Albuquerque: University of New Mexico Press, 1976.

Bach, Wilfrid. Atmospheric Pollution. New York: McGraw Hill Book Co., 1972

Barnes, Irston R. The Economics of Public Utility Regulation. New York: F. S. Crofts, & Co., 1947.

Bauer, John. Public Organization of Electric Power, Conditions, Policies, and Program. New York: Harper & Brothers Publishers, New York, 1949.

__________. Transforming Public Utility Regulation: A Definite Administrative Program. New York: Harper & Brothers Publishers, 1950.

__________. Updating Public Utility Regulation: Assuring Fair Rates and Fair Returns. Chicago: Public Administrative Service, 1966.

Berlin, Edward; Cicchett, Charles J.; and William J. Gillen. Perspective on Power: A Study of the Regulation and of Electric Power. Cambridge, MA: Ballinger Publishing Company, 1974.

Blum, John M.; Morgan, Edmund S.; Rose, Willie Lee;

Schlesinger, Jr., Arthur M.; Stampp, Kenneth M.; Woodward, C. Vann. The National Experience: A History of the United States since 1865. fourth edition, New York: Harcourt Brace Jovanovich, Inc., 1977.

Bonbright, James C., and Means, Gardiner C. The Holding Company, Its Public Significance and Its Regulation. New York: McGraw-Hill Book Co., Inc., 1932.

________. Principles of Public Utility Rates. New York: Columbia University Press, 1961.

Brooks, John. Telephone the First Hundred Years. New York: Harper & Row Publisher, 1978.

Brownlee, W. Elliot. Dynamics of Ascent: A History of the American Economy. New York: Alfred A. Knopf, 1974.

Bryant, John Myron. Elements of Utility Rate Determination. New York: McGraw-Hill, 1940.

Cabot, Philip, and Malott, Dean W. Problems in Public Utility Management. New York: McGraw-Hill Book Company, Inc. 1930.

Bush, George. Future Builders: The Story of Michigan's Consumer Power Company. New York: McGraw Hill, 1973.

Byers, William N. Encyclopaedia of Biography of Colorado: History of Colorado. Four volumes Chicago: The Century Publishing and Engraving Company, 1901.

Cicchetti, Charles J., and Jurewitz, John L. eds., Studies in Electric Utility Regulation. Cambridge, MA: Ballinger Publishing Co., 1975.

Clark, James Anthony. The Chronological History of the Petroleum and Natural Gas Industries. Houston: Clark Book Co., 1963.

Clay, Cassiums M. Regulation of Public Utilities: A Crucial Problem in Constitutional Government. New York: Henry Holt and Company, 1932.

Clemens, Eli Winston. Economics and Public Utilities. New York: Appleton-Century-Crofts, Inc., 1950.

Cochran, Thomas C. American Business in the Twentieth Century. Cambridge, MA: Harvard University Press, 1972.

Cole, Arthur H. Business Enterprise in its Social Setting. Cambridge, MA: Harvard University Press, 1959.

Committee for Economic Development. Social Responsibilities of Business Corporations. New York: Research and Policy Committee, Committee for Economic Development, 1971.

Cooke, Morris L. ed., Public Utility Regulation. New York: Ronald Press Company, 1924.

Dawson, Frank G. Nuclear Power: Development and Management of a Technology. Seattle: University of Washington Press, 1976.

"Doherty, Henry Latham." Robert L. Schuyler and Edward T. James, eds. Dictionary of American Biography. XXII, supplement two, New York: Charles Scribern's Sons, 1958.

"Doherty, Henry Latham." The National Cyclopaedia of American Biography: Being a History of the United States. XXXIV New York: James T. White & Company, 1948.

Doyle, Jack. Lines Across The Land: Rural Electric Cooperatives, the Changing Politics of Energy in Rural America. Washington, DC: The Rural Land and Energy Project Environmental Policy Institute, 1979.

Duffy, Joseph W. Power: Prime Mover of Technology. Bloomington, IL: McKnight & McKinght Publishing Co., 1964.

Dunsheath, Percy. A History of Electrical Power Engineering. Cambridge, MA: The MIT Press, 1962.

Edison Electric Institute. Historical Statistics of the Electric Utility Industry. volume I 1902-1950, volume II 1951-1963, New York: EEI, 1963.

Eisenman, H. J. III. Charles F. Bush: Pioneer in Electrical Technology. New Jersey: Case Institute of Tehnology, 1967.

"Electricity: Hydroelectric Generation." Encylopaedia Britannica. 15th ed. Vol. 6.

Ellis, Clyde T. A Giant Step. New York: Vintage Books, 1966.

Ellis, William D. On the Oil Lands with Cities Service. Tulsa, OK, 1983.

Environmental Action Foundation. Resource Guide on Electric Utility Issues, Utility Project. Washington, DC: Environmental Action Foundation, n.d.

"Faller, Guy." The National cyclopaedia of American Biography:Being a History of the United States. G 1943-46 New York: James T. White and Co., 1946.

Farris, Martin T. and Roy J. Sampson. Public Utilities: Regulation, Management, and Ownership. Prospect Heights, IL: Waveland Press, 1973.

Ferril, Will C. Sketches of Colorado. I Denver: The Western Press Bureau Co., 1911.

The First Fifty Years: A Romance of Electricity on the Western Slope. The Western Coke Power Co., n.d. 17 pages.

Fleming, Thomas. The Man Who Dared the Lightning, A New Look at Benjamin Franklin. New York: William Morrown and Co., Inc., 1971.

Floy, Henry. Valuation of Public Utilities Property. New York: McGraw-Hill Book Company, 1912.

Frank, Sullivan. Crisis of Confidence: Utilities Public Relations and Credibility. Canaan, NH: Pheonix Publishing, 1977.

Frankfurter, Felix, and Hart, Henry M., Jr. "The Reasons and methods of Regulation," in MacAvoy, Paul W., ed. The Crisis of the Regulatory Commission: An Introduction to a Current Issue of Public Policy. New York: W. W. Norton and Company, 1970.

Frueauff, Charles A. The Denver Gas and Electric Company and its Subsidiary Companies, Their Power Organization, Franchises, Property, Mortgages and Business. (Denver: The Smith Brooks Co., Printers, 1 May 1905.

Funigiello, Philip J. Toward a National Power Policy: The New Deal and the Electric Utility Industry, 1933-1941. Pittsburgh: University of Pittsburg Press, 1973.

Garfield, Paul J., and Lovejoy, Wallace F. Public Utility Economics. Englewood Cliffs, NJ: Prentice Hall, Inc., 1964.

Garwood, John D., and Tuthill, W. C. The Rural Electrification Administration: An Evaluation. Washington, DC: The American Enterprise Institute for Public Policy Research, 1936.

Glaeser, Martin G. Public Utilities in American Capitalism. New York: The MacMillan Company, 1957.

Golze, Alfred R. Reclamation in the United States Caldwell, ID: The Caxton Printers, Ltd., 1961.

Goodman Louis J.; Hawkins, John; and Love, Ralph N., eds. Small Hydroelectric Projects for Rural Development, Planning and Management. New York: Pergamon Press, 1981.

Gordon, Myron J. The Cost of Capital to a Public Utility. East Lansing: Michigan State University Press, 1974.

Gormley, William T., Jr. The Politics of Public Utility Regulation. Pittsburgh: University of Pittsburgh Press, 1983.

Groner, Alex. The American Heritage History of

American Business and Industry. New York: American Heritage, 1972.

Groninger, Taylor G., Public utility Rate Making. Indianapolis: The Boos Merrill Co., 1928.

Gruening, Ernest. The Public Pays: A Study of Power Propaganda. New York: Vanguard Press, 1964, reprinted from 1931.

Guide to National Archives of the United States. Washington, DC: General Service Administration, 1974.

Hession, Charles H., and Sardy, Hyman. Ascent to Affluence, A History of American Economic Development. Boston: Allynand Bacon, Inc., 1969.

Hughes, Thomas P. Networks of Power: Electrification in Western Society 1880-1930. Baltimore: The John Hopkins University Press, 1983.

Hughes, Thomas P. Thomas Edison: Professional Inventor. Chatham,, England: McKay, Ltd., 1976.

Hungerford, Edward. The Story of Public Utilities. New York: J.P. Putnam's Sons, 1978.

Hunt, Florine E. Public Utilities Information Sources. Detroit: Gale Research Company, 1965.

Hunt, Inez, and Draper, Wanetta W. Lightning in His Hand, the Life Story of Nikola Tesla. Denver: Sage Books, 1964.

Hyman, Leonard S. America's Electric Utilities: Past, Present and Future. Arlington, VA: Public Utilities Reports, Inc., 1983.

Jones, Alton W. "The Cities Service Story." Cities Service Company: A Case History of American Enterprise. New York: The Newcomen Society in North America, 1955.

Jones, Eliot and Bigham, Truman C. Principles of Public Utilities. New York: The MacMillan Company, 1931.

Josephson, Mathew. Edison. New York: McGraw-Hill Book Co., Inc., 1959.

Keily, William E., ed. Public Utilities in Modern Life: Selected Speeches (1914-1923) by Samuel Insull. Chicago: privately printed, 1924.

Kendrick, John W. Productivity Trends in the United States. Princeton, NJ: Princeton University Press, 1961.

King, Clyde. The History of the Government of Denver, with Special Reference to Its Relations with Public Service. Denver: The Fisher Book Co., 1911.

_________. The Regulation of Municipal Utilities. New York: D. Appleton and Company, 1912.

Kohlmeier, John M., Jr. The Regulators: Watchdog Agencies and the Public Interest. New York: Harper & Row Publishers, 1969.

Kolb, Burton and Lipstream, Otis. New Concepts and Current Issues in Public Utility Regulation. Denver: Mountain States Telephone and Telegraph, 1963.

Larson, Henrietta M. Guide to Business History. Cambridge, MA: Harvard University Press, 1948.

Leeston, Alfred M., John A Chricton and John C. Jacobs. The Dynamic Natural Gas Industry. Norman, University of Oklahoma Press, 1963.

Leonard, John W., et al., eds. Romance of American Petroleum and Gas. II New York: J. J. Little and Ives Company, n.d.

Lindsey, Ben B., and O'Higgins, Harvey J. The Beast. New York: Doubleday, Page & Company, 1910.

"Lighting and Lighting Devices." The New Encyclopaedia Britannica. Vol. 10, 1978.

"Loiseau, John E." The National Cyclopaedia of American Biography. LII, New York: James T. White & Co. 1970.

Loth, David. Swope of General Electric. New York: Arno Press, New York Times Co., 1976.

MacAvoy, Paul, ed. The Crisis of the Regulatory Commission, an Introduction to a Current Issue. New York: W. W. Norton & Co., Inc., 1970.

McCracken, Paul W. Economic Progress and the Utility Industry. Michigan Business Paper No. 38, Ann Arbor,, MI: Graduate School of Business Administration, University of Michigan, 1964.

McDonald, Forest. Insull. Chicago: University of Chicago Press, 1962.

McNellis, Dan, "Heat, Light and History." The Colorado Cattleman's Centennial Commission, The Cooperative Century. Denver, n.p., 1967.

Makar, James F. Economic Forces Behind Colorado's Growth, 1870-1967. Denver: Denver Research Institute, 1963.

Martin, Albro. James J. Hill and the Opening of the Northwest. Cambridge, MA: Harvard University Press, 1981.

Metcalf, Lee, and Reinemer, Vic. Overcharge. New York: David McKay Co., Inc., 1967.

"McMillin, Emerson." The National Cyclopaedia of American Biography: Being a History of the United States. XXIV New York: James T. White and Company, 1935.

Miller, Mabel. Michael Faraday and the Dynamo. Philadelphia: Chilton Book Co., 1968.

Moody's Manual of Investments. New York: Moody's Investors Service, 1900-1985.

National Electric Manufacturers Association, A Chronological History of Electrical Development from 6000 B. C. New York: National Electric Manufacturers Association, 1946.

Nelson, Ralph L. Merger Movements in American Industry 1890-1956. Princeton, NJ: Princeton

University Press, 1959.

New Challenges to Public Utility Management. Institute of Public Utilities, Proceedings of the Sixth Annual Conference 24-25 April 1973. East Lansing, MI: Graduate School of Business Administration, Michigan State University, 1974.

Pachauri, R. K. The Dynamics of Electrical Energy Supply and Demands: An Economic Analysis. New York: Praeger Publishers, 1975.

Passer, Harold C. The Electrical Manufacturers 1875-1900, A Study in Competition, Entrepreneurship, Technical Change, and Economic Growth. New York: Arno Press, A New York Times Company 1972.

Phillips, Charles L., Jr. The Economics of Regulation, Theory and Practice in the Transportation and Public Utility Industries. Homewood, IL: Richard D. Irwin, Inc., 1969.

Pomerantz, Laurence S. Allowance for Funds During Construction. East Lansing, MI: Michigan State University Press, 1978.

Research Center in Entrepreneurial History. Change and the Entrepreneur: Postulates and Patterns. Cambridge, MA: Harvard University Press, 1949.

Ritchie, Robert F. Integration of Public utility holding Companies. Ann Arbor: University of Michigan Law School, 1954.

Roberts, Marc and Bluhm, Jeremy S. The Choices of Power: Utilities Face the Environmental Challenge. Cambridge, MA: Harvard University Press, 1981.

Ruggles, C.O. Public Utilities: A Survey of the Extent of Instruction in the Field of Public Utilities in Colleges and Universities; the Industries Demand for College Graduates; the Character of Opportunities in the Industry Open to College Men; and the Willingness and Ability of the Utilities to Cooperate with Colleges and Universities in the Training of

Men for the Industry and in the Study of Public Utility Problems. New York: National Light Association, 1929.

Salmonson, Roland F., ed. Public utilities Accounting: Models, Mergers and Information. East Lansing, MI: Michigan State University Press, 1971.

Sayre, Kenneth., ed. Values in the Electric Power Indstry. Notre Dame, IN: University of notre Dame Press, 1977.

Schlesinger, Arthur M., Jr. The Crisis of the Old Order: 1919-1933. Boston: Houghton Mifflin Company. Boston, 1957.

Schulze, Suzanne, compiler. A Century of the Colorado Census. Greeley: Univeristy of Northern Colorado, 1976.

Schuyler, Robert L. and Edward T. James, eds. Dictionary of American Biography. XXII, Supplement Two New York: Charles Scribner's Sons, 1958.

Sharlin, Harold I. The Making of the Electrical Age: from the Telegraph to Automation. New York: Abelard-Schuman, 1964.

Shepherd, William, and Gies, Thomas. Utility Regulation.. New York: Random House, 1966.

Shrader-Frechette, K.S. Nuclear Power and Public Policy: The Social and Ethical Problems of Fission Technology. Dordrecht, Holland: D. Reidel Publishing Company, 1980.

Sichel, Werner, and Gies, Thomas G., eds. Applications of Economic Principles in Public Utility Industries. East Lansing: Michigan State University Pres, 1981.

Sichel, Werner, and Gies, Thomas, eds. Public Utility Regulation, Change and Scope. Lexington, MA: Lexington Books, 1978.

Smiley, Jerome C. History of Denver. Denver: Times Sun Publishing Company, 1901.

Southern Illinois University Conference on Current Issues in Public Utility Regulation and Management. 1972.

Spron, Philip. The Social Organization of Electric Power Supply in Modern Societies. Cambridge, MA: MIT Press, 1971.

Spurr, Henry C. Guiding Principles of Public Service Regulation. I, Rochester, NY: Public Utilities Reports, Inc., 1924.

Starr, Chancey. "Energy and Power, the Role of Energy in Human Life: Past, Present, and Future," in Energy and Power. San Francisco: W. H. Freeman, 1971. It originally appeared as an article in the September, 1971 issue of Scientific American.

Stigler, George J., and Friedland, Clair. "What Can Regulators Regulate? The Case of Electricity." in MacAvoy, Paul, ed. The Crisis of the Regulatory Commission, an Introduction to a Current Issue. New York: W. W. Norton and Company, Inc., 1970.

Stone, Wilbur. History of Colorado. I and IV, four volumes, Chicago: The S. J. Clarke Publishing Company, 1918.

Stobaugh, Robert, and Yergin, Daniel, eds. Energy future: Report of the Energy Project at the Harvard Business School. New York: Random House, 1979.

Stotz, Luis and Alexander Jamison. History of the Gas Industry New York: Press of Stettnier Bros., 1938.

Technology Futures, Inc., and Scientific Foresight, Inc. Principles for Electric Power Policy. Westport, CT: Quorum Books, 1984.

Thompson, Charles W. and Smith, R. Wendell. Public Utility Economics. New York: McGraw Hill, 1941.

Thompson, Robert Thuther. Wiring of a Continent, the History of the Telegraph Industry in the United States 1832-1866. New York: Arno

Press, New York Times Co., 1972.

Trachsel, Herman H. Public Utility Regulation. Chicago: Richard D. Irwin, Inc., 1947.

Trebing, Harr M., ed. Essays on Public Utility Pricing and Regulation. East Lansing, MI: Institute of Public Utilities, Michigan State University, 1971.

Troxel, Emery. Economics of Public Utilities. New York: Rinehart & Company Inc., Publishers, 1947.

Turk, Amos; Turk, Jonathan; and Wittes, Janet T. Ecology, Pollution, Environment. Philadelphia: W. B. Saunders Co., 1977.

Ubbelohde, Carl; Benson, Maxine; and Smith, Duane A. A Colorado History. revised centennial edition. Boulder: Pruett Publishing Company, 1976.

Urquhart, Lena M. Glenwood Springs, Shoshone Spa in the Mountains. Boulder: Pruett Press, 1970.

Varnum, Charles and J. Frank Adams. Franchises and Special Privileges of the City and County of Denver. Denver: Smith Books,1907.

Vennard, Edwin. The Electric Power Business. second edition. New York: McGraw Hill book Co., 1970.

__________. Management of the Electric Energy Business. New York: McGraw Hill Book Co., 1979.

Wainwright, Nicholas G. History of the Philadelphia Electric Company 1881-1961. Philadelphia: Philadelphia Electric Company, 1961.

Weiss, Leonard W. Regulation: A Case Approach. New York: McGraw-Hill Book Company. 2d ed., 1982.

William J. Barker, Compiled and Published by His Associates of Many Years in Denver Gas and Electric Light Company. Denver: privately published, 1922.

Wilcox, Delos F. The Administration of Municipally Owned Utilities. New York: Municipal Administration Service, 1931.

Wilson, Mitchell and the editors of Life. Energy. New York: Life Science Library, Time, Inc., 1963.

Zajac, Edward E. Fairness or Efficiency An Introduction to Public Utility Pricing. Cambridge, MA: Ballinger Publishing Company, 1978.

ARTICLES AND PERIODICALS

Air Pollution in the Denver Area. Denver: Public Service Company, Denver, Colorado, no date.

Barb, Clark F. "The Oil and Gas Industry in Colorado." Colorado School of Mines Quarterly, XXXVII (April, 1942), pp. 13-24.

"Behind the Power Lobby." Nation. 18 July 1928, p. 57.

Boffrey, P. M., "Energy Crises: Environmental Issues Exacerbates Power Supply Problems," CLXVII Science (26 June 1970), pp. 1554-59.

"Cabin Creek Pumped Storage Hydroelectric Project." Denver: Public Service Company of Colorado, 1968.

DeLorme, Roland L. "Turn-of-the-Century Denver." Colorado Magazine. XLV (Winter, 1968), pp. 6-7.

Bitner, M. S. "The Colorado-Big-Thompson Project." Reclamation Era. XXX (September, 1940), pp. 267-269.

Chandler, Alfred. "Entrepreneurial Opportunities in Nineteenth Century America." Explorations in Entreprenurial History. I, 1963/1964, pp. 75-92.

Colorado State Planning Division, Colorado Year Book, (Denver: Colorado State Planning Division), 1933-1969.

"Corporate Contribution." Denver: Public Service Company of Colorado, n.d.

Commercial and Financial Chronicle, LXXIV (May, 1902), p.990.

Davenport, John. "Industry Starts the Big Cleanup." Fortune Magazine, LXXI, No. 2 (February 1970), 114-117 and 174-178.

Denver Municipal Facts. II (Denver: City and County, July, 1919).

Duesenberry, J. S. "Some Aspects of the Theory of Economic Development." Explorations in Entrepreneurial History, 1968/1969. pp. 3-12.

Edison Electric Institute. The Electric Utility Industry. an annual publication, New York, 1950-1969

Electrical Review and Western Electrician. LXVII (22 April, 1916), 705.

Electrical Review. XLVII (14 July 1906) p. 672.

Electrical West, 1927-1970.

Emery, Wilson B. "Natural Gas in the Rocky Mountain Areas." The Oil and Gas Journal, G, XXVI (16 June 1927), pp. 24.

Explorations in Economic History, 1947-1960.

Explorations in Entreprenuerial History, 1945-1947.

"From Arrows to Atoms. Denver: Public Service Company of Colorado, n.d.

"Fort St. Vrain Nuclear Generating Station." Denver: Public Service Company of Colorado, n.d.

"Fort St. Vrain." General Atomic Company, n.d.

Gas Facts, an annual publication of the American Gas Association, New York, 1960-1969.

Gasser. The publication of Colorado Interstate Gas, 1978.

Hale, Irving. "Influence of Electricity on Colorado's Progress."c. 1890 (reprinted from an unkown source, Denver Public Library Western History Department, Denver, Colorado.

Heilbroner, Robert. "The Energy Revolution." American Petroleum Institute Quarterly, Centennial Issue, Spring/Summer, 1959, pp. 60-72.

"How to Shuffle U.S. Utilities." Business Week, 16 August 1952, pp. 167-69.

"Insulls Methods Were Not Unique." Christian Science Monitor. 28 September 1932, pp. 115-57.

"John Franklin Shafroth, Reform Governor of Colorado, 1909-1913." Colorado Magazine, XXIX (January, 1952), pp. 37-52.

Journal of Economic History, 1961-1963.

Journal of Electricity, 1927-1970.

"Just and Reasonable, Supreme Court Precedent-Smashing Decision on Battle between the Hope Natural Gas Co. and the FPC." Time Magazine, 17 January 1944, pp. 81-82.

King, J. "Next Phase of the Power Fight." New Republic, 10 December 1930, pp. 91-93.

Lines, 1939-1969.

Literary Digest LXXCII (2 June 1923), pp. 56-58.

"Million Dollar Lobby." Nation. 16 May, 1928, pp. 554-55.

Miller, Peter G. "HTGR, A Safe Way to Nuclear Power." Popular Science, (February, 1975), pp. 66-68 and 138-29.

Mills, J. Warner. "The Economic Struggle in Colorado." Arena. XXXIV (November, 1905), pp. 36-38.

Moorehouse, E. W. "Public Utilities in the Depression: Rate Making and Credit." American Economic Review, supplement March, 1934, pp. 10-20.

"Nuclear Power Turns Up the Juice." Business Week,"

(March, 1967), pp. 64-66.

Poor's Register of Corporations, Directors and Executives, United States and Canada, 1928-1969.

Progressive Age, 1901-1969.

Public Service Bulletin. II (2 June 1942), 1.

Public Service Company of Colorado. An Analysis of Colorado's Economy. Public Service Company of Colorado, 1965.

Public Service Company of Colorado, Providing Energy for More than a Century. Denver: Public Service Company.

Public Service Company of Colorado, Annual Reports, 1943-1988.

"Public Utilities and Public Opinion." New Republic, 27 June 1928, pp.67-72.

Public Utility Compendium, 1928-1941.

Riply, W. Z. "Public Utilities Insecurities." Forum, August, 1932, pp. 66-72.

Rocky Mountain Committee on Public Utilities Bulletin. No. 1, 15 November 1920, no pagination. Denver: 302 Gas and Electric Building.

Rukeyser, Merryle Stanley. "Is There a Power Trust?" Nation. CIIVIII (6 March 1929), pp. 281-283.

"Serving the West: Valmont Plant." Denver: Public Service Company of Colorado, 1947.

San Luis Valley Historical Society. XIV, No. 4, p. 3.

Smith, Robert E. "Senator T. M. Patterson, the Colorado Supreme Court and Freedom of the Press." Colorado Magazine, LIV (January, 1977), pp.58-71.

Standard and Poor's trade and Securities Statistics, 1969-1988.

Time Magazine, (13 February 1984), pp. 34-45.

"Utilities Face Generation Gap." Business Week, 2 August 1969, p. 301.

"Utilities Prospects." Newsweek, 6 December 1937, pp. 44-46.

Western Electrician, 5 August 1893.

NEWSPAPERS

Cervis News Service, 1947.

Colorado Springs Gazette, 1902.

Colorado (Denver) Tribune, 1870-1882.

Denver Daily Tribune, 7 June 1879.

Denver Democrat, 7 July 1939.

Denver Post, 1909 to 1988.

Denver Republican, 1906-1922.

Denver Times, 1899-1922.

Denver Tribune, 1872-1898.

Fort Lupton (Colorado) Press, 4 July 1940.

Pueblo Chieftain, 31 January 1960

Rocky Mountain Herald, 9 June 1860.

Rocky Mountain News, 1867 to 1988.